Becoming Confident Teachers

CHANDOS
INFORMATION PROFESSIONAL SERIES

Series Editor: Ruth Rikowski
(email: Rikowskigr@aol.com)

Chandos' new series of books are aimed at the busy information professional. They have been specially commissioned to provide the reader with an authoritative view of current thinking. They are designed to provide easy-to-read and (most importantly) practical coverage of topics that are of interest to librarians and other information professionals. If you would like a full listing of current and forthcoming titles, please visit our web site www.chandospublishing.com or email info@chandospublishing.com or telephone +44 (0) 1223 499140.

New authors: we are always pleased to receive ideas for new titles; if you would like to write a book for Chandos, please contact Dr Glyn Jones on email gjones@chandospublishing.com or telephone number +44 (0) 1993 848726.

Bulk orders: some organisations buy a number of copies of our books. If you are interested in doing this, we would be pleased to discuss a discount. Please contact us at e-mail info@chandospublishing.com or telephone +44 (0) 1223 499140.

Becoming Confident Teachers

A guide for academic librarians

CLAIRE MCGUINNESS

CP

CHANDOS
PUBLISHING

Oxford Cambridge New Delhi

Chandos Publishing
Hexagon House
Avenue 4
Station Lane
Witney
Oxford OX28 4BN
UK
Tel: +44 (0) 1993 848726
E-mail: info@chandospublishing.com
www.chandospublishing.com

Chandos Publishing is an imprint of Woodhead Publishing Limited

Woodhead Publishing Limited
80 High Street
Sawston
Cambridge CB22 3HJ
UK
Tel: +44 (0) 1223 499140
Fax: +44 (0) 1223 832819
www.woodheadpublishing.com

First published 2011

ISBN: 978 1 84334 629 6

© C. McGuinness, 2011

British Library Cataloguing-in-Publication Data.
A catalogue record for this book is available from the British Library.

Typeset by RefineCatch Limited, Bungay, Suffolk
Printed in the UK and USA.

Contents

List of tables

About the author

Claire McGuinness is a part-time lecturer in the School of Information & Library Studies at University College Dublin, and has been conducting research into Information Literacy since the late 1990s. After completing a BA in International Marketing and Languages in 1993, Claire moved into the field of Information & Library Studies, graduating with an MLIS degree in 1996, followed by 3 years in professional practice in the library of the Dublin Dental Hospital. Returning to academia in 1999, Claire's PhD, which was funded by a scholarship from the Irish Research Council for the Humanities and Social Sciences and awarded in 2005, explored curriculum-integrated information literacy and barriers to faculty-librarian collaboration. Since then, Claire has remained in the School of Information & Library Studies, first as post-doctoral fellow in 2006–2007, and then as part-time lecturer. Over the years, she has published continuously in Information Literacy and learning, including book chapters and peer-reviewed articles based on her research, and has presented at several international conferences, including three times at LILAC (Librarians' Information Literacy Annual Conference). Claire is also module designer and coordinator of two Information Literacy modules at undergraduate and postgraduate level in the School of Information & Library Studies, in which she endeavours to combine theory with practice, and to use active and e-learning methods to engage her students and encourage them to learn. She is particularly interested in instructional training for librarians, and since 2004, her advanced "Teaching Librarian" module has aimed to prepare trainee professional librarians on the Masters and Diploma programmes for the teaching work that they are often expected to undertake in the professional workplace. Claire is often invited to give talks and seminars to professional librarian groups in Ireland, where Information Literacy has been high on the agenda for the past number of years. She was also the academic representative on the Working Group on Information Literacy in the Library Association of Ireland, which was convened in 2006 to advise on best practice for information literacy across all library sectors in Ireland.

Since completing her PhD, Claire's research interests have expanded into other areas of Information Literacy and learning, including the use of reflective learning journals and portfolios to teach the research process to students, the development of reflective practice among teaching librarians, and exploring the concept of "teacher identity" as it applies to librarians. Recently, she has been a team member on a number of interesting teaching and learning projects in the School of Information & Library Studies, including the development, use, and evaluation of interactive e-practicums to teach information research concepts to undergraduate students.

Claire can be contacted at:

School of Information & Library Studies
University College Dublin
Belfield
Dublin 4
Ireland

claire.mcguinness@ucd.ie

Acknowledgements

My sincere thanks to all who have supported and facilitated me, both in my career and the writing of this book. Special thanks to Chandos Publishing, especially Dr Glyn Jones and Jonathan Davis, for the opportunity to undertake this project.

In the School of Information & Library Studies, UCD, I would like to express particular gratitude to Professor Mary Burke, Dr Ian Cornelius, and Professor Diane Sonnenwald who have provided a stimulating and encouraging environment for me to explore and expand my interest in information literacy and teaching.

And to other SILS colleagues and friends with whom I have worked and laughed over many years: Jessica Bates, Crystal Fulton, Claire Nolan, Clare Thornley, Judith Wusteman, Shane McLoughlin and Nuala Connolly, to name but a few.

A special thanks to the many students I have taught and supervised in UCD and who have, in turn, taught me so much about education, information literacy and achieving goals.

I am also greatly indebted to the wonderful community of academic librarians in Ireland, particularly the UCD librarians with whom I collaborate every year, and to all those who participated in the survey carried out for this book.

My wonderful circle of non-LIS friends who are there with me every step of the way.

My husband Karl, and my precious boys, Luke and Emmet – thank you, with love.

Finally, I dedicate this book to my mother, Susan, and to my late father Vincent McGuinness – there are no words to express my gratitude.

Introduction

This book is for, and about, the unsung yet critically important group of professional academic librarians, who strive to facilitate learning among students and library users, and who frequently do this whilst juggling a range of other library tasks and responsibilities. The world of the Teaching Librarian is diverse, challenging and often contrary. Sometimes, the role is barely recognised; at other times is it all encompassing, and viewed as the cornerstone of information service provision. Sometimes librarians feel confident and well-prepared for this role; often, they feel intimidated, ill-equipped and insufficiently trained. It is a job that can be maddening, rewarding, arduous, exciting and transformative – all at the same time. It is also a job that remains curiously undefined and poorly understood outside of librarianship. It is a job that many librarians both dread and embrace, while there are those within the profession who do not believe that librarians should teach at all. Whether you are a librarian who only teaches occasionally, or whether teaching is the activity that occupies virtually all of your working hours, this book is for you. If you are a student of information and library work, you will also find much of interest here, as you develop an understanding of the diverse nature of academic librarianship, and the inextricable link between information literacy and learning, which informs your role. And for those whose task it is to prepare professional librarians for the workplace, this book offers useful insight into the skills, knowledge and expertise that Teaching Librarians require to perform the instructional role confidently and effectively.

The book has emerged from more than a decade's involvement in information literacy, as a practising librarian, student, academic, researcher, faculty member and author. Research has shown that the role of Teaching Librarian is viewed as important, and that information skills are considered essential within higher education; yet, in practice, librarians find that they must continually engage in marketing, promotion and outreach, to ensure that they reach their target student base. The embedding of information literacy instruction in academic curricula is inconsistent; while there are many successful programmes, there are also many which are beset by difficulties, and some which enjoy initial success, only to fade away when circumstances change. Much depends on the cooperation and support of academics and administrators in the librarians' institutions. While "information literacy" is now widely recognised as an important research domain and area of professional practice within Library and Information Science (LIS), communicating this agenda effectively to other disciplines and professions has proved challenging. However, a sign that this is beginning to change was evident in the US Presidential Proclamation on Information Literacy in late 2009 (White House, 2009).

This book has a number of objectives. First, as a practical primer, it is designed to support Teaching Librarians at all levels of experience; for instance, those who are confident instructors, but who wish to advance their skills and knowledge and to explore, in depth, the concepts of professional development and reflective practice. Equally, it is aimed at librarians who perhaps feel that they have not received sufficient training to perform the role as they would wish, and who are uncertain about what is expected of them. Lack of confidence in one's own ability to teach is a known cause of stress among academic librarians (Davis, 2007), especially when it is considered that instructional training is still not a core component of pre-service professional education in many Schools of Library and Information Science. In this book, the skills, tools, and methods of instruction are set out and discussed in the specific context of information literacy instruction. Recognised instructional and implementation challenges are also addressed, with suggestions for how Teaching Librarians might overcome difficulties through reflection, research and the practical application of knowledge.

However, although important, the book is not solely concerned with the "mechanics" of teaching and learning, and seeks to address a wider agenda. Self-development and self-understanding in the role of Teaching Librarian is seen as crucial to effective performance and perception of self-efficacy (Jacobs, 2008). An additional aim of the book is, therefore, the encouragement of reflective practice among Teaching Librarians, and the development of a "teacher identity", which can inform, and serve as the basis for, all teaching and learning activities that are undertaken. In the book, the nature and responsibilities of the Teaching Librarian role are discussed and analyzed, along with the internal and external factors that influence and shape it. Individual and group-based strategies for professional self development are presented, while end-of-chapter exercises and reflection give readers the opportunity to think about their own roles and responsibilities in the spirit of constructive self-analysis.

The book has six chapters. The first two chapters provide the context for consideration of the Teaching Librarian role. Chapter 1 explores the relationship between librarians' professional identity and the evolution of the information literacy instruction. Asking "who is the Teaching Librarian?", the chapter examines the various factors and trends that have influenced the development of the role, including the rise of the information literacy movement, the progressive, though sometimes limiting effect of academic librarians' *own* role conceptions, as well as the strong influence of academics' conceptions and attitudes on how the role is perceived, and integrated within higher education. The chapter also analyses the educational requirements of librarians with teaching responsibilities, suggesting a range of topics, skill sets and strategic concerns which could be included on pre-service professional education programmes. Chapter 2 takes a wider view, outlining ten significant trends and concepts that are influencing the development of the Teaching Librarian role in academia, ranging from internal factors, such as personal pedagogical philosophy and reflective practice, to external trends, including the diversification of the student body, the importance of information literacy for researchers, and the need for new strategies for collaboration and advocacy.

Chapters 3, 4 and 5 are concerned with the "nuts-and-bolts" of teaching, learning, and reflective practice, and are designed to furnish Teaching Librarians with the basic knowledge, skills, and strategies to confidently handle any teaching situation in which they find themselves, as well as the means to constructively evaluate their own performance and to progress in their careers. Chapter 3 works through eight key areas of competence which aim to provide a thorough grounding in the techniques of teaching and learning, with specific reference to the context of information literacy instruction. All stages of the teaching and learning process are covered, from planning, to the selection and design of teaching methods, to the implemention of appropriate assessment and evaluation tools. Chapter 4, by contrast, takes a problem-based approach, and suggests solutions to some of the real-life challenges or "confidence zappers" that crop up frequently in information literacy teaching, from unmotivated students to the limitations of the "one-shot" session. Chapter 5 focuses attention on the "reflective" librarian, and discusses the practical means of professional development and advancement, including evaluation of teaching performance, peer-mentoring, creating teaching portfolios and writing grant applications, amongst other methods.

Finally, Chapter 6 presents the results of a qualitative survey which was carried out among 38 Irish academic librarians in October 2010. To provide some favour of the real lives of Teaching Librarians, the survey participants were invited to share their personal experiences of teaching, their conceptions of "teacher identity," the challenges and motivations of their work, and their overall feelings about the role they play in their institutions. The themes discussed in this chapter will hopefully offer some reassurance to you, as fellow Teaching Librarians, that your experiences are universal, and that the Community of Practice is, indeed, as worldwide one.

The overarching objective of this book is to help to instil confidence, and to offer a clear guide for Teaching Librarians in terms of the knowledge, skills and tools required to perform the role. Although challenges exist, it is hoped that the knowledge and tools described here will equip Teaching Librarians with the means to face these challenges effectively.

The evolving role of the teaching librarian

Abstract: This chapter explores the origins of the academic teaching librarian role and describes how the development of the role has been shaped by librarians' own conceptions of their professional teaching identity, as well as the conceptions and attitudes of academics. The chapter also explores the rationale for the teaching role, as well as the barriers encountered by teaching librarians in their efforts to integrate with the curriculum. Finally, the instructional knowledge and skills that teaching librarians require in their pre-service and continuing professional education are discussed, including the importance of reflective practice.

Key words: teaching librarian, teacher identity, information literacy, professional education, academics.

Who are we? Where did we come from? The teaching librarian is something of an outlier in library and information work; unlike cataloguers, systems analysts or reference librarians, teaching librarians have only recently been recognised as a specialist sub-group within library and information services (LIS). Mysteriously, the role seems to have evolved and emerged independently, rather than been consciously developed and nurtured; in some respects, the library profession seems to have been almost caught by surprise by the realisation that teaching is a central part of what we do, although the many librarians who have been developing and delivering instruction for all of their professional lives might have a different perception. In recognising the significance of the teaching role, both now and for the future development of the profession, the time has come to seriously address what being a teaching librarian means, from both a practical and philosophical perspective. The first step is to explore some of the key influences which have converged to shape the role, and what they mean to practising librarians, such as you. This chapter presents the bigger picture, and is intended to encourage teaching librarians to think about how their work fits in with the overall mission of library and information work, and what their contribution means to the educational experience of students.

Teaching librarians and the information literacy revolution

It is generally accepted that the term 'information literacy' (IL) was first coined in the early 1970s by Paul Zurkowski in his report to the US National Commission on Libraries and Information Science (Zurkowski, 1974; Bruce, 1997; Webber and Johnston, 2000; Pinto et al., 2010). This first use of the term was anchored in Zurkowski's proposal for a ten-year national IL programme and referred to one's ability to problem-solve effectively, through optimal use of available information tools and resources. The term itself was used only sporadically during the latter years of the 1970s and early 1980s in different contexts, ranging from the ability to locate and retrieve information, to the capacity of the individual to participate fully in the democratic process (e.g. Burchinal, 1976; Owens, 1976; Taylor, 1979). Since then, the phrase has become more mainstream, and the information literacy 'movement' has gained pace in the past two decades, during which time a series of predominantly US-based publications and events have converged to establish and advance the IL agenda, and to gradually extend its reach beyond the politically limited library sphere to the point that it is now recognised as an essential life skill by the President of the US (Spitzer et al., 1998; White House, 2009).

While the origins of information literacy reach back to the early library instruction and bibliographic instruction movements of the nineteenth and twentieth centuries (Weiss, 2004), it is only since the beginning of the IL movement in the late 1980s that the potential role of libraries in *facilitating*, rather than just supporting, learning has received any sort of consideration in domains outside of librarianship. But this has not been without its challenges. Cynical contributors to the debate have suggested that the promotion of the movement constitutes a strategic attempt by librarians to increase their status and visibility, and to ensure a continuing role for themselves in times of uncertainty; for example, Foster (1993) suggests that it represents 'an effort to deny the ancillary status of librarianship by inventing a social malady with which librarians as "information professionals" are uniquely qualified to deal' (p. 346), views which have been more recently echoed in Wilder (2005). However, dissenters are relatively few, and it is a more widely held view that it is predominantly the technological revolution, in particular the pervasiveness of the Internet/World Wide Web and its effect on information work, that has stimulated the re-imagining of the role served by librarians, and the growth of the movement. The document that is often cited as the touch-paper of the movement is the American Library Association's (ALA) *Presidential Committee Report on Information Literacy* (1989), which produced the most frequently quoted definition of IL:

> To be information literate, a person must be able to recognise when information is needed and have the ability to locate, evaluate and use effectively, the needed information. . . . Ultimately, information literate people are those who have learned how to learn.

Along with Breivik and Gee's seminal book from 1989, *Information Literacy: Revolution in the library*, this report was one of the first documents to suggest that the existing learning process should be rethought and restructured to incorporate the principles of IL, such as critical thinking and problem-solving, rather than create a new information studies curriculum. Competency in six information-related areas is deemed to be the essential outcome of the general educational process. Following the report, the establishment of two key organisations in the US – the National Forum on Information Literacy (NFIL) in 1989, and later, the Institute for Information Literacy (IIL) in 1998 – was viewed as a significant step forward in the promotion of the IL movement.

Teaching librarians should be aware of the context that has shaped and moulded the role; having a sense of the history of instruction in library work contributes to a greater sense of identity. To this end, it is instructive to examine the key trends and concepts that have characterised the information literacy revolution since the 1980s. They are discussed below.

Information literacy and learning

The link between the concepts of IL and learning has been a consistent theme, and has strongly influenced how the term is conceptualised and understood. Many definitions of IL centre on its relationship to the learning process. While the various definitions tend to reflect the interests and concerns of the different groups involved in implementing programmes of instruction, there seems to be at least a basic consensus that information-literate individuals are those who have the ability to recognise an information need or a gap in their knowledge; can formulate appropriate questions; can construct and execute effective search strategies, using a variety of media; can evaluate, use and present information. Becoming information literate as part of the formal education process is seen as essential, in light of the 'dynamic and changing information environment of the last quarter of the century' (Bawden, 2001). Virkus (2003) points out how IL has 'permeated strategic thinking' in the industrialised, English-speaking world, and has been highlighted in several major reports emanating from government and the higher education sector. In the main, IL is viewed not as an isolated skill-set, but as a formative agent central to the whole educational process – a conceptual framework upon which to base the development of general educational models and curricula to foster information competence across society as a whole (Bruce, 1997).

Lifelong learning

The global emphasis on 'lifelong learning' has been a key political catalyst behind calls to incorporate IL into educational curricula. Central to the lifelong learning agenda is a conceptualisation of learning and upgrading of one's skills that continues throughout the individual's lifetime and does not cease once the formal education system is left behind. Underpinning the lifelong learning ideology are the information society imperatives of eliminating social division and increasing democratic participation through the provision of equal access to information, of building and maintaining economic competitiveness through a highly educated workforce, and of empowering individuals by equipping them with the means to deal efficiently with the information they encounter on a daily basis. Lifelong learning currently represents a major strategic objective for all Western nations (e.g. OECD; European Commission Lifelong Learning Programme; Coalition of Lifelong Learning Organisations, US). Other factors that have contributed to the growth of the IL movement within education are identified as the rapid spread of information technology, and the transformation of libraries, which has led to the replacement of 'tool-based' instruction, designed to show users how to effectively use library-based tools and sources, with 'concept-based' instruction, which instead emphasises processes and general research principles that can be transferred across different contexts (McCartin and Feid, 2001).

Information literacy in education

In recent times, there has been plenty of evidence that IL activity in educational institutions at all levels is increasing and expanding, although higher education is considered to be the most progressive sector and is the domain in which most IL research is carried out: 'academic institutions have been engaged in efforts to define information competencies, and integrate information skills instruction' (Spitzer et al, 1998: 52). However, IL developments in Europe are not considered to have kept pace with those in Australia and the US (Webber and Johnston, 2000). Research on information literacy is also emerging from other sectors, including IL at school level (Thomas, N.P., 2004), in the workplace (Kirton and Barham, 2005) and as a public library function (Eve et al., 2007; O'Beirne, 2006).

Curriculum-integrated instruction

There is a strong emphasis on the need to integrate IL into subject-specific teaching, which involves a restructuring of the existing learning process. This is based on the notion that students will learn skills more effectively if taught as part of a subject, rather than as a separate course. However, a contrasting viewpoint is that IL should be taught as an academic discipline in its own right. In 1996, Shapiro and Hughes suggested that information literacy should be defined broadly, 'so as to constitute both a liberal as well as a technical art', and that this definition should be turned into a curriculum. By liberal art, the authors mean 'knowledge that is part of what it means to be a free person in the present historical context of the dawn of the information age' (ibid.). Webber and Johnston (2000; 2006) also argue persuasively for the development of IL as a separate discipline, with its own curriculum; specifically, they assert that it should be considered a soft-applied discipline 'rather than a set of personal attributes' (2006: 109). This is an interesting polarity, which continues to influence the modes of ILI(information literacy instruction) that are implemented in practice.

Information literacy models and standards

Many IL programmes are designed according to prescribed IL models and standards, which suggest content areas, objectives and learning outcomes to guide curriculum design and evaluation of student learning, such as the ACRL *Information Competency Standards for Higher Education* (2000). Models usually describe the information problem-solving process in terms of six to ten steps, and variations of the basic model have been developed in many countries. They 'provide educators with a framework within which specific information skills can be targeted and their coordination can be fostered' (Moore, 2002: 2). However, a number of commentators have argued against this primarily quantitative view of IL. Webber (2003) suggests that this may lead to a 'tick the box' approach to IL education, as the student moves through each standard, although at each stage, the issues may not have been addressed in sufficient detail (p. 7). This is supported by Bruce (1997), who contends that IL or 'information use' is a phenomenon experienced by individuals in unique ways, and is not, as such, a measurable or observable entity. More recently, Walton (2010) argues that models such as the Seven Pillars are 'dangerously oversimplified' and convey an inaccurate picture of information-seeking behaviour to those using it to develop their programmes. In particular, the affective and social dimensions of learning tend to be omitted from these models.

Continuing innovation in use of technology for IL

Information literacy and technology are inextricably linked. Librarians continue to display inventiveness as they experiment with new and emerging technologies for information literacy instruction. An increasing number of publications are devoted to showcasing the various tools and learning objects designed by teaching librarians to complement the traditional teaching approaches (Godwin and Parker, 2008; Mackey and Jacobson, 2008). In recent times, Web 2.0 applications have attracted particular attention because of their collaborative and interactive possibilities.

Who is the 'teaching librarian'?

'Librarians teach. [. . .] the subject of much angst, soul-searching and self-justification by academic librarians [. . .], this statement would now be accepted almost without argument both within the library world and largely by our colleagues in the wider academic community' (Powis, 2008: 6).

When women and men choose librarianship as a career in the twenty-first century, what do they believe the role will entail? What motivates them to choose this type of work? While it is safe to say that the modern librarian is far removed from this stereotypical image described by Luthmann (2007): '[A]n older, single, white woman, generally accoutred with one or more of the following: cardigan, pearls, tweed skirt, hair in a bun and spectacles perched on the nose' (p. 775), the question of what roles a librarian is typically expected to fulfil proves difficult to answer, particularly in a world where boundaries are constantly shifting and technology acts as an ever-present catalyst for change (Fourie, 2004; Biddiscombe, 2002). The lack of emergence of a 'new stereotype', a more positive evocation of the realities of the day-to-day responsibilities of an information professional, has meant that, to outsiders at least, the old image still maintains a grip of sorts; Fourie (2004) notes that 'librarians seem to have a poor public image' and continue to be tarred with overtly negative attributes such as 'introversion, lack of confidence and poor communication skills' (p. 65). However, Davis (2007) suggests that, to an extent, librarians are themselves responsible for the perpetuation of the stereotypical image, which has a limiting effect on their own role conceptions. Oen and Cooper (1988), amongst others, have described this role uncertainty as a type of identity crisis: 'Because it is hard to establish a long-lasting identification with a moving target, information professionals have not yet established a strong identity for themselves or even a uniform definition of their field' (p. 357). Arguably, the seismic shifts in how information is created, stored, transmitted and used, even in the two decades since Oen and Cooper made their assertion, have only exacerbated this problem (Dillon, 2008). Doskatch (2003) affirms this when she refers to a claim, made by members of the profession itself, that 'a lack of professional self-understanding and self-definition has contributed to an inability to communicate to the academic community what it is we do, and what we stand for' (pp. 113–14).

The question of the teaching librarian is framed within the broader context of librarians' professional identity and role, and adds a further layer to what is a much-debated issue (Davis, 2007). Historically, the provision of instruction, although manifestly a part of what librarians have been doing since at least the 1800s (Weiss, 2004; Thomas, 1999), was not fully acknowledged as an important library function until the 1970s, when librarians who were active in bibliographic instruction, as it was then known, decided to establish a forum for collaboration and support, and 'banded together [. . .] to talk and share ideas and approaches to teaching and learning' (Grassian and Kaplowitz, 2009: 19). It was only during this period that teaching librarians developed a unified voice, and national umbrella organisations, such as the California Clearing House on Library Instruction in the US, began to spring up. Arguably, it was at this point that instruction was finally recognised as a core service element in libraries; that alongside collection management, acquisitions and reference services, teaching was something that librarians *did*.

Defining the teaching librarian role

So, who is the teaching librarian? If the role of the librarian is difficult to define, then that of a teaching librarian is perhaps even more so. There is no model, no prototype, of a typical teaching librarian to guide us. Doskatch (2003) observes that the LIS discourse 'constructs a complex picture of the educative role of librarians' (p. 113). The question of whether 'teaching librarian' even refers to a specific type of defined role immediately arises, and indeed, the question of whether we ought to attempt to define it at all. The label itself appears interchangeable and arbitrary, with 'instruction librarian' at least as popular and used in a number of recognised capacities, including the *ACRL Standards for Proficiencies for Instruction Librarians and Coordinators* (2008). The latter document defines instruction librarian as 'any librarian with teaching responsibilities' (p. 4). However, it also distinguishes between librarians with teaching responsibilities and the coordinators who manage the overall instructional programmes, and separate proficiencies are listed for them. 'Professor librarian' is yet another label, suggested by Douglas (1999). However, notably, none of those terms currently appear as descriptors in the online thesaurus of the CSA database Library and Information Science Abstracts; instead, the terms 'teacher librarian' and 'tutor librarian' are listed as descriptors to enable users to refine their searches. In developing an interview guide for their study of librarians, Julien and Pecoskie (2009) note that they use the terms 'teacher', 'instructor' and 'educator' interchangeably, 'since librarians use various labels for their educative positions' (p. 153). The post of 'learning support librarian' in the UK has also been advertised recently on the website *LISJOBNET.com*.

The role is nebulous and difficult to define in terms of specific activities, skills and attributes, although several authors have tried (Kilcullen, 1998; Peacock, 2001; Meulemans and Brown, 2001). It is difficult to say whether teaching librarian is viewed as a defined and viable career path – it's doubtful that budding information professionals embark on their careers with the specific objective of becoming teaching librarians, although a prospective instructional role may appeal to some (Walter, 2008). Rather, anecdotal evidence has shown that it is more often the case that librarians 'find' themselves having to provide instruction, perhaps unexpectedly and, in some cases, unwillingly. Occasionally, in fact, the opposite holds – some individuals seem to become librarians specifically in order to *avoid* having to teach: 'Many of us became librarians precisely because we wanted to avoid getting up in front of groups' (LaGuardia and Oka, 2000: 3). Walter (2005) suggests that despite a long history of involvement in the provision of instruction, and the current demand for the kind of teaching that librarians can provide, 'few librarians are ever formally prepared to teach as part of their professional education' (p. 1). A personal account by a librarian at Lincoln Memorial University illustrates the apprehension often experienced by librarians who discover that classroom teaching is part of their job:

> When I looked out at the classroom full of students, I could not help but think that it was never my intention to teach [. . .] I've spent over six years of my career in technical services departments. My experience with reference and bibliographic instruction was limited.
> (Slavin and Mead, 2008: 1)

Thus, a strange kind of dichotomy appears to have emerged, between the acknowledgment and acceptance of the librarians' teaching role in the professional discourse, and the reality of the novice information professional who is somewhat bewildered to find themselves in a classroom or information skills laboratory, surrounded by expectant faces waiting to be taught. Although it is an unproven assertion, Davis (2007) refers to a 'general rejection of teaching roles among the ranks' (p. 81). She also suggests that this is not just the case for novice librarians; that many experienced information professionals 'have lamented the expansion of their duties into an active teaching role' (p. 78). Many librarians still tend to distinguish between the 'traditional' librarian role they expected to fulfil and the instructional duties they are required to. Douglas (1999) describes this phenomenon succinctly:

> I tell people that I am a librarian, but then I hastily add that I teach courses in computer applications [. . .] Teaching credit bearing computer courses is not what people expect librarians to do. Even

when I meet fellow librarians, they are surprised by my unusual position. (p. 25)

Davis's study of teacher anxiety in librarians (2007) revealed that just over one-third of respondents found that they had had to defend their teaching duties to other librarians at some point. Much has also been written about librarians who find themselves to be poorly equipped to deal with the teaching duties that they are required to fulfil (Walter, 2005, 2006; Liles, 2007). Walter (2005: 3) describes the knowledge and skills gap experienced by teaching librarians as 'mystifying', observing that it has remained a problem for more than three decades, without ever having been seriously addressed.

It is perhaps helpful, at this point, to distinguish the teaching librarian, as we conceptualise it here, from the quite specific role of the 'teacher librarian', 'school librarian,' or 'school library media specialist', which is defined as a person who 'holds recognised teaching qualifications and qualifications in librarianship' (ASLA Standards of Professional Excellence for Teacher Librarians, n.d.). The role of teacher-librarian is officially recognised and incumbents gain certification through fulfilling state or national training requirements. Very clear guidelines exist to explain how one may become a teacher-librarian and obtain certification; for instance, the route to teacher-librarian in the US is usually via a nationally recognised NCATE-AASL (National Council for the Accreditation of Teacher Education/American Association of School Librarians) reviewed and approved School Library Media Education Programme – it is a well-defined career path (AASL, 2003). However, outside of the school library setting, an equivalent career path does not appear to exist; rather, the teaching librarian is a construct which might be described more accurately as a 'librarian with diverse teaching responsibilities', akin to the ACRL definition referred to above; similarly, Julien and Pecoskie's study of librarians' teaching experiences refers to the participant population as 'library staff with instructional responsibilities' (2009: 150). Every librarian who facilitates learning in their institution most likely has a unique story to tell – about their work, their status in their library, relationships with their colleagues, the client-base they serve and the path which led them to that position.

Do we need to define 'teaching librarian'?

Why do we need to define the role at all? Colbeck (2008) suggests that labels are important, in the sense that they are inextricably tied up with role expectations: 'Role labels convey meanings and expectations for behaviour that have evolved from countless interactions among people in a social system' (p. 10). In their study of convergence and professional identity in academic libraries, Wilson and Halpin describe the frustration of librarians, who had acquired new job titles, such as 'learning adviser' and 'information officer', which were intended to reflect the professional identity associated with the new, hybrid library: 'it is generally felt that job titles do not communicate the extent of their skills and experience' (Wilson and Halpin, 2006: 88). So, role labels matter, both from the perspective of communication to outsiders and the sense of professional identity that a job title conveys.

In the absence of a defined role, there are a number of possible ways to describe a teaching librarian:

- **A librarian whose principal role is the facilitation of classroom-based or virtual learning support activities** – i.e. who spends the majority of their time involved in the planning, design, delivery, evaluation and promotion of information literacy instructional activities, and who is involved in other library services only to a minor degree, or not at all. Some librarians have job titles which reflect this responsibility – e.g. instructional librarian, information skills librarian.

- **A librarian who is actively engaged in learning support activities, of varying formats and durations, but who also performs other library services, such as circulation desk or reference, on a regular basis** – this is more reflective of the traditional 'jack-of-all-trades' library role, which sees librarians turn their hands to multiple library functions as required. It can also be a challenging position, which requires a considerable amount of juggling, as librarians attempt to reconcile the varying demands on their time (Walter, 2008).

- **Any working academic library professional in the twenty-first century** – Walter's study of teacher identity (2008) revealed that the librarians who were interviewed felt that the teaching function pervades every aspect of their work – that it is impossible to divorce their other library responsibilities from their instructional roles (p. 61). One view of academic librarianship is that it is inherently educative – that as the library exists to support the educational mission of the parent institution, it is natural for academic librarians to consider themselves to be educators, regardless of the changing nature of service provision. So, perhaps it is accurate to state that all academic librarians are, in fact, teaching librarians to one degree or another? With this in mind, Webb and Powis (2004) suggest that teaching and learning do not necessarily have to be rigidly defined: 'Learning is learning, wherever it happens; teaching is teaching, whoever does it. You just have to do it well' (p. 17).

The following section examines the arguments in favour of a teaching role for librarians.

Should librarians teach?

'When academic librarians are presenting in an educative environment, are they teaching, informing, or responding?' (Davis, 2007: 82). The question of whether librarians should teach – or whether the instruction they already provide can be classified as 'teaching' in the traditional sense – has also been a topic of debate among the profession. Not all commentators – or librarians – believe that librarians should have a teaching role. A number of arguments have been advanced which support the idea of the teaching librarian. Several of them are explored below.

Librarians 'get' information literacy

One argument in favour of a teaching role for librarians suggests that, as a profession, they are more attuned to the needs and requirements of the information society than any other group in the academic community, and are in a strong position of advocacy: 'To us [librarians] it is obvious that bibliographic instruction merits an important place in every college and university' (McCarthy, 1985: 142). It is true that librarians have been in the vanguard of the information literacy movement since the 1970s, and have propelled it forward with notable success, building a strong case for the necessity of information literacy in all walks of life – recently, October 2009 was declared National Information Literacy Awareness Month by the US President, Barack Obama, 'to recognize the important role information plays in our daily lives, and appreciate the need for a greater understanding of its impact' (White House, 2009). This represents a level of recognition that would have been unthinkable just a few years previously. However, despite the rising profile of information literacy, resistance from academics continues to be a strong theme: 'Librarians face a constant struggle to convince students and subject faculty that information skills are important and needed by students' (Fosmire and Macklin, 2002: 1). The argument suggests that if information literacy is to be integrated successfully into academic curricula, librarians are needed to proactively move the agenda forward and to convince faculty that it is crucial to embed instructional programmes where they are likely to be most effective (Orr et al., 2001).

Librarians understand how students really do research

According to this viewpoint, librarians' long years of experience at the reference desk, dealing with student queries and observing their difficulties, place them at an advantage when it comes to identifying instructional needs: 'Librarians have always been aware of the problems of information overload and the need to evaluate information according to a client's specific needs' (Estrin, 1998: 2). Abson (2003) suggests that academic librarians have developed a special insight into students' information-seeking and study patterns, as they observe students working in the library: 'not just the books on the reading list, but the ways they study – the group work, their presentations' (p. 14).

Allied to this is the long-held notion that academics have unrealistic expectations of students when it comes to doing research and that the assignments they set for students are frequently too complex, in terms of the knowledge of scholarly communication that is required to complete them. Leckie (1996) explores this notion more fully, claiming that the gap between academics' own experiences of research and the students' limited conceptions of the scholarly publication and dissemination process increases the degree of information anxiety experienced by students in completing assignments that have been designed by academics. The 'expert researcher' model described by Leckie portrays a system of shortcuts, honed by long years of research experience and networking, with a heavy reliance on personal contacts and citation trails, methods which are alien to the student researcher (p. 202). Ellis's widely cited model of the information behaviour of social scientists supports this image, emphasising the importance of informal contacts, browsing of known journals, and 'chaining', which involves following citations from one journal to another (Case, 2007: 260). McCarthy (1985) suggests that faculty do not perceive the value of the library in relation to student work, since they themselves tend not to rely on it as a prime resource for their own research: '[Academics] seldom use the library, except perhaps through browsing, to extend the sources of their information . . . they do not often use indexes, abstracting services or the library's subject catalogue' (p. 143). In this context, teaching librarians are seen to act as a bridge between the 'expert' and 'novice' researchers; while on the one hand, they can assist students in solving the problems set by the academics, they are also in a position to offer advice to the academics regarding the feasibility of their assignments.

Librarians have been teaching for decades anyway

'Librarians, of course, have always taught' (Wilkinson, 2000: 37). Although not recognised as a core library function until relatively recently, librarians have a long history of involvement in teaching, stretching back to at least the nineteenth century (Weiss, 2004), and the nature and form of that teaching has evolved alongside the information revolution. For instance, Dennis (2001) suggests that the evolution of library instruction from basic demonstration of bibliographic research tools to a broader conceptualisation of information use, involving the development of critical thinking and evaluation skills, has created an opportunity for librarians to become involved in developing inquiry-based exercises to foster information literacy in students (pp. 124–5). McCartin and Feid (2001) note that the traditional form of bibliographic instruction, defined as a limited form of 'tool-based' instruction, has been replaced with 'concept-based' instruction that emphasises processes and general research principles which can be transferred across different contexts. Douglas (1999) points out that librarians' technological expertise combined with years of experience makes teaching a natural occupation: 'We are expert technology users and we already teach in many capacities. So I believe that the librarian as professor is the next step in the evolution of the profession' (p. 26).

Librarians are trained information experts

'Librarians are uniquely situated to collaborate with academics to implement the information literacy agenda – they "live" the information problem solving process; they understand information organisation, access and use' (McLaren, 1999: 7). Although librarians do not usually have academic qualifications in the subject areas they manage, their role as generalists encompasses a broad knowledge of the structure of scholarly communication in specific disciplines, and they are well equipped to advise on appropriate information sources for a desired purpose: 'When asked to speak to a class that will shortly be doing term paper research, the reference librarian will probably think immediately of half a dozen basic sources important for research in the field' (McCarthy, 1985: 144). Rader (1997) observes that it is the librarians' lengthy experience with the organisation and use of information that has accorded them 'expert' status in this regard: 'Librarians' experience and expertise in the area of information handling position them uniquely to work with teachers and faculty in the nurturing of student learners so they become critical users of information' (p. 49).

Academics can't – or won't – teach information literacy

In the past, a small number of authors have suggested that *academics*, rather than librarians, should assume responsibility for teaching research and information skills to students (Lester, 1979; Smith, 1997). From one perspective, it might make sense; students' motivations and information behaviour are greatly influenced by academics, who set and grade assignments, develop reading lists for their courses, and communicate their expectations about how students should do research. Librarians' response to this, however, usually centres on the notion that academics have misguided and unrealistic perceptions of how students approach research tasks, a theme touched on earlier (Leckie, 1996): 'If faculty lack an understanding about the need to develop a progression from elementary to advanced research techniques, then librarians must work to reorient them' (Carlson and Miller, 1984: 489). Academics' own lack of expertise with the most up-to-date information resources is often touted as another reason for librarian involvement:

> The idea that lecturers should teach library skills seems impractical. Librarianship is a profession; those of us who practice it have years of training and experience behind us: why do we imagine that academic colleagues should add these skills to their own considerable experience when they seldom need or use them? (Price, 1999)

Moore (2002), writing about the school sector, speaks of the sometimes erroneous assumption that the teachers are themselves information literate, and that 'they apply higher order thinking skills when undertaking complex information tasks' (p. 8). She describes the results of a study carried out among 91 practising teachers in Australia by Henri (2001), which indicated comparatively poor IL practices among the participants and low confidence levels when confronted with non-traditional information tools. Other studies, such as Starkweather and Wallin's (1999) research into academics' attitudes to library technology, reveal a considerable lack of uniformity in their knowledge and use of resources. While some academics are sophisticated and forward-looking users of multimedia formats, others still prefer the traditional mode of print-based information-seeking. A study of academics' attitudes towards information literacy instruction in Ireland found that many academics believe that they *already* teach information literacy skills to students and that no additional instruction is necessary; there is a perception that simply through doing assignments, working collaboratively with other students and receiving feedback from their lecturers, students will indirectly develop as competent information users (McGuinness, 2006). Markless and Streatfield (1992) describe this belief as a 'common trap', suggesting that a lack of skill support, coupled with unclear course work guidelines, may in fact 'reinforce inappropriate or incorrect execution of the skill' (p. 23).

Complex new scholarship practices

Through the application of technology, scholarly publication and dissemination has changed radically over the past two decades. Now, new scholarship practices have changed the face of research and academic librarianship. Dillon (2008) outlines several of the changes that have been wrought:

- large data repositories in some disciplines;
- many students never visit a physical campus;
- libraries assume the role of publishers;
- tenure decisions 'loosened' from the traditional documentary formats;
- special collections become indistinguishable from museums;
- scholars working in remote teams, sharing server space;
- convergence between text, graphics, audio and video.

Biddiscombe (2000) suggests that librarians, who are at the centre of the changing scholarly paradigm, are best equipped to guide others through the problem-solving process in the new scholarly landscape: 'Librarians' training in the organisation of knowledge, matching of need with solution, and a positive and professional approach to the service ethic, provide essential elements that are important in the era of information technology' (p. 65).

Farber (1995) also asserts that it is the librarians' technological expertise, and willingness to impart these skills to students, that will lead academics to accept them as having a teaching role in the academic community: 'Because librarians are the ones to show their students how to gain access to these (technological) sources, and to demonstrate what they provide, academics are much more willing to accept librarians as teaching colleagues' (p. 432).

Teaching brings librarians closer to the heart of the institution

A common challenge for academic librarians is that they often appear to lack decision-making power and influence within their institutions, and have little or no say in educational and strategic policy-making: 'Librarians' sphere of influence may be limited in comparison with that of academic staff, and thus information literacy may be marginalised and trivialised' (Webber and Johnston, 2000: 384). In developing and promoting their teaching role, Kemp (2006) suggests that librarians can avail of a number of wider advantages in their institutions at large. In the first instance, teaching offers an opportunity for librarians to forge an improved client relationship with students, and to gain deeper insight into their information-seeking and research processes. This has the potential to develop into a symbiotic relationship, insofar as the students may come to see librarians as *educators*, as well as support staff, and to develop an appreciation for the library as a place where learning is facilitated, rather than a static collection of resources. Another potential benefit of the teaching role involves librarians' relationships with academic faculty. Kemp suggests that teaching is a form of academic apprenticeship for librarians, through which they can be socialised to the scholarly community; she observes that through their involvement in teaching and learning activities, librarians 'become sensitized to the issues important to teaching faculty' (p. 19), including administration, the demands of students, managing workloads and developing effective teaching strategies. Another suggestion by Kemp focuses on improvement of library service; she comments that librarians may choose to adapt their collection development policies, through first-hand observation of students' actual resource use. Finally, Kemp proposes that the teaching role serves to enhance librarians' faculty status, which is a long-held goal (Bryan, 2007). The ACRL, which has been extremely active in attempting to set guidelines and standards for the award to faculty status for librarians, views the educational role as key to gaining this status: 'the function of the librarian as participant in the processes of teaching and research is the essential criterion of faculty status' (2007a). Kemp suggests that, through engaging in teaching activities, librarians can gain increased recognition and respect from their academic colleagues and reap the benefits of equality of status.

Teaching librarians – what do academics think?

'Conflicts and tensions underlie the relationship between teaching faculty and academic librarians, between the desired recognition sought by the library and the limited role university administrators will have it play' (Owusu-Ansah, 2001: 282).

What academics think and believe about the teaching role of librarians is important. If librarians could facilitate student learning in a vacuum, *removed* from students' academic curricula, the issue of how they work and collaborate with academics would not be so crucial. However, the desirability of the curriculum-embedded model for information literacy instruction has meant that librarians need to find ways of forging productive, collaborative relationships with academics, to ensure that students see information skills as relevant and meaningful in the context of their education, and beyond. Curriculum-integrated instruction (CII) requires close, long-term collaboration between academics and teaching librarians. Articulations of 'best practice' in information literacy instruction routinely list academic–librarian collaboration as an essential criterion for success. One such list is the Final Report of the UK-based 'Big Blue' Information Skills project (Manchester Metropolitan University, 2002). The review of the literature which informed the project outlined a set of conditions deemed critical for success in the implementation of information literacy programmes, including:

- the need for information skills training to be integrated into the curriculum, rather than be treated as a separate subject removed from the subject content;

- the need to establish collaborative working partnerships with all those involved in the teaching and learning process;

- the need to engage students in the process through such means as highlighting the transferability and attractiveness of skills both to themselves and to future employers, or by making courses credit bearing;

- the need for library and information service staff to feel that they have a relevant role to play;

- information skills programmes can provide opportunities for staff training and development activities.

Holtze (in Kraat, 2005: 2) asserts that faculty–librarian collaboration is at the centre of CII: 'It all comes down to the relationship you have with other faculty at your institution.' The question of academic–librarian collaboration has dominated the discourse on information literacy instruction. From a practice-oriented perspective, recent research into the subjective experiences of teaching librarians in the US (Julien and Pecoskie, 2009) also demonstrates the extent to which librarians perceive that academic support is the most important factor, which determines whether their programmes will be effective or not: 'The faculty/librarian relationship is so critical that sometimes instructional "success" was defined by these study participants as successful faculty negotiation and relations, rather than in terms of students' learning.' (p. 151)

The 'faculty problem'

The 'faculty problem', as it has been described (McCarthy, 1985), is a common theme in the literature and has grown out of librarians' dependence on academics for access to subject curricula and their frustration when collaboration fails to happen. Evidence has shown that collaborative working arrangements are difficult to achieve in practice; as Donnelly (2000) points out, the likelihood that students will have the opportunity to develop their information and research skills during their education often depends on the efforts of individual staff members, or 'academic champions', and is largely a matter of chance: 'Most current campus information literacy or bibliographic instruction initiatives are hit or miss. By luck of the draw, some students participate in multiple library instructional sessions because they take courses from professors who value research skills, and who make time for in-class instruction by librarians' (p. 60). This dependence on 'academic champions'

(McGuinness, 2007) or 'library active faculty' (Hardesty, 1991) is unsustainable, however, since cooperative arrangements may collapse as the academic moves to a different institution, or finds that they no longer have time to devote to information literacy. Loomis (1995) suggests that such short-term collaborations often prove to be 'shaky foundations for our programs in terms of long-term planning, for they are *personality*, not program, dependent' (p. 130). So, while working with supportive, enthusiastic academics might offer a chance for librarians to gain a foothold within the academic curriculum, a longer-term collaborative strategy is required to ensure that information literacy becomes embedded in the curriculum.

Why do librarians need to work with academics, and what are the barriers that prevent them from doing so? The problem has been explored at length by LIS researchers and practitioners. Academics act as the 'gateway' to subject curricula for librarians, for a variety of reasons, and are the key to curriculum-embedded instruction. Some of the reasons are outlined below:

- Professional autonomy dictates that academics have control over their own teaching and learning environments (Hardesty, 1995; Jenkins, 2005), and are therefore in a position to create learning situations which encourage information-seeking as an element of problem-solving (Smith, 1997). As Chiste et al. (2000) note: 'Bibliographic instruction is unlikely to find itself ensconced in the academic curriculum without people in positions of power having a very good reason for wanting it there' (p. 204).

- In the context of their academic studies, students' information needs are, to a large extent, prompted by academics through the assignments they set and the expectations they raise regarding the time and effort a student should devote to course work. Students' information-seeking and research strategies are also dictated somewhat by their lecturers, who create expectations, and sometimes offer direction about how and where to search for information (Nimon, 2000; Haynes, 1996).

- Academics are responsible for grading students' assignments and determining the rewards of the system; generally speaking, the 'strategic student' tends to respond only to course requirements that are set by academic teaching staff, with the aim of getting a good grade, or even just passing the course (Nimon, 2000). Librarians who wish to evaluate the impact of their instruction must, therefore, work with academics on course assignments.

- The value that academics attach to library use and information skills can determine how important students subsequently perceive them to be; if an academic is enthusiastic about the library, and links library use to good academic performance, students may be more likely to visit the library than if left to their own devices (Lipow, 1992; Maynard, 1990).

- Librarians, as generalists, do not possess enough in-depth subject knowledge to be able to fully integrate information literacy into different subject curricula; therefore, they need to collaborate with academics and to blend their information expertise with the academics' subject knowledge to create curriculum-integrated programmes (Hepworth, 2000; Jobe and Grealy, 2000).

However, while the reasons for collaboration might seem clear, the task of actually engaging academics in joint teaching and learning partnerships has proved difficult; as Jenkins (2005) points out: 'Though . . . many are willing converts, collaborating with librarians is something faculty think about rarely and act on even less frequently' (p. 23). As a result of their frustration, librarians have frequently branded academics dismissive or apathetic, as research by Julien and Given (2003) has demonstrated; their analysis of librarians' postings on the ILI-L listserv revealed that librarians have a poor perception of their relationships with academics, suggesting that academics are difficult to work with and deliberately obstructive to their instructional endeavours. In the study, academics were perceived as being territorial and possessive about their courses, as well as being rude, uncooperative, arrogant and uncaring with regard to their students' needs. However, at the same time, a number of posters were critical of their library colleagues, suggesting that they are unwilling to embrace a wider role for themselves outside of the traditional library functions, or that they hold limiting perceptions of themselves, which reinforce those that are imposed on them from outside.

What do academics think?

Academics' attitudes to librarians, including their teaching role, have not been exhaustively investigated, but various studies over the years have offered some insight. Studies include research by Cook (1981); Divay et al. (1987); Oberg et al. (1989); Ivey (1994); Maynard (1990); Hardesty (1991); Cannon (1994); Thomas (1994); Dilmore (1996); Leckie and Fullerton (1999); and McGuinness (2006). A summary of the research reported in these papers reveals several themes:

- Academics generally think highly of librarians and value their work; they perceive them as professionals, although not as academic equals. The main reason for this is the librarians' lack of research publications and teaching experience.

- Librarians are valued by academics primarily for the support services they provide, including reference assistance, collection development and computer-mediated searching. Academics do not generally rate librarians' teaching activities as important.

- Most academics perceive that librarians make a limited contribution to students' overall education.

- There is some evidence that academics' perceptions of librarians' role and status in the academic community differ according to the discipline.

- On the whole, academics view information literacy as important to undergraduate education.

- However, the teaching methods that they employ to encourage the development of these skills among students often do not involve library staff in design or delivery. Comparatively few academics regularly invite librarians to give a talk to their students.

- The main reason that academics do not seek teaching assistance from librarians is that they are not aware that librarians can provide this type of service.

- Teaching approaches which require academic–librarian collaboration are viewed as less desirable by academics than methods which are delivered by librarians alone.

- Academics believe that 'we're already doing it!' when it comes to information literacy, and that students will develop information skills indirectly through completing course work, researching dissertations, taking advice from lecturers, collaborating with classmates, attending class and generally just in resolving information problems by themselves.

- Academics' perceptions of library service are influenced by the nature of their relationship with library staff. Frequent contact with librarians results in more positive perceptions of library service; equally, positive service perceptions lead to increased use of the library by academics.

Barriers to collaboration

The key to identifying the real barriers to academic–librarian collaboration lies in understanding the demands and attributes of the academic profession, as well as academics' attitudes towards the library and information literacy.

Hardesty (1995) and Jenkins (2005) suggest that a number of factors relating specifically to 'faculty culture' explain the difficulties other groups, including librarians, experience in attempting to forge collaboration with academics. Hardesty, in particular, identifies five attributes of 'faculty culture':

- *An emphasis on research, content and specialisation.* The primary occupation of academics is the pursuit, creation and dissemination of knowledge, and they are expected to spend the majority of their time engaged in research activities.

- *A de-emphasis on teaching, process and undergraduates.* In academia, teaching activity is not valued to the same extent as research accomplishments when it comes to recruitment and promotion.

- *The centrality of professional autonomy and academic freedom.* Academics expect to retain full control over their pedagogical practices and research directions

- *Lack of time.* Academics are typically overburdened with professional responsibilities ranging from heavy teaching loads to the pressure to publish that determines promotional opportunity and recognition from their peers in the field.

- *Resistance to change.* Academics are frequently perceived as hostile towards proposals that involve restructuring and redistribution of their time.

Jenkins (2005) also highlights other stressors in the lives of academics, including dealing with their administrative burden, balancing teaching and scholarship, and handling the demands of committee work, which can be numerous. All of these factors add up to a heavy, demanding workload, coupled with a need for and expectation of autonomy – a combination which can certainly militate against venturing into collaboration with librarians.

Recent research (McGuinness, 2004) explored faculty culture and academics' pedagogical practices as potential barriers to collaboration for curriculum-integrated information literacy. The findings of the study, which was carried out among Irish university-based academics in the disciplines of sociology and civil engineering, pointed to a number of additional factors that can act as obstacles to working together:

- Academics have a limited conception of 'information literacy', focusing on finding and locating information, or using information technology, at the expense of 'higher-order' perspectives, such as knowledge construction.

- Academics believe that it is the *students'* own responsibility, rather than that of teaching or library staff, to ensure that they develop information literacy skills during their education.

- Academics' interactions with library staff focus mainly on collection matters, such as acquisitions, inter-library loans and making course materials available to students, rather than on teaching and curriculum-related matters.

- Academics face many challenges when attempting to introduce innovative teaching methods, including logistical difficulties of managing large student numbers, overwhelming staff and student workloads, a belief among the academics that students will not respond positively to more interactive, independent modes of learning, and fears relating to students' trustworthiness, particularly with regard to matters such as plagiarism.

- Academics are locked into the traditional didactic, lecture-based mode of teaching in higher education, which does not encourage independent student activity and information-seeking, but rather assimilation and regurgitation of set content. Many academics try to 'package' course material for students, rather than encourage independent research.

Although many of these barriers seem insurmountable, there is much that teaching librarians can do to engage the support of academics and instil a culture of collaboration in their institutions, if none existed before. Strategies for outreach and promotion will be discussed later in this book.

Teaching librarians and professional education

'Instructional librarians find themselves thrown in at the deep end as they do not understand, or they lack knowledge of, the educational theories and methodologies that can be applied to information literacy instruction' (Selematsela and du Toit, 2007: 119).

It is unreasonable to expect librarians to engage in instructional activities without being properly trained; we would not expect a cataloguer to have no knowledge of metadata or a reference librarian to be unfamiliar with key reference sources. Yet, evidence has shown that this is precisely what has been happening for many years within the profession. Until relatively recently, the small number of core, or even elective, modules on pedagogical practice in many LIS professional programmes around the world has meant that librarians frequently have had to 'go it alone' when it comes to developing the skills and knowledge required to effectively facilitate teaching and learning (Walter, 2005, 2006; Peacock, 2000; Kilcullen, 1998). This is a cause for concern; as Peacock (2000) observes, while teaching might come naturally to some librarians, 'many are unprepared theoretically, technically, and practically for the role, and the experience can lead to frustration and prove detrimental to their self-esteem, confidence and enthusiasm' (p. 182).

The relatively low level of pre-service training opportunities for student librarians has been fairly well documented. Both Meulemans and Brown (2001) and Walter (2005) highlight studies as far back as the late 1970s, which suggest that it has been a gap in the LIS professional curriculum for quite some time. They refer to several surveys (Mandernack, 1990; Shonrock and Mulder, 1993; Sullivan, 1997; Westbrook, 1999) which show that librarians have been forced to 'turn to self-study, workshops and short courses . . . to meet their needs for continuing professional education' (Walter, 2005: 3). In the UK, the issue of 'who trains librarians in their role as trainers' was also addressed in the Big Blue Information Skills project (Manchester Metropolitan University, 2002). As part of their nationwide survey of information skills practices in the higher education and post-16 sectors, the project group included a brief survey of LIS schools across the country to establish the extent to which undergraduate and postgraduate LIS students received training, in order 'to prepare them for their future role as trainers'. The results of the survey, which was based on responses received from 17 LIS schools, indicated that although most students receive *some* degree of training with regard to general learning styles, presentation and communication skills, only one of the schools included teaching methods and curriculum design in their course content. A survey of information literacy practices in higher education institutions carried out in Ireland in 2007 found that just 11 of the 77 academic librarian respondents had received instructional training as part of their pre-service professional LIS programme; one-third had received no training at all in how to teach (McGuinness, 2009). Research carried out in 2007 across the entire LIS sector in the UK found a similar pattern – out of 463 responses, 59 per cent of the librarians across all sectors confirmed that they had received teacher training 'on the job', while just 31 per cent had done either an accredited or non-accredited course. Significantly, 72 per cent revealed that they had developed their teaching competence through 'trial and error' (Conroy and Boden, 2007).

While self-study, short courses and intensive workshops can be effective ways of developing and honing instructional skills, Meulemans and Brown (2001) suggest that many librarians who have been self-taught 'would have preferred to have more opportunities for course work and practice in teaching during their graduate education' (p. 256). Acquiring a basic grounding in the theories and methods of teaching and learning offers fledgling librarians in their first jobs a distinct advantage over those who find themselves in at the deep end and struggling to catch up.

More recently, however, there have been signs of change. Walter (2008) suggests that the availability of formal course work on instruction in LIS pre-service curricula is now 'inconsistent' rather than lacking entirely (p. 57). Many LIS schools in the US now offer instruction-related modules – a frequently updated list of full library instruction courses that are available in accredited master's programmes in library and information studies is maintained in wiki form by the Instruction Section of the ACRL.[1] In Europe, a survey carried out among LIS schools in June 2005, under the auspices of the project 'Library and Information Science Education in Europe: Joint Curriculum Development and Bologna Perspectives',[2] showed that 'information literacy and learning' was covered in the curriculum in 76 per cent (n = 38) of the LIS schools surveyed (n = 50), although it was included as a *core* component in just 45 per cent (n = 21) (Larsen, 2005). It is unclear, however, how much of this referred to specific content on instructional planning and design.

The desirability of flexible, on-the-job learning options for librarians has also been recognised in two relatively recent instructional initiatives in the UK – both 'SirLearnaLot' and 'Pop-i/Lollipop' comprise suites of freely available online modules, designed to teach librarians in the public and academic library sectors how to design, deliver and assess information literacy programmes in their institutions. In the case of SirLearnaLot, which was funded by the Higher Education Academy Subject Centre for Information & Computer Sciences (HEA ICS), and the information literacy section of the Community Services Group in CILIP, the eight units focus on areas such as 'Understanding Learning', 'Planning a Learning Event' and 'Delivering a Learning Event'. The course is delivered via the learning management system 'Moodle', and institutions can download the files and deliver the course themselves, as all are freely available under Creative Commons Licence. The online instructional model could represent a real solution for teaching librarians who wish to develop or upgrade their instructional skills and continue to carry out their jobs.

What should be included in LIS instructional modules?

The conference arising from the European curriculum project described above was held in August 2005. Members of the Information Literacy and Learning Group gathered to discuss and debate the kind of instructional content that could be included in LIS curricula. The group proposed that it is essential for LIS students:

- to be aware of information literacy as a concept;
- to become information literate themselves;
- to learn about some key aspects of teaching information literacy (Kajberg and Lørring, 2005: 67).

In essence, there are two key elements that come into play when a teaching role of the librarian is considered – one concerns the librarian's *own* personal development and level of confidence as an information-literate individual; the second relates to their ability to conceptualise the learning process and engage the appropriate strategies and methods to facilitate student learning. In many ways, this mirrors the expectations that are laid upon academics, who must demonstrate a high level of subject expertise *in addition to* teaching competence, to be able to deliver a course effectively. It can be an erroneous assumption that LIS students are skilled information users, although it is a common one; as is pointed out in the report by Kajberg and Lørring, 'LIS students need to understand *themselves* as information literate people, and understand IL holistically, before they can start teaching someone else about it' (2005: 68). How to incorporate both elements into a single module in the LIS curriculum, in light of time restrictions, is a challenge.

Walter (2008) also highlights the importance of focusing on the development of the pre-service librarian's professional identity as a teacher, rather than just on the mechanistic, pedagogical skills that underpin the teaching and learning process; he notes that 'how one thinks of oneself as a teacher can affect everything from successful induction into the profession to effectiveness in the classroom to the ability to cope with change and to implement new practices in one's instructional work'

(p. 55). The notion of *professional identity development* has been generally neglected in pre-service teaching modules for librarians, while curriculum content has tended to address issues such as instructional design, presentation techniques and design of evaluation instruments.

In terms of what could ideally be included in an instructional module within the LIS curriculum, the European group reached consensus on a set of relevant topics, which they divided into four categories, each with a number of sub-topics (pp. 71–2):

- **curriculum design and planning:** identifying learners' needs, developing learning outcomes, assessing learning outcomes, alignment of teaching, learning and assessment, use of technology in learning environments, course evaluation;

- **understanding learners and learning theory:** models and theories of learning, different learning styles, needs and characteristics of student groups, information behaviour research;

- **understanding basic concepts, theories and practice of teaching:** concepts of and approaches to teaching, methods, tools, collaborative learning;

- **understanding the context for teaching and learning:** educational policy, lifelong learning, teaching in different sectors, the role of information literacy in LIS profession, role of the teaching librarian, promotion and advocacy for information literacy.

From a general perspective, there is a wide range of opinion, regarding both the competencies required by teaching librarians and the content that could be included in the LIS curriculum to prepare librarians as teachers. Two early studies (Shonrock and Mulder, 1993; Larson and Meltzer, 1987), which attempted to identify required competencies for teaching librarians, are mentioned by Walter (2008). He notes that the competencies rated most highly in the Shonrock and Mulder study 'relate to principles of instructional design, pedagogical skills and basic instruction in information retrieval' (p. 58). These were similar to findings in the Larson and Meltzer study. More recently, several authors and groups have attempted to create competency and curriculum frameworks, including Kilcullen (1998), Peacock (2001), Selematsela and du Toit (2007), ACRL (2008) and the European consultation group described above (2005). In particular, the *ACRL Standards for Proficiencies for Instruction Librarians and Coordinators* (2008) is a detailed document, the outcome of four years of consultation by the ACRL Instruction Section Proficiencies for Instruction Librarians Task Force. It constitutes the first official set of guidelines on competencies for teaching librarians and 'can be used as standards to create professional development opportunities for librarians with teaching responsibilities in order to improve or expand their skills' (p. 4), in a similar manner to the *Information Literacy Competency Standards for Higher Education* (ACRL, 2000), which are used for IL programme planning.

Having collated and compared the guidelines proposed by the different authors, it is possible to categorise the skills and competencies under three broad headings:

1. pedagogical/andragogical adult learning knowledge and skills and instructional design;
2. political and strategic skills;
3. professional development and competency.

Below each category are listed areas of competence which could form the basis for a teaching module in LIS curricula. However, due to time and resource restrictions, it is likely that not all of the competencies can be included in a single module.

1. **Pedagogical/andragogical knowledge skills and instructional design**
   - theories of learning (e.g. behaviourism, constructivism);
   - different learning styles;
   - understanding of, and ability to gather information on, the characteristics of different student groups, including adult learners;
   - identifying the instructional needs of different student groups;
   - composing instructional goals, objectives and learning outcomes;
   - knowledge of different teaching approaches, methods and tools, various media;
   - knowledge of when and how to use technology appropriately for teaching; skills in using various e-learning technologies;
   - assessment and evaluation techniques and tools, aligning assessment to learning outcomes and teaching approaches;
   - ability to facilitate collaborative learning;
   - presentation and delivery skills, using visual media, etc.

2. **Political and strategic skills**
   - communication skills, including negotiation, conflict resolution, leading discussions;

- promotional skills – advocacy for information literacy, promoting instruction to academics and students, initiating collaboration with academics, representation at local, national and international level;

- leadership – proactively seeking out instructional opportunities, instigating discussion and debate with colleagues.

3. **Professional development and competency**

- understanding and development of oneself as an information-literate individual;

- knowledge and understanding of theories of human information behaviour (HIB);

- keeping current within relevant subject areas;

- participation in continuing professional development activities to keep skills fresh;

- engaging in reflective practice, understanding oneself as a teacher;

- understanding the wider context of teaching and learning – lifelong learning, educational and public policy, etc.;

- understanding one's own role (and the role of the library) in the educational process.

How these topics might be included and taught within a pre-service teaching librarian module is discussed in Chapter 3.

Exercises and reflections

Exercises can be carried out individually or, better still, in groups:

1. Develop a fictional timeline for a typical day in the working life of an academic teaching librarian. What kinds of problems and stress-points do you believe could arise during the day? Discuss ways in which a teaching librarian can meet the challenges of the day.

2. Identify and discuss the attributes of a 'teaching librarian' using the following headings: **Key duties of role; Skills and knowledge required to fulfil the role; Pre-service training needs; Appropriate criteria for advancement/promotion.** With regard to the skills and knowledge elements, rank your list according to which skills/knowledge you believe are most important for the role and which are of lesser importance.

3. **Scenario 1:** Your library is currently advertising the position of Instruction Librarian, which has opened up recently in your institution. Your task is to write the advert that will appear in national newspapers and professional journals and websites. Naturally, you wish to recruit the best candidate for the position. What criteria should the job advert specify?

4. **Scenario 2:** You (or your group) constitute an interview committee for the position of 'Instructional Librarian' that has opened up in your library. You task is to develop an interview schedule with the questions you believe should be asked in order to identify the best candidate for the job.

5. **Scenario 3:** In your library, you have been invited to create a 10-minute promotional video, the purpose of which is to 'sell' your instructional services to academics and students. Your task is to create an initial 'storyboard' for the video. What are the key messages that you should try to get across, and what kinds of visual images would help you to do it?

Notes

1. *http://wikis.ala.org/acrl/index.php/IS/Library_Instruction_Courses.*
2. *http://www.db.dk/LIS-EU/project.asp.*

Teaching librarians: 10 concepts shaping the role

Abstract: This chapter explores and discusses 10 key trends and concepts that are currently influencing the shape and future development of the teaching role in academic libraries. The 10 concepts described are: developing a teacher identity; reflective practice; developing a personal teaching philosophy and knowledge base; the virtual learning environment (VLE); teaching a diverse student base; information literacy for graduate students and researchers; instructional training for librarians; action research in practice; reinvigorated strategies for collaboration; and advocacy.

Key words: reflective practice, virtual learning environment, student diversity, action research, advocacy, collaboration.

While the unstoppable march of technology is the dominant factor influencing the evolution of the teaching librarian role, librarians should also be aware of other phenomena which are shaping and moulding instruction in libraries. This chapter examines 10 emerging concepts which are determining the direction of teaching and learning in the academic library setting.

Developing a 'teacher identity'

'Once an individual has accepted and internalised expectations for a role as part of his or her identity, that identity becomes a cognitive framework for interpreting new experiences' (Colbeck, 2008: 10).

In Chapter 1, we observed that 'teaching librarian' remains a varied and subjective role that defies a 'one-size-fits-all' description and is heavily influenced by the tremendous changes occurring within the profession and society at large; however, it was also noted that it is important for a professional who is currently filling that role to develop a clear sense of purpose, an understanding of how the role fits with other information work, and feelings of competence and confidence in order to perform effectively. To teach well, librarians benefit from constructing a personal 'teacher identity', which could best be described as an individual framework of beliefs, values and attitudes that offer a context for evaluating and developing your instructional work. Not having such a framework can have a negative effect. As Walter states, 'Lack of a consistent teacher identity among academic librarians may hinder their effectiveness in meeting these expanding instructional responsibilities in a changing organisational environment' (2008: 65). It is also important to try to resolve any conflict between the 'teaching' and 'librarianship' roles, where it exists – Colbeck suggests that 'when two identities with contrasting meanings and expectations are activated at the same time, an individual is likely to experience stress' (2008: 10).

So, is fostering a teacher identity among librarians essential, or does it really make a difference? There are a number of strong arguments in favour of encouraging teaching librarians to think about what their role means:

- *Confidence.* Librarians who are clear about their sense of purpose, and who experience no conflict or ambiguity about their role, are more likely to feel positive about their job performance and their ability to handle the tasks required of them.

- *Motivation.* Librarians who have a strong sense of what their role entails, as well as the degree to which their efforts support student learning and serve the needs of society at large, are more driven to develop goals and learning objectives and to deliver programmes which align with the overall educational mission of their institutions and which are satisfying on a personal level.

- *Communication with outsiders.* Librarians who have the ability to clearly and unambiguously describe what they do and the contribution that they make are better prepared to identify shared goals and common concerns with outside parties, such as academics, and to suggest collaborative arrangements which are of benefit to both sides. They are also more adept at marketing and promoting their services to potential users.

- *Professional identity.* A stronger image of the instructional role in librarianship contributes to the reshaping and clarification of the overall identity of the profession, which is undergoing significant changes in the light of the technological revolution and users' changing information habits and preferences.

- *Identification of training needs.* A greater understanding of the day-to-day experience of being a teaching librarian helps to highlight the challenges of the role and to identify areas in which training is most needed, at both pre-service and in-service level.

The daily experiences of teaching librarians are only partly understood. To date, there has been very little research into librarians' 'teacher identity', and the general conceptualisation of the role is largely shaped through anecdotal evidence or expert analysis and predictions about the 'future of the librarian'. However, two very recent empirical studies offer welcome insights into the perceptions and subjective experiences of teaching librarians in practice. Walter's study (2008) analysed the interview testimony of six academic librarians who were heavily involved in instruction in their institutions, while Julien and Pecoskie's research (2009) engaged a wider sample of 48 librarians, who participated in semi-structured interviews. In both studies, the findings show that the teaching librarian's experience can be rewarding, although equally challenging and frequently stressful.

The first, Walter's study (2008), discovered five key themes which ran through the experiences of the librarians who were interviewed. These themes are likely to be familiar to practising librarians, who undoubtedly experience the same challenges and rewards:

- *The centrality of teaching.* The librarians explained how their teaching role tended to flow into everything else they did – they saw themselves as 'always teaching' and had accepted their jobs because of the teaching opportunities attached to the posts.

- *The importance of collegial and administrative support.* The librarians emphasised the importance of supportive colleagues and supervisors who allowed them to pursue their teaching duties unobstructed.

- *The stress of multiple demands.* All of the librarians experienced personal stress due to competing demands on their time – they worried that they were unable to give 100 per cent to each task and felt conflicted with regard to their various responsibilities.

- *Deficiencies in professional education.* As we observed in Chapter 1, this is a widespread problem. The librarians in the study felt unprepared for their teaching work, as they had not received sufficient training in pre-service education.

- *Stereotypes and misperceptions.* The librarians spoke of a feeling that those outside the profession do not understand or appreciate the role and function of libraries, and that the traditional librarian stereotype does not include the teaching aspect. This was personally frustrating for them.

Julien and Pecoskie (2009) found that the librarians in their study were wholly preoccupied by their relationships with the *academics* in their institutions, rather than the mechanics of teaching or their own information skills: 'the faculty/librarian relationship is so critical that sometimes instructional success was defined ... as successful faculty negotiation and relations, rather than in terms of students' learning' (2009: 151). Their research points to three major themes which characterise this relationship:

- *The 'gift of time'.* The librarians spoke of a sense of *dependence* on the academics, who had the power to grant or to refuse them the 'gift of time' of a slot in their modules to teach information literacy. Access to the curriculum for the librarians is entirely dependent on the academics' attitudes and 'generosity'.

- *Deference to academics.* This theme was revealed through the librarians' use of language when describing their relationships with the academics. They seemed hesitant, using terms like 'sort of' and 'kind of' when referring to their involvement with the academic curricula, and appeared overly grateful for any support received.

- *Incidences of disrespect.* Several incidents recounted by the librarians pointed to difficult and unequal power relationships between the two parties – the librarians testified to feeling exploited and 'used' by the academics in some situations. They felt marginalised, unappreciated and frustrated by the lack of recognition.

While these studies represent the first systematic forays into the subjective world of the teaching librarian, they offer an initial, although limited, framework for exploring and understanding the role. As the teaching role expands, it will become ever more crucial to deepen this sense of identity. Understanding how professional identity is constituted is a necessary first step. In writing about school teachers, Beijaard (1995) conceptualises traditional teacher identity through the intersection of three distinct categories, namely:

1. the subject one teaches;
2. the relationship with students;
3. the teacher's role and role conception.

For teaching librarians, the complexity is increased by the multidisciplinary nature of the work, the inconsistency of the teaching schedule itself and the underlying need to 'prove' oneself as a bona fide teacher. The process of identity formation has largely been neglected in pre-service LIS education. Reflective practice, discussed below, offers a means for exploring these issues further. Other means of identity construction will be discussed later in this book.

Reflective practice

'If we are going to address the issues of librarians' roles within educational endeavours systematically, we, as a discipline, need to foster reflective, creative, critical habits of mind regarding pedagogical praxis within ourselves, our libraries and our campuses' (Jacobs, 2008: 256).

In Chapter 1, the dual elements of becoming a teaching librarian were described – namely, the importance of understanding and developing one's *own* information-literate identity, as well as the pedagogical skills and knowledge required to foster an IL identity in students. Despite their training as information professionals, many librarians lack confidence in their own information expertise and wonder how they can possibly be qualified to instruct students in this area. Focusing on the tools and mechanics of teaching is unlikely to resolve any confusion they are feeling about their instructional role: 'Simple mastery of basic instructional competencies [. . .] will not help librarians to develop the sort of teacher identity that research in teacher education suggests is important to their ongoing professional development' (Walter, 2008: 60). This is echoed by Jacobs (2008: 257), who suggests that, unless the pedagogical skills and knowledge gained 'are used in relevant ways, and developed in reflective, creative environments', they may not help librarians feel any more prepared for the teaching they have to do. Teaching librarians, Jacobs argues, should also develop an understanding of pedagogical theory, as well as the broader educational objectives in their institutions in order to contextualise their work more effectively and provide a greater sense of purpose.

The desirability of a holistic approach to one's work as a librarian, not just as a teaching librarian, is a topic of increasing interest to the information professions – looking inwards, as well as outwards, is now viewed as a critical component of professional development. Several recent publications have called for those involved in the information professions to construct a 'theoretically informed praxis' to inform the work of the profession (Elmborg, 2006; Jacobs, 2008). As a result of this recognition, 'reflective practice' is a theme which features more and more in the library discourse, especially in relation to teaching (Thomas et al., 2004; Grant, 2007; Jacobs, 2008). Borrowed from the field of education, reflective practice 'involves thoughtfully considering one's own experiences in applying knowledge to practice while being coached by professionals in the discipline', and has a long history in both pre-service and in-service teacher training (Ferraro, 2000).

Andrew Pollard (2008), who has written extensively about reflective teaching in the school context, notes that the concept derives from the work of Dewey in the 1930s, who described the difference between 'routine action' and 'reflective action'; while the first tends to be static and guided by tradition and habit, the latter 'involves a willingness to engage in constant self-appraisal and development [and] implies flexibility, rigorous analysis and social awareness' (p. 14). The term itself was defined by Schön in the 1980s, and the concept was developed more fully; Baker (in Thomas et al., 2004) articulates Schön's idea of reflective practice as a 'way of being professional that looks much more like artistry than science' (p. 2). Defined in this way, reflective practice encompasses a rolling, continuous process of self-questioning and observation, framed by an honest awareness of how one deals with the daily anomalies that crop up in teaching. Pollard (2008) describes teaching as a series of frequent dilemmas, requiring the execution of judgement on the teacher's part. He explores the possibilities of using *evidence* to resolve such dilemmas, suggesting that 'a practical problem in the classroom can helpfully be considered in terms of the issues that might underlie it' (p. 10). For the teaching librarian, dilemmas can arise in a number of distinct dimensions, which are not quite the same as those faced by school teachers:

- *Teacher identity.* Do librarians teach? Should *I* teach? What qualifies me to teach? Am I competent to teach?

- *Personal information literacy.* How can I develop others as information-literate individuals, if I am uncertain about my own information literacy skills? Should I bluff? Will the students find me out?

- *Classroom skills.* How do I handle unexpected or awkward situations which arise in my classes? How do I make information literacy relevant to today's students? Do they care?

The tools of reflective practice, such as teaching portfolios, when adopted wholeheartedly, offer the means for teaching librarians to learn how to resolve dilemmas more effectively. These will be explored in Chapter 5.

Developing a personal teaching philosophy and pedagogical knowledge base

According to Liles (2007), effective teaching does not derive from individual mastery of methods and tools, but is based instead on an 'understanding of how learners learn' (p. 116). *How* the student learns determines everything that a teacher must do to facilitate and foster this learning; absolutely everything flows from this basic understanding. Biggs and Tang (2007) describe this as a 'student-centred model of teaching', which focuses on what the *student*, rather than the teacher, does and whether the intended learning outcomes are achieved (p. 19). So, while teaching librarians might be, and often are, tempted to measure their teaching competence in terms of the methods and tools they have mastered, unless their use is accompanied by a solid understanding of how *learning* occurs, they only tell part of the story. The key message must always be: *start with the student.*

This is a crucial observation. Liles (2007: 116) suggests that teaching librarians should reflect on three key questions to provide a basis for their instruction, namely:

- *What is learning?*
- *How do humans learn?*
- *How do we know when someone has learned something?*

Biggs and Tang (2007) also recommend a period of personal reflection on one's *own* teaching and learning philosophies, in order to uncover beliefs and attitudes that may be subconscious, but which have the potential to influence all instructional decision-making. They suggest that a teacher should simply ask themselves '*What is learning?*' and '*What is teaching?*' Bruce et al. (2006) propose that teaching librarians should also ask themselves '*How is information literacy seen in your context?*' as the variation in perception can also differ widely here.

What do librarians believe and understand about teaching and learning? Is it possible to identify a common conceptual framework? This question has been explored by a number of authors. In 1999, Leckie and Fullerton compared the different 'pedagogical discourses' of academics and librarians as one means of explaining the role misconceptions that exist between them. Through analysing the literature relating to academic librarianship and information literacy, they identified five dominant librarian pedagogical discourses, which they suggest represent the differing perceptions of IL instruction held by librarians. Each discourse heavily influences the teaching approaches employed by its adherents. The discourses are described as follows. Readers of this book should examine their own beliefs and conceptions about pedagogy in the light of the authors' frameworks:

1. *Pedagogy as disciplinary integrity* – the importance of teaching the 'core concepts' of information literacy. Focuses on librarians' beliefs about what 'should' be taught.

2. *Pedagogy as meeting users' needs* – the responsibility of librarians to discover their users' instructional needs and knowledge or skills gaps, and to teach accordingly, rather than attempt to predict what those needs might be.

3. *Pedagogy as generic skills* – the responsibility of librarians to teach generic skills for lifelong learning, e.g. critical thinking, research.

4. *Pedagogy as efficiency* – the notion that information literacy instruction is a more efficient means of dealing with repeat queries and problems that arise among library users.

5. *Pedagogy as peer status* – the belief that librarians teach in order to attain equal status to their academic colleagues.

While some of these conceptions might still persist, it is likely that they have evolved over time, as the student body and instructional approaches have changed. Seven years later, Bruce et al. (2006) proposed their 'Six Frames for Information Literacy Education' model as a framework for interpreting and understanding the different ways in which individuals perceive information literacy, learning and teaching. The six frames were developed as a 'conceptual tool to help participants in the IL education arena to reflect on, and analyse, the varying implicit or explicit theoretical influences on their contexts' (p. 3). Each frame represents a different view of teaching and learning, information, content and assessment:

1. *The Content Frame* – similar to the disciplinary integrity discourse above, the focus is on *what* students need to know about information literacy and has a discipline orientation.

2. *The Competency Frame* – here, the focus is on what students should be able to *do* as a result of instruction and the level of skill they should attain.

3. *The Learning to Learn Frame* – focuses on the question of what it means to think like an information-literate professional and how information processes can be applied to problem-solving.

4. *The Personal Relevance Frame* – focuses on learners' conceptions about what information literacy can do for them and relates to motivation and personal meaning.

5. *The Social Impact Frame* – focuses on the question of how information literacy impacts on society and how it can help to solve problems.

6. *The Relational Frame* – focuses on helping learners to conceive of information literacy in more powerful and complex ways.

Bruce et al. observe that the aim of teaching librarians should be to help students in 'developing new and more complex ways of experiencing information literacy' and should focus on both content and process (2006: 6).

Although not aimed specifically at librarians, Biggs and Tang's 'levels of thinking about teaching' constitutes another framework for interpretation (2007). However, they suggest that, rather than categorising the differing views held by individual teachers, each level represents a point in the evolution of *all* teachers' thinking and practice, moving from a relatively limited viewpoint to a more balanced one, which happens over the course of a career:

1. *Level 1 Focus: What the student is.* This way of thinking about pedagogy places the responsibility for learning firmly on the *students*; teachers who think this way believe that there are 'good students' and 'poor students' and engagement with learning activities depends on the choices, motivations and inherent abilities of individuals. As such, teachers see their own role as transmitting information, rather than 'facilitating learning'. A student's failure to learn is perceived as a lack of motivation or ability, rather than a problem in the learning environment.

2. *Level 2 Focus: What the teacher does.* This conception focuses on the skills and competence of the teacher – the responsibility for whether learning takes place depends on what the teacher *does* in the classroom to facilitate this learning. Similar to above, therefore, there are 'good teachers' and 'poor teachers' and those who have a larger and more

varied portfolio of instructional tools and methods are often perceived as more competent.

3. *Level 3: What the student does.* In this framework, the focus is on the student's engagement with learning activities, their *understanding* of concepts and achievement of learning outcomes. This is a wholly student-centred view of pedagogy – learning is not viewed as solely the responsibility of student or teacher, or as transmission of content, but rather the creation of appropriate learning activities designed with regard to specific learning outcomes.

As teaching librarians, you can use these frameworks to enhance your understanding of your *own* pedagogical conceptions and beliefs. They are not definitive, but offer a basis for contemplation. Understanding basic pedagogical philosophy is a first step in developing a sense of oneself as an effective teacher that should not be skated over.

The virtual learning environment

There is widespread consensus in the literature and amongst the profession that the role and function of libraries has changed radically, and that the chief driver of this change has been technology (Biddiscombe, 2000; Wilson and Halpin, 2006). The digital revolution has the potential to change the way in which learning is facilitated, but the pedagogical uses and applications of technology are still being debated. The increasing popularity of social networking applications in recent years has opened up yet more possibilities within the field of education. At the same time, the danger of appropriating 'technology for technology's sake' is stressed by some authors; for example, Grassian and Kaplowitz (2009) warn against adopting new technologies 'without careful consideration of why we would want to use them for ILI and how they may or may not enhance teaching and learning' (p. 294). No matter what methods you use, the message is always the same – *Start with the Student.* In their book, Webb and Powis deliberately decline to differentiate face-to-face teaching from e-learning, as they believe that 'the principles of good teaching apply as much in the virtual arena as they do in the physical classroom' (2004: 118). Advocates of e-learning tools stress their potential for enhancing and deepening students' learning experience, freeing the learning experience from the restrictions of time and location, increasing active engagement and motivation through the implementation of novel learning activities (e.g. wikis, blogs, chat), and serving as a strategic means for librarians to improve and consolidate their educational role in their institutions (Roes, 2001; Mackey and Jacobson, 2008: 83). A key development, originating in the 1990s, has been the evolution and integration of virtual learning environments (VLEs), defined by Stiles (2000) as web-based systems which are 'designed to act as a focus for students' learning activities and their management and facilitation, along with the provision of content and resources required to help make the activities successful'. Well-known VLEs include Blackboard and Moodle. To date, much of the discussion surrounding the relationship between VLEs and libraries has focused on how library and information services can be effectively integrated with virtual classrooms, rather than on how librarians can use them for information literacy instruction. Masson (2009) highlights several of the benefits to library users with respect to VLE library integrations; they include increased awareness of available resources and services, simplification of the user experience, and improved relationships between academics and librarians (p. 220).

However, the teaching librarian's role involves a much deeper examination of the potential for VLEs, which reaches beyond the question of resource integration. Roes (2001) suggests that library involvement in educational innovation has already resulted in the creation of new jobs, such as *academic technology specialist*, a 'hybrid function, combining library and ICT expertise' (p. 7). Such a role requires a combination of skills and knowledge that has not traditionally been included in pre-service library training, including mastery of e-learning tools, and more importantly, understanding of how learning can be facilitated more effectively in the virtual environment.

Stiles (2000) outlines the most serious missteps that hamper effective learning in VLEs:

- a failure to engage the learner;
- mistaking 'interactivity' for engagement;
- focusing on content rather than outcomes;
- mirroring traditional didactic approaches on the technology (p. 3).

All of these errors point to instruction that is planned and delivered without reference to the basic principles of learning; they also warn against simply transferring traditional teaching approaches, such as lectures, into the virtual system – for example, merely uploading PowerPoint slides, class notes and other static pieces of content. However, others describe a strategy in which the VLE is actually used to *free up* face-to-face classroom time for interactive learning activities; Briggs and

Skidmore (2008) refer to the 'classroom flip' (also known as the 'inverted classroom'), which involves 'moving everything possible from a standard lecture course into the online setting [whereby] class time would be freed up for revision, practice and more active and deeper learning' (p. 96). This approach subtly endorses the importance of social learning and the personal touch in learning situations, which some feel are lacking in the online environment (Stiles, 2000).

For teaching librarians, technology is important for two reasons:

1. *It's part of **what we teach***. Information literacy, which is what we ultimately wish to foster in our students, is inextricably linked with information technology. While early commentators took pains to distinguish between information literacy and computer literacy, it is now virtually impossible 'to develop one set of skills without the other' (Mackey and Jacobson, 2008: xvi). If teaching librarians are to reach their teaching goals, we must accept ICTs as inherent to our educational mission – as part of the 'content' of our programmes. This is **technology *in* learning**, and requires us to develop a good awareness and understanding of the IT skills and knowledge that students need to acquire to function effectively in the modern information environment.

2. *It's part of **how we teach***. Technology, when applied in accordance with sound learning principles, can be used to enhance and revitalise the learning experience and improve the effective use of digital resources, and the potential for creating interactive learning opportunities for students is exciting. This is **technology *for* learning**, and requires us to develop our own knowledge and mastery of e-learning tools, coupled with an awareness and understanding of learning theories and styles.

Teaching a diverse student base

'Today's undergraduates are a diverse group of people from a wide range of ages, cultures, languages and socio-economic backgrounds. This diversity calls for a variety of instructional strategies that apply a range of contemporary learning theories' (McCartin and Feid, 2001: 25)

Much is now written about the increasing diversity of the academic student body (McCartin and Feid, 2001; Grassian and Kaplowitz, 2009: 247; Biggs and Tang, 2007). Librarians, especially teaching librarians, are cautioned against imposing a singular model of teaching and learning which may suit some students, but not others. The tendency, in Western nations, has been to focus pedagogically on what we know as the 'traditional' student, described by Gold (2005) as arriving on campus 'at age 18 with a carload of sophisticated technology and supportive family members eager to see their son or daughter take the first transitional steps toward independence' (p. 467). The image of the young student, making the difficult transition from second-level to higher education, dominates discussions of how best to facilitate learning at this level, and assumptions about their motivation and abilities, positive and negative, heavily influence the instructional approaches that are used.

What are our assumptions and beliefs about the traditional student body? Teaching librarians should examine their own perceptions and beliefs about traditional undergraduates. They might include, amongst others, a conceptualisation of the typical student as:

- young, aged between 17 and 19;
- directly transitioning from second-level education, sometimes with a 'gap year' in between;
- accustomed to didactic, highly directive teaching and rote learning;
- exam-focused, having completed public examinations to gain entry to higher education;
- technologically savvy, having grown up in the age of the Internet, but mainly use ICTs for leisure;
- strategic learners, extrinsically motivated by the desire to 'pass' or fulfil the instructor's expectations;
- reluctant to engage in active learning, preferring to receive 'packaged' course material;
- highly sociable, and focused on networks of friends;
- comparatively free of responsibilities, other than their studies, and perhaps part-time work;
- viewing higher education as an opportunity to become involved in many extra-curricular and social and sporting activities.

A general consensus has been that young undergraduates require a stimulating, sensory learning experience, where instructors 'break material into modules, maintain a brisk pace, include real-life anecdotes and humour, and encourage a high level of interactivity', as well as providing information in multiple ways, including orally, visually, online and in print (McCartin and Feid, 2001: 13).

Today, however, the picture is further complicated by the perception that the profile of the 'traditionals' is *also* changing, and that instructors must now deal with the 'new traditionals', a group whose rapid uptake and use of new technologies in the past decade, particularly social networking and gaming, is perceived to have had a significant impact on their learning and information behaviour and, consequently, on the quality of their academic work. This image is perpetrated in numerous publications and has been given multiple labels: Google Generation, Generation Z, Digital Natives, Millennials, to name but a few (Behen, 2006; Geck, 2006; Guevara, 2007; Barnes, 2009). But are today's young undergraduates so different from previous generations? In recent years, a number of studies have been carried out in an attempt to understand the current information behaviour and needs of school-goers and traditional undergraduates, including the University of Washington's *'Project Information Literacy'* (2009–present) and University College London's CIBER[1] Report on the *'Information Behaviour of the Researcher of the Future'* (Rowlands et al., 2008). The latter, in particular, has attempted to examine some of the assumptions about the behaviour of the so-called 'Google Generation' (those born after 1993), and the report's findings made some interesting observations about the information behaviour and technology use of this demographic.

Part of the project involved the researchers in examining the veracity of a number of popular 'myths' that circulate about the Google Generation (GG) (Williams and Rowlands, 2007):

- *GG are more competent with technology.* The researchers agree with this, but observe that young people prefer to use more simple applications than presumed.

- *GG prefer interactive systems over passive absorption of information.* Again, the researchers generally agree and note that television and newspapers are used much less frequently.

- *GG expect 'edutainment'.* The researchers are ambivalent about this suggestion, noting that *all* information media must be engaging, or they will not be used.

- *GG turn to their peers instead of authority figures for information.* The researchers believe that this is a myth; research has shown that young people in fact turn to teachers, relatives and textbooks in the first instance.

- *GG are the 'cut-and-paste' generation.* The researchers believe this to be largely true and that plagiarism has become a significant problem.

- *GG prefer quick 'chunks' of information, rather than full-text.* The researchers believe this to be a myth; their own deep-log analysis of web-based information resources showed that users of *all* generations and at all levels displayed shallow 'flicking' and 'power browsing' behaviour, with abstracts being chosen in favour of full-text even by older researchers.

- *GG are expert searchers*. The researchers suggest that this belief is 'dangerous', noting that there has been no apparent improvement in young people's information skills in several decades.

- *GG do not respect intellectual property*. The researchers suggest that although GG are *aware* of it, they believe copyright to be unfair and feel justified in challenging it.

Overall, the CIBER report concludes that the information behaviour exhibited by the 'Google Generation' is not so radically different from previous generations of undergraduates – the challenges that existed then still exist now and are not exclusive to younger information users. This conclusion is supported by the *Project Information Literacy* researchers, who explored the information behaviour of university students; they note that 'when it comes to finding information and conducting research, today's students clearly favour brevity, consensus and currency in the information sources they seek. This may have been the criterion for some students 20 years ago, too' (Head and Eisenberg, 2009: 33). Therefore, although information formats are changing, teaching librarians must still deal with the challenges that they have always dealt with – for instance, authority and evaluation of sources, plagiarism and *using* information, not just accessing it.

Today, although 'traditional' students are still in the majority on campuses, the profile of the student body is changing, and more-diverse, 'non-traditional' groups are growing in number. Information behaviour notwithstanding, different student bodies have particular instructional needs, based on various contextual factors, including age, ability, culture, language and external life responsibilities. Broadly, it is useful to categorise the student body according to these different groupings, which are defined based on attributes such as nationality/culture, age and special needs.

1. **The 'traditionals'** – the young school-leaver group described above.

2. **Adult or mature learners** – this rapidly growing population comprises mature students, usually aged 23 or over, who have chosen to return to education after a period of absence from the formal education system, at undergraduate or postgraduate level.

3. **International students** – students who have travelled to the country in question with the specific aim of enrolling in an educational programme. This group might now also include recent immigrants, who are in the process of integrating with the culture of the host nation.

4. **Students with special needs** – this group includes students with both physical and learning challenges, which mean that they find it difficult to participate in learning activities without some degree of assistance.

5. **Flexible or distance learners** – students who have chosen to pursue their programmes on a part-time or flexible basis, which can include any of the student types described above. Often, a great deal of their learning takes place remotely, in the virtual learning environment, and they visit the physical campus infrequently.

Each group brings its own set of challenges for the teaching librarian, who must think creatively about how to construct suitable learning activities that will engage and motivate. While each group, naturally, consists of unique individuals, all with their own personalities and preferences, it is possible to identify some characteristics that are common to more or less all members of the group – Grassian and Kaplowitz refer to this as the 'modal personality' of a group, which they define as 'traits that occur most often in a sample of the population' (2001: 315). Understanding the attributes of each group is a necessity; knowing how to find information about their needs and particular situations is an essential first step.

Adult learners will be discussed in more detail later in this book, along with suggestions about how to incorporate their needs and preferences in learning situations.

Information literacy for graduate students and researchers

'Graduate students have unique needs with respect to library research, and it can be challenging for librarians to develop instruction programs to meet those needs' (Hoffmann et al., 2008: 2).

To date, information literacy research and practice in academia has been largely focused on the needs and behaviour of undergraduate students – as the largest cohort, and the group which is typically perceived as having the lowest level of information skill, they comprise a natural target population. A substantial amount is known about their information behaviour and the ways in which they learn (Case, 2007: 301). By contrast, 'comparatively little study has been done of graduate students as a discrete group' (Fleming-May and Yuro, 2009: 200), although this is increasing (Hoffmann et al., 2008: 2). A recent report on information training for graduate students, which was commissioned by the Research

Information Network in the UK (RIN, 2008), suggests that the role of libraries and librarians in the research activity of their institutions has not been clearly defined; while information training for graduate students does take place, it is often on a 'piecemeal' basis and developed 'as an extension of the provision they offer to undergraduates' (p. 8) – an approach that may not always be suitable, considering the significantly different information needs that exist between the two groups.

Hoffmann et al. (2008) highlight some of the common themes that have emerged from research into postgraduate students' information behaviour. They include the findings that:

- Postgraduates have more complex research and information needs, and consequently need to employ more sophisticated information strategies than undergraduate students.

- Postgraduates often lack awareness of the full range of library services offered in their institutions.

- Postgraduates often display a preference for consulting with supervisors or lecturers over visiting the library for their information needs.

- Academics frequently assume that postgraduates already know how to carry out research and that they are information literate, although this is not always the case.

- Postgraduate students sometimes overestimate their own level of research competence.

Fleming-May and Yuro (2009) point out that even within the generic group of 'graduate students', expectations and needs vary considerably according to sub-group; in particular, they note that PhD students 'differ significantly enough from other constituents of academic libraries, including other graduate students, to justify their study as a separate group' (p. 200). Graduate students, particularly those who are pursuing research-based rather than taught programmes, undergo a process in which they ultimately learn to behave as *researchers* – Fleming-May and Yuro refer to this as a 'transformation from student to scholar; a process that includes initiation into faculty and larger academic culture' (ibid.).

The work of academic researchers, both professionals and graduate students, is guided by a number of criteria, chief among them the need to make an *original* contribution to the body of published knowledge in their disciplines; their information behaviour is heavily influenced by this requirement. Leckie (1996) suggests that the need for originality 'requires a thorough knowledge of the conceptual and theoretical dimensions of the chosen field of study, and a strong sense of the various research paradigms evident in the discipline' (p. 202). Graduate students aspire to the 'expert researcher model', also described by Leckie (ibid.), which differs radically from the information strategies required at undergraduate level. The 'expert researcher' displays a number of attributes:

- is a sophisticated information user;
- often maintains own personal subscription to key journals;
- spends considerable time browsing the literature;
- tends to follow citation trails, rather than carry out a literature review, as they are familiar with the key researchers within their disciplinary areas;
- often does not see a need to use the library, as resources are available electronically at the desktop, or can be accessed via a personal network of contacts.

David Ellis's well-known model, which was originally derived from a study of the information behaviour of social science and humanities researchers (1989), outlines several different features of the research process at this level. The different features are described as follows – although in real-world research settings, they are not necessarily followed in sequence:

- *Starting* – how the researcher begins to look for information, for example, identifying a key paper on the topic. Ellis's research found that informal contacts were particularly important during this phase of the process.
- *Chaining* – the process of following citations, or other pointers, such as book reviews in scholarly material, or chaining forward from papers to citation indexes. This presupposes a comparatively thorough knowledge of the key researchers and publications in the field.
- *Browsing* – involves semi-directed searching of scholarly material. Serendipitous findings sometimes result from this process.
- *Differentiating* – here, the researchers uses their knowledge of the differences in information sources – for example, publishers, generalist/specialist sources, etc. – as a way of filtering the information retrieved.
- *Monitoring* – keeping current with developments in the field.
- *Extracting* – being selective and identifying relevant material in information sources.
- *Verifying* – checking the trustworthiness and accuracy of the information.
- *Ending* – making a final search of the literature to ensure that all relevant information has been obtained.

However, the changing information environment is affecting the ways in which researchers carry out their work. A discussion panel on the future role of research libraries, which was convened by the Council on Library and Information Resources in 2008 (CLIR, 2008), highlighted many current and emerging trends in research practice, which have significant implications for library support. They include an increase in collaborative and cross-disciplinary research projects, a greater reliance on large data sets, and radical changes in digitisation and scholarly communication (p. 2). Courant (2008a) expresses concern that easy and ubiquitous access to information might mean that 'the special character of scholarly work and understanding can often be skipped altogether, because it is now easy to obtain answers to questions that are "good enough" via any number of tools that are immediately, freely and conveniently available on the web' (p. 202). He argues that a role of academic libraries should be the fostering and support of 'scholarly literacy', defined as an understanding of sources, methods and their use. The RIN report referred to above (2008) suggests that the information skills of researchers have not kept pace with the proliferation of available resources and the changes in scholarly communication; however, the findings of the RIN survey showed that, in their training, most libraries tended to focus only on information-seeking, source citation and the services offered by the library, rather than on the more complex and higher order competencies, such as 'evaluating, organising, managing, transforming, or communicating information, or cf key underpinning issues such as copyright and open access' (p. 14).

While there is some discussion in the literature about the threat to the library profession as a result of the new research paradigm in academic institutions, for the most part, discussion focuses on a reframing of service provision and what academic libraries must now do to support and foster excellence in research. Alongside evolving functions such as data curation and digital information management, *training* features again and again as a key element of the service offering in the 'new' research library (RIN, 2008; Courant, 2008b; CLIR, 2008).

Instructional training for librarians

'On-the-job training remains the most common approach to professional development activities among academic librarians, and a number of studies have demonstrated this to be the case for instructional improvement activities' (Walter, 2005: 7).

In Chapter 1, we saw how, despite librarians' increasing commitment to their instructional activities, and the rising demand for that teaching in their institutions, 'teacher training' for librarians remains primarily an elective option within pre-service professional education, if it is available at all (Walter, 2005). As the instructional role expands, it is likely that the demand for comprehensive and flexible training opportunities will be driven by teaching librarians themselves, who no longer wish to rely on self-teaching and on-the-job training for the skills and knowledge they need to fulfil their roles. Powis (2008) speaks of the responsibility for teaching librarians to 'be fully engaged in training for, and maintaining competence in, this aspect of our professional identity' (p. 1). Teaching librarians require very specific and focused instruction (Powis, 2008); while we can, and do, borrow from the pedagogical knowledge base that informs teacher training for schools, as Liles points out, 'there is a dearth of teaching information designed specifically with librarians in mind and directed toward the unique circumstances of information literacy instruction' (2007: 114). Some of the differences between information literacy instruction, and teaching in school and higher education, are outlined in Table 2.1.

The structure of teacher training for librarians is likely to expand to include a combination of formal and informal opportunities, remote and in-person (F2F), synchronous and asynchronous, pre-service and CPD. Teaching librarians will be required to manage their own training and development, while managers have the responsibility to ensure that their staff are aware of, and can avail of, the opportunities that exist: '[Managers] can alert staff to appropriate, stimulating learning opportunities, including in-house training, classes, local, state and national conferences, workshops, Web casts, and other online instructional opportunities. They can offer financial support to staff members who wish to improve their skills in relevant arenas' (Grassian and Kaplowitz, 2005: 117). At present, teaching librarians can develop and augment their pedagogical skills base through direct instructional opportunities, or through the less concrete, self-development approach which often has the advantage of helping to foster 'teacher identity', an aspect that is frequently neglected during formal education.

The direct instruction menu ideally available to teaching librarians could consist of:

- *A full teaching module (core or elective) within pre-service library training*: As we saw in Chapter 1, the availability of teaching modules on LIS pre-service programmes is improving, and the content that

| Table 2.1 | Differences between teaching librarians, school teachers and academics |

Teaching librarians	School teachers	Teaching faculty
Instruction one of a number of core activities	Instruction the primary professional activity	Instruction one of three core areas of activity, alongside research and administration/service
Instruction not carried out by all members of the profession	Instruction carried out by all members of the profession	Instruction carried out by vast majority of the profession, with occasional breaks (sabbaticals, etc.)
Pre-service instructional training not compulsory, and not always accessible	Pre-service instructional training compulsory	Pre-service instructional training not compulsory, and not always accessible
Instructional approaches frequently learned on the job	Instructional approaches acquired during pre-service training, and developed on the job	Instructional approaches often developed during graduate education teaching assistantships, and further developed on the job post-graduation
Instruction often takes place on a 'one shot' basis – little opportunity for rapport with students	Instruction is ongoing over time, allowing build-up of rapport with student groups	Instruction ongoing, but frequently distance maintained between staff and students
Content and format depend on context and resources. Often instigated in response to a request	Content and format based on set curricula	Content and format based on teaching faculty's interests, departmental/school priorities, institutional structures and policies, and requirements of professional bodies
Teaching performance not regularly evaluated	Teaching performance monitored and evaluated	Teaching performance not regularly evaluated

should be included in these types of modules is being debated at a high level (e.g. ACRL Standards for Proficiencies for Instruction Librarians and Coordinators, 2008; Foster, 2006).

■ *Non-LIS teaching qualification – e.g. postgraduate diploma, certificate or master's in teaching and learning.* Although they do not deal specifically with information literacy instruction, librarians are increasingly enrolling themselves in general teaching and learning courses. According to Powis (2008), these formal qualifications 'have the advantage of fixing librarians into the same training for teaching as their academic colleagues' (p. 3), which can enhance their credibility.

- *In-house training programmes.* Many libraries, where there is an active interest in the professional development of their staff, will continue to offer tailored in-house training opportunities, often arranged with external agencies.

- *External CPD opportunities.* Walter (2005) notes that there is an 'active market for continuing education in this area', due to the relative lack of training opportunities in pre-service training. Many teaching librarians continue to avail of workshops, short courses and distance modules that are often facilitated by professional organisations or provided by commercial entities to fill the market need.

- *E-learning (e.g. SirLearnaLot).* As most librarians work full-time, flexible learning opportunities will continue to increase in popularity. Remote, asynchronous e-learning packages allow librarians to fit their learning around the working day. SirLearnaLot is one example of an e-learning package that is specifically designed for teaching librarians.

Less obvious, but equally powerful, are the indirect, self-development approaches to learning that contribute to a sense of 'teacher identity' in librarians, as well as imparting the practical skills and knowledge required to facilitate student learning. They include: peer-mentoring and/or peer review of instruction; teaching portfolios; self-instruction; availing of grant opportunities for research and instructional innovation; and collaboration with other institutional teaching and learning experts. These and other methods for self-development will be discussed in detail in Chapter 5.

Walter (2005) also refers to the desirability of establishing a 'culture of teaching' in academic departments, as a means of fostering instructional improvement. An idea which has been borrowed from the literature on college teaching, a 'culture of teaching' creates an environment in which teaching and learning are viewed as central to departmental operations, and around which a number of stimulating activities are established to foster instructional development. He notes that there are a number of elements that define a 'culture of teaching', including:

- a commitment by senior administrators to supporting instructional development in staff;

- the close involvement of academics in the development of programmes designed to improve teaching;

- a frequent and ongoing dialogue among academics about instructional issues;

- the availability of resources on campus to support instructional development, including a teaching and learning centre;

- the inclusion of teaching as a criterion in appointment, promotion and tenure decisions (p. 5).

Thus, while formal instructional training is likely to become a core element of pre-service professional education for librarians, a parallel focus on the *indirect* development of teacher identity will help to bolster librarians' confidence and sense of self-efficacy as they go about their teaching work.

Action research in practice

'Critical reflection and systematic investigation of our own practice should become an integral part of our daily classroom lives. In this way, we build professional expertise' (Pollard, 2008: 49).

The evidence-based library and information practice (EBLIP) movement constitutes an approach to information work that 'promotes the collection, interpretation and integration of valid, important and applicable user-reported, librarian-observed, and research derived-evidence' to improve librarians' judgements and decision-making on a day-to-day basis (Wallace and Carter, 2008: 1). A problem-oriented model that has been applied for many years in the health sciences, and other disciplines such as business and engineering, as well as education, the call for EBLIP is an attempt to ground the practice of librarianship more deeply in the research base which informs it – to make research 'useful', so to speak. It also aims to encourage librarians *themselves* to carry out formal studies, in order to strengthen the research base of LIS, which has historically been focused on descriptive rather than systematic accounts of practice – this is similar to the notion, within education, of promoting teachers' *direct* involvement in classroom inquiry, so that they can 'take control of their own research and development' (Pollard, 2008: 8). The practice of EBLIP has been structured in quite a formal way, with Booth and Brice (2004) outlining it as a five-step process:

1. Define the problem/formulate the question.

2. Locate the evidence.

3. Critically evaluate the evidence.

4. Apply the selected evidence to the problem.

5. Evaluate the plan – quality assurance.

Librarians can seek evidence from three sources: (1) we can turn to studies that have already been carried out, or other official documentation, to inform our decision-making; or (2) we can engage in a range of informal observational and reflective activities in the classroom, such as journal-keeping, systematic observation, audio/video recordings of sessions, active listening, questioning and concept-mapping (Pollard, 2008: 64–75); or 3) we can undertake the research ourselves. Action research is concerned with the latter; but rather than assuming the traditional researcher's role as 'disinterested observer', the librarian is fully a participant in the process, with the specific aim of resolving a problem that has been identified (Pickard, 2007: 134) – for example, you might notice that a student group seems bored and unmotivated, and wonder if the use of a classroom response system might improve engagement? Action research is particularly suited to teaching environments, where it is important to evaluate the impact of new methods and interventions; for teaching librarians, it has the additional benefit of offering a means of formally documenting the impact of our instruction and, in that way, gaining credibility for our programmes.

Action research can be defined as 'systematic observations of tests of methods conducted by teachers or schools to improve teaching and learning for their learners' (Woolfolk et al., 2008: 19). It differs from traditional research in the sense that it is focused on immediate and ongoing action – normally, 'theoretical' research includes recommendations for future action that may or may not be implemented. By contrast, in action research 'practitioners attempt to study their programmes scientifically in order to guide, correct, and evaluate their decisions and actions' (Pickard, 2007: 134). Action research also differs from the day-to-day formative processes of 'trying different approaches', which we all engage in – rather, it is a highly systematic and rigorous approach which offers valid and reliable findings. However, unlike most published research, it has an immediate practical application.

The 'action research cycle' describes the various steps in the process (Pickard, 2007); it is similar to the EBLIP process outlined above:

1. *Identify problems.* In most cases, the problem concerns a situation that is causing difficulty for the teacher, which they wish to resolve. As

with all forms of research, the first step is to gather as much information as possible from existing sources, to provide a conceptual framework for analysing the problem – akin to carrying out a literature review, except that your strategy might also include talking to colleagues or discussing ideas with experts. So, to use our earlier example, you might become concerned about your students' lack of engagement in a course and wonder what you can do to improve this situation. This stage involves careful documentation of all the evidence – in action research, the issues are treated as *research problems*, which require a systematic approach at all stages.

2. *Action planning*. Based on what is discovered in the first phase, the planned intervention is selected. In the example above, the evidence may have indicated that classroom response technology might offer a way of stimulating interest among class groups, so it is chosen as a possible solution to the problem.

3. *Implementation*. The intervention is put in place; in our example, a classroom response system might be used in one or two of the sessions to see what kind of effect it has on the students' levels of attention and engagement with the class topic.

4. *Evaluation*. As the teacher-researcher, you must choose how you are going to formally evaluate the impact of the intervention. The methods used are the normal tools of the researcher – questionnaires, interviews, focus groups, documentary analysis and product or performance appraisal, etc. You choose whichever is most appropriate to your needs.

5. *Reflection*. On completion of the research, a period of reflection follows, during which you decide how to proceed in the next cycle – for instance, you might ask yourself was the intervention successful? Were there other factors that influenced the outcome? Were my assumptions about this situation misguided?

A similar notion to action research is the idea of using the outcomes from student assessments to inform the development and modification of learning activities; Grassian and Kaplowitz (2009) refer to assessment as an opportunity for 'improving both learning and teaching' (p. 199), in the sense that it should not be viewed as just being about student performance. Avery (2003) suggests that the results of student assessment 'should be used to implement positive changes in the teaching of information literacy' (p. 2), while Sonntag and Meulemans (2003) view assessment as a cycle, whereby the evaluation of student learning is used to inform and improve the instructional process.

For teaching librarians, research is becoming a core competence, whether it is secondary evidence-gathering through literature searching or undertaking action research projects as described above. Knowing how to use the results of such investigations to inform practice and to promote your work will have a significant influence on the shaping of the instructional role.

Reinvigorated strategies for collaboration

'The cornerstone of an information literacy program that flourishes and endures on a campus is the powerful partnership between faculty and librarians' (Curzon, 2004: 29).

Collaboration with academics is at the heart of any serious discussion about curriculum-integrated information literacy instruction; as we concluded in Chapter 1, establishing a functional and enduring working relationship with the academics is the only way for librarians to gain access to the curriculum and to create instructional opportunities that are fully embedded and student-centred: 'To be truly integrated throughout the teaching and learning activities of our campuses is the core of being a truly embedded librarian' (Dewey, 2004: 12). We saw how the librarians interviewed in Julien and Pecoskie's study of teacher identity (2009) defined their successes almost wholly in terms of the extent to which they managed to establish successful relationships with their academic colleagues; equally, a *lack* of success was also attributed directly to them. The ACRL *Standards for Proficiencies for Instruction Librarians and Coordinators* (2008) lists 'information literacy integration skills' as a core proficiency set, which includes the objectives:

- 'The effective instruction librarians collaborates with classroom faculty to integrate appropriate information literacy competencies, concepts and skills into library instruction sessions, assignments, and course content
- The effective instruction librarian communicates with classroom faculty and administrators to collaboratively plan and implement the incremental integration of information literacy competencies and concepts within a subject discipline curriculum' (p. 7).

Similarly, the ACRL *Guidelines for Instruction Programs in Academic Libraries* states that 'planning such active learning strategies and techniques should be carried out collaboratively with faculty in order to increase overall student engagement in the learning process' (2003). For teaching librarians, the drive to enter into collaborative teaching arrangements with academics is based to a significant extent on the desire to reduce their dependence on so-called 'academic champions' and to establish a more consistent approach to information literacy instruction that can continue without the support of individual academics (Loomis, 1995; Grassian and Kaplowitz, 2005; McGuinness, 2007). Traditionally, the majority of information literacy programmes have been founded on a *coordinated*, rather than a fully collaborative approach. Raspa and Ward (2000) distinguish between the two forms of working arrangement; in coordination, both parties share a common goal (e.g. fostering better information skills in students), but work separately and independently towards the achievement of that goal, with only perfunctory consultation. While a teaching librarian might use course-related examples, instruction is not generally aligned with the learning objectives of the course, and the learning activities can seem de-contextualised and lacking in relevance. This is seen most often in the 'one-shot' single information skills session, slotted into a course, and delivered by a librarian. By contrast, in collaborative instructional development, both parties are committed to the development of aligned instruction from the beginning, and a consensual approach to the creation of learning activities and assignments ensures that the contributions of both academics and librarians are directed towards the attainment of the learning outcomes. However, this type of approach requires a level of commitment from both parties that can be challenging to establish.

A great deal has been written about academic–librarian collaboration, primarily from the viewpoint of librarians, and we have already seen how the working relationship is often framed in a negative light, with academics perceived as either apathetic or hostile (Julien and Given, 2003). The barriers to collaboration have been explored in several studies, and have been outlined in Chapter 1. However, underpinning all of the barriers is a fundamental *disconnect* between the two parties, in terms of how they understand and conceptualise information literacy, and in their beliefs about how learning activities can be designed to foster information literacy in students. Renon et al. (2008) describe this as 'perceptual dissonance', which is defined by them as the different ways in which both parties may view the librarian's role, information literacy and pedagogical practice (p. 36) Academics often believe that students can develop information skills with a minimum of intervention, and that students largely progress through simple engagement with the curriculum as it is, particularly through doing research-based assignments (Markless and Streatfield, 1992; Manuel et al., 2005; McGuinness, 2006). Curzon (2004) illustrates how faculty conceive of collaboration in a much less intense way than librarians: 'Most faculty feel that they have established a partnership with librarians, if they have thought about it at all, when they have requested a one-hour bibliographic instruction session for their students and given class reading lists to the bibliographers' (p. 30). Long-term collaboration with librarians is not a priority for academics, but unlike librarians, they do not see this as problematic; Christiansen et al. (2004) refer to an 'asymmetrical disconnection' between librarians and academics, whereby 'faculty perceive no serious problems in relations between the two groups, nor do they identify any negative consequences arising from this disconnection' (p. 118).

The term 'faculty problem' was coined by McCarthy in 1985; 25 years later, there is no real evidence that relationships between the two groups have changed radically (Stevens, 2007: 255). Rentfrow (2008) points out that faculty perceptions have remained constant: 'The seismic changes that have affected librarianship and the ways in which the profession can and should be intimately involved with advanced research and undergraduate education have, for the most part, not changed how scholars think of the library' (p. 60).

That said, there have been many more examples of successful collaborations described in the literature, many of them now based on the use of up-to-date ICT and social networking applications (Renon et al., 2008; Briggs and Skidmore, 2008). However, as was the case with most previous collaborations, the interest and motivation of individual academics is almost always a key factor in success – a strategy which we know to be unstable and not conducive to long-term programmes.

Teaching librarians and coordinators tend to move between several different strategic approaches when trying to establish collaborative partnerships with academics:

- Targeting and working with individual 'academic champions', which can develop from serendipitous meetings, long-standing working and/ or social relationships, the academic's personal desire to remedy a perceived shortcoming in their student groups, or a general interest in innovative approaches to pedagogy.

- Adopting a position of advocacy and outreach, which involves persuading academics and other stakeholder groups of the importance of information literacy, and the contribution that information literacy instruction – and the librarian – can make to the students' learning experience. This can be rather an uphill struggle, although showcasing impressive learning innovations, sharing reusable learning objects (RLOs), devising interesting 'mini-collaborations', or clearly demonstrating the impact of instruction on students' work in other courses via rigorous assessment practices, can be powerful motivators. (Grassian and Kaplowitz, 2005: 88–94). If choosing this route, Terri Holtze's '100 Ways to Reach your Faculty' (2002) is a comprehensive starting point.

- The third approach takes a 'top–down' view and aims at aligning information literacy outcomes with the overall learning goals of the institution (McGuinness, 2007). This is a much more strategic approach, which envisions information literacy as a core educational competency and integral to the institutional mission. If successful, it establishes librarians as key players in the institution's teaching and learning strategy and places them on a more equal footing with academics.

It is clear that the issue of academic–librarian collaboration is just as pressing – and challenging – as it was a quarter of a century ago. If teaching librarians are to fulfil their mission, they should focus on the strategic approach (Rockman, 2004: xiii) and reflect on how their instructional practices align with the critical issues, not just within education, but in society at large. A reliance on collaborations with individual academics has been shown to be an unstable model for a number of reasons: (1) much depends on the nature of the interpersonal relationship between the academic and librarian, which is a matter of chance, more than anything else; (2) it is difficult to identify those academics who are both 'library friendly' and who have the actual leverage to instigate a collaboration; (3) although they are responsible for their individual courses, academics may have very little control over *programme* structure and face the same barriers as librarians at this level. Bruce (2001) referred to the need for librarians to identify and exploit 'hooks' that can capture the imagination of academics and administrators and result in collaborative programmes. Some examples of the general areas in which librarians can forge collaborations with academics include:

- dealing with the issue of plagiarism and lack of evaluative skills among students, a problem that has been exacerbated by the web (Grassian and Kaplowitz, 2005; Stubbings and Franklin, 2006);

- emphasising the connection between 'critical thinking' and information literacy: 'Make a powerful link between critical thinking and information literacy as part of the conversation to interest faculty in the need for student information literacy skills' (Curzon, 2004: 33);

- linking information literacy to the broader, more political agenda of 'lifelong learning', which is a key target of all institutions of higher education (Bruce, 2001; Curzon, 2004; Grassian and Kaplowitz, 2005: 111);

- positioning information literacy as a core skill for students who are transitioning from second-level to higher education, and who struggle with the different demands and workload, e.g. as part of the 'freshman seminar' or as a component of general writing skills programmes (Rockman, 2004);

- contributing to and supporting institutional strategic goals, such as a focus on graduate qualities and competencies, or the overall concept of 'graduateness' (Doskatch, 2003);

- embracing the potential for e-learning, and developing and contributing to innovative digital and blended learning initiatives. Librarians are in a good position to assume a leadership role in this area (Doskatch, 2003).

Ideally, creating an institutional environment that encourages and supports academic–librarian collaboration should be the goal of teaching librarians, rather than depending on strategies that focus on trying to cajole and persuade academics to join forces with them or endeavouring to enhance their *own* status in the academy, in order for academics and administrators to 'take them seriously'. Doskatch (2003) suggests that such an environment requires multiple alliances across campus and that 'librarians need to think and act strategically' (p. 118). Both Grassian and Kaplowitz (2005: 50) and Doskatch (2003) stress the need for librarians to frame their requests for collaboration in terms of the needs and interests of the desired *partners*, particularly those issues of mutual concern, rather than focusing solely on their own needs.

Advocacy – spreading the word

'The library believes that academic librarians have to be the main advocates to further the information literacy agenda across campus, and that they need certain skills and hooks to help them achieve this' (Stubbings and Franklin, 2006: 2).

The literature on curriculum-integrated information literacy indicate that, in the main, the agenda has largely been driven from the *bottom–up*, based on the efforts and promotional activities of librarians at grassroots level; for instance, Stevens (2007) observes that 'information literacy remains of interest primarily to librarians, and . . . the term has little cultural currency among the teaching faculty with whom so many librarians would like to collaborate' (p. 255). Librarians are viewed, from both a positive and negative angle, as the chief drivers of the information literacy movement, and virtually all progress on this front over the past two decades is as a direct result of their activities. Rockman (2004) refers to the convening of the ALA Presidential Committee on Information Literacy, and the subsequent issuing of their seminal report, as a 'turning point in the visibility and advancement of information literacy' (pp. 4–5), which ignited an explosion of activity, leading to an increasingly global recognition of the concept, by organisations such as UNESCO and IFLA. However, efforts to have information literacy recognised as an essential educational and life competency have had mixed success, although a significant victory in recent times was the proclamation of National Information Literacy Awareness Month 2009 by the US President, Barack Obama. In the proclamation, which was issued in October 2009, the President refers to a 'crisis of authenticity' which has arisen due to the opportunities for personal publishing that have been afforded by new technologies; the proclamation also links information literacy to effective and informed citizenship, stating that 'the ability to seek, find, and decipher information can be applied to countless life decisions, whether financial, medical, educational, or technical.' There have been other notable successes in the US, including the inclusion of information literacy as an accreditation standard by the Middle States Commission on Higher Education (Thompson, 2002), and the recognition of the concept as a learning objective and required standard in a variety of educational policies nationwide (Rockman, 2004). In the UK, a survey carried out by Sheila Corrall (2007) aimed to 'investigate the extent and nature of strategic engagement with information literacy in UK higher education institutions' (p. 1). Through examining institutional documents, such as mission statements, from 114 universities, the survey found 'evidence of engagement' at 75 institutions, although the specific term 'information literacy' was located primarily in LIS documents.

A recent success in Europe has been the extensive work and awareness-raising performed by the members of the *Scottish Information Literacy Project*, which concluded in 2010 after a five-year span. Based at Glasgow Caledonian University, the original aim of the project was to develop an information literacy framework linking secondary and higher education in order to 'produce secondary school leavers with a skill set which further and higher education can recognise and develop or which can be applied to the world of work directly' (Information Literacy Skills Project, 2004–5[2]). However, the project expanded to include a range of research, development and strategic activities, which are documented in the *Scottish Information Literacy Project Weblog*, located at *http:// caledonianblogs.net/information-literacy/*. One of the key strategic achievements of the team has been the creation and development of a National Information Literacy Framework, covering all educational sectors, including lifelong learning, learning in communities and within the workplace. Advocacy and promotion accounted for a great deal of the project members' time and an important outcome has been the creation of a 'community of information literacy activists' in Scotland, which arose through the identification of project partners within the various sectors to contribute to the project's aims. Advocacy work carried out within the project included a host of outreach activities, including presenting at national and international conferences, seminars and workshops, writing articles for relevant publications, holding face-to-face meetings with interested individuals and groups, facilitating visits from external parties and participating in remote, electronic discussions. Although the project ended in April 2010, work is continuing and various forthcoming publications will describe elements of the project in greater detail.

Teaching librarians, thus, are required to engage in promotion and advocacy for information literacy on two levels:

1. They are the drivers of integrated information literacy at the local, or institutional, level, as they seek to persuade faculty and administrators of the strategic importance of information literacy to the learning experience of students.

2. They are the national and international advocates for information literacy on the global stage, as they attempt to enshrine information literacy within policies, frameworks and strategic initiatives at the level of government and society at large.

While the challenges of promoting information literacy internally have been extensively debated in the literature, the teaching librarian's role as global advocate has not been addressed to the same extent. Yet, it is clear that librarians have been filling this role for many years, even before the information literacy movement became visible at the beginning of the 1990s. However, librarians' activism for information literacy has been dismissed by some as an attempt to increase their *own* status and visibility, 'by inventing a social malady with which librarians as "information professionals" are uniquely qualified to deal' (Foster, 1993: 346). More recently, Wilder reiterated the sentiments expressed by Foster, suggesting that librarians have exaggerated the challenges posed by the Internet: 'Simply put, information literacy perceives a problem that does not exist' (2005: B13). In spite of these, and a small number of other dissenters (e.g. Williams, 2006; Eadie, 1990), it is now widely accepted that the challenges are real (Powis, 2008) and that information literacy is an important tool for empowerment. However, as no other groups have taken up the mantle of advocacy, librarians still find that they must promote the agenda as before, but in the context of a changing infosphere, which raises both challenges to, and opportunities for, reinvigorated promotional strategies.

How can librarians effectively advocate for global recognition of information literacy? Key strategies they have used in the past, and continue to use today, include:

- showcasing their information literacy programmes through the publication of journal papers which describe 'How we did it!' and discussing the benefits that resulted for the students of the programmes;

- sharing experiences and resources through websites and digital repositories (e.g. SOS for Information Literacy, NDLR Information Skills Community of Practice, Ireland);

- presenting research findings, showcasing innovations and running practical workshops at national and international conferences and seminars;

- organising high-profile think tanks and colloquia to debate the meaning and impact of information literacy for society at large (e.g. Information Literacy Meeting of Experts, Prague, 2003; High-Level Colloquium on Information Literacy and Lifelong Learning, Alexandria, 2005);

- lobbying government for the inclusion of information literacy in national policy and strategy documents – as part of the Scottish Information Literacy Project described above, a petition was submitted to the Scottish Parliament, 'to urge the Scottish Executive to ensure that the national school curriculum recognises the importance of information literacy as a key lifelong learning skill'. Following a lengthy process, response to the petition was deemed to be favourable, and members intend to use the positive responses to support future advocacy;

- occasional contributions to popular media, including newspapers, radio/television broadcasts and audio/videocasts on the web.

A major criticism of librarians' promotional strategies has been that they focus almost exclusively on the library and information community. Weetman Dacosta (2007) and Stevens (2007) discuss the relative lack of articles about librarians and information literacy in publications outside the LIS field, as well as the absence of material on information literacy that is authored or co-authored by academics. Librarians appear to be talking primarily to *each other*, rather than attempting to establish a presence in journals and newsletters that may be read by those with whom they are trying to collaborate. Stevens suggests that 'perhaps . . . it is also necessary for librarians to go beyond preaching to the choir, reaching out to faculty rather than lamenting that faculty do not understand what they "have not been taught" and "never had a reason to think about"' (2007: 257). Stevens' own study of 54 non-library journals reported in the paper revealed that of the content searched 'only a tiny fraction of them mentioned libraries, and fewer still focus on IL and library instruction' (p. 261). Weetman Dacosta (2007) suggests that librarians should target both educational and discipline-specific journals with their papers on the pedagogy of information literacy, as well as case-study descriptions that will showcase their work. Educational conferences are suggested as another potentially useful channel that is not currently being exploited by librarians. She also suggests that teaching librarians should put themselves forward for institutional and national teaching awards and fellowships, in order to demonstrate their expertise and commitment to non-library colleagues who might not be aware of the teaching work that they do. These points are reinforced by Powis (2008), who emphasises *visibility* as an important strategy for teaching librarians, through sitting on panels and committees, applying for awards and fellowships, and obtaining teaching and learning qualification equivalent to the academics – 'In short, become visible, collaborate, demonstrate your competence in your subject and make teaching and learning a key element in your continuing professional development (CPD)' (p. 2).

Social networking applications offer teaching librarians another channel with a potentially global reach. Blogs and RSS feeds are already used by many librarians to promote information literacy (e.g. Sheila Webber's *Information Literacy Weblog*, Peter Godwin's *Information Literacy meets Web 2.0* blog). Facebook, YouTube and other social media are increasingly being used to support and promote libraries and education, and to create vibrant interest groups. An extremely interesting use of Twitter has been the trend for 'live tweeting' from conferences, which non-attendees can follow through using the hashtag search function that conscientious tweeters attach to their conference updates. All of these efforts, and more, will continue to enhance the global profile of information literacy; as teaching librarians, the role of advocate is an important one for us, and exploiting any and all possible channels of communication will help to ensure the inclusion of information literacy as a strategic priority in multiple contexts.

Exercises and reflections

1. Based on your own experience, consider the ways in which your job has changed since you entered academic librarianship. What new skills and knowledge have you acquired along the way? What skills and knowledge do you believe that you *should* acquire? Are there any aspects of your job that have become obsolete during your employment? What has replaced them?

2. Ideally in groups and using a flipchart or whiteboard, **brainstorm** the skills and competencies that you believe an academic librarian requires in the twenty-first century. Then, taking all suggestions, whittle them down to create a definitive list. Rank the skills and competencies from the most important to least important, based on your conception of the academic librarian's role.

3. Imagine the role of academic librarian is to be gradually phased out, as the current holders of the position retire. Individually or in groups, your task is to create an **Academic Librarians' Manifesto**, stating why the role should be preserved, and showing how it contributes to educational attainment and to society at large.

Notes

1. Centre for Information Behaviour and the Evaluation of Research
2. *http://www.gcu.ac.uk/ils/Informationliteracy-thelinkbetweensecondaryand tertiaryeducation.html.*

3

Preparing teaching librarians for practice: focusing on the basics

Abstract: This chapter explores the skills and knowledge required by teaching librarians to perform their instructional duties and suggests eight key areas of competence which constitute a basic knowledge base for instructional librarianship. The eight areas of competence include: conceptualising information literacy; articulating the instructional mission of the library; learning theories; broad learning frameworks; instructional needs assessment; writing goals, objectives and intended learning outcomes; selection of teaching and learning activities; creating effective learning materials; aligning assessment with learning outcomes and activities; and promotion and outreach. The areas of competence described could be used by LIS trainers to structure an instructional curriculum for pre-service librarians.

Key words: professional education, instructional training, pedagogy, teaching and learning methods, learning theories.

A teaching programme aimed as a preparation for professional practice has [. . .] to accommodate more than a definitive statement of the subject, it must be an introduction to thinking, asking questions, and interpreting, and should instil the same critical thinking skills that are prerequisites for information literacy.   (Foster, 2006: 492)

Unlike school teachers, librarians do not have the luxury of specialised, prolonged training in how to teach and facilitate learning. The body of knowledge and skills that are deemed essential for excellence in teaching can seem overwhelming, as book after book and workshop after workshop promote emerging tools and techniques, which must be mastered and added to the basics. For teaching librarians who are struggling with lesson plans and learning outcomes, pressure to use a classroom response system or to create slick Adobe Flash presentations can leave them feeling stressed and inadequate. In truth, the main question for most teaching librarians is, 'Where do I start? What are the basic knowledge and skills that will enable me to carry out my teaching work to the best possible level, given the current circumstances of my job?' Librarians have many competing demands on their time (Walter, 2008) and must continually choose which tasks to prioritise. Confidence is defined by the *Oxford English Dictionary* (2001) as 'self-assurance arising from an appreciation of one's abilities' – in order to feel confident that the teaching and learning tasks which are encountered on a daily basis can be tackled without stress, teaching librarians must perceive that they possess a sufficient body of knowledge and skills that enables them to handle 'ordinary' teaching situations, as well as offering a framework for future development and more advanced skills. Advanced teaching methods and techniques can be acquired gradually at the discretion of the librarian and according to their circumstances. However, alongside the 'content' of teaching and learning, it is arguably *more* important for teaching librarians to develop a sense of self-development, to provide them with the tools to reflect on their teaching approaches, to identify their own learning needs and to explore training opportunities which will fill the gaps in their knowledge.

In Chapter 1, the question of what could ideally be included on a teaching librarian curriculum was discussed, and the skills and knowledge were categorised under three broad headings:

1. pedagogical/andragogical knowledge, and skills and instructional design;

2. political and strategic skills;

3. professional development and competency.

Under each category is an array of sub-categories, pointing to various areas of competence that a teaching librarian could ideally develop – more than 20 in total, and with the probability that more could be added. However, given the relatively short length of most training opportunities for teaching librarians (a semester-long pre-service module is generally the most that teaching librarians receive, if at all), covering all of this content in detail is simply not possible. In designing their modules, instructors of teaching librarians must be strategic, focusing on key basic components which will enable their students to perform competently – and confidently – when out in the 'real world'.

The purpose of this chapter is to suggest and elaborate a basic framework of knowledge, skills and reflective practice which every teaching librarian could acquire and which empowers them to immediately engage with 'real world' teaching and learning situations. Pre-service teaching librarian instructors can use this framework to develop their curricula; practising teaching librarians and students of LIS can use it to identify the gaps in their knowledge and to perhaps fill some of those gaps, although it is not a substitute for active training. Providers of CPD for librarians can also use the content to devise short modules and workshops for their professional clients.

What are the basics?

Instructional training for librarians needs to prepare them for the frontline work that they will actually be doing on a day-to-day basis. Therefore, from a practical perspective, we need to ask what are the actual tasks that teaching librarians regularly engage in? In their quantitative survey of 82 UK subject librarians, Bewick and Corrall (2010) found that the main teaching activities that occupy the librarians are as follows:

- providing on-the-spot support (94 per cent);
- writing guides and training materials (93 per cent);
- teaching small groups (91 per cent);
- giving pre-arranged one-to-one instruction (90 per cent);
- teaching large groups (79 per cent).

If we were to compile a list of teaching librarian tasks, a typical workload might consist of some or all of the following:

Daily/weekly

- facilitating face-to-face or remote learning activities – lectures, demonstrations, seminars, video-conferencing, remote online chat, etc.;
- providing individual support and advice to students, e.g. at the reference desk, or through appointments;
- communicating with students, academics, library colleagues and other non-library colleagues; responding to queries, discussing possible learning sessions, attending meetings;

- familiarising oneself with the specific needs and characteristics of particular student groups; examining subject curricula and module assignments to determine how to integrate IL instruction (if possible);
- planning broad approaches to learning sessions – sketching outline lesson plans, choosing an overall approach, e.g. problem-based learning, selecting areas to cover;
- creating print and/or digital content for learning sessions – PowerPoint presentations, handouts, exercise sheets, assignments, quizzes, bibliographies, podcasts, videos, etc.;
- grading assignments, analysing course evaluations, preparing reports;
- creating promotional materials for the library's instructional services – flyers, posters, e-mailshots, website content, bookmarks, social networking, etc.;
- updating blogs, Twitter, Facebook, etc.

Monthly/annually

- writing broad mission statements, policy documents or strategic plans;
- keeping oneself up to date with new resources and developments in scholarly communication;
- updating one's teaching and learning skills portfolio;
- thinking broadly about how to improve one's own teaching and learning skills;
- attending conferences, seminars, training programmes;
- writing papers for publication or for conference presentations; writing grant applications.

Teaching librarians might engage in some or all of these activities on a regular, semi-regular or infrequent basis, depending on the amount of time they have to devote to instructional tasks. Using the above list as a guide, a basic body of knowledge and skills, or 'building blocks', needed by teaching librarians might consist of the following:

1. **Core concept.** Knowing the different ways in which 'information literacy' is conceptualised, defined, articulated through 'models', and how it relates to human information behaviour; being aware of one's own experience of IL; helping students to explore and articulate

their own experiences of information literacy, and to be able to draw on the most suitable conception of IL for any given circumstance.

2. **Mission.** Being able to articulate the educational mission of the library and reflecting on one's own role within it.

3. **Theory.** Knowing the key principles of the major learning theories and applying theory to practice when creating learning activities to address defined instructional needs.

4. **Needs.** Being able to identify the instructional needs of diverse student groups; knowing the modal characteristics of traditional and non-traditional students and being able to vary one's teaching approach to best facilitate each group.

5. **Broad approaches.** Knowing when and how to employ different broad learning frameworks, such as active learning, problem-based learning, enquiry-based learning.

6. **Outcomes.** Being able to write effective programme goals, learning objectives and intended learning outcomes (ILOs).

7. **Methods.** Selecting appropriate instructional methods and tools.

8. **Content.** Creating effective content for learning sessions in a range of media.

9. **Assessment.** Aligning assessment with learning activities and outcomes. Using the results of assessment and evaluation as a basis for instructional improvement.

10. **Promotion and outreach.** Selecting and designing effective promotional methods – marketing the instructional services of the library. Being able to communicate effectively with non-library colleagues, especially academics; maintaining a broader view of the impact of information literacy in society and advocating for greater inclusion of IL in institutional, national and international policies.

Each of the sections which follow explores each 'building block' in greater detail. An important aspect of each section is the discussion about *why* teaching librarians need to acquire the knowledge and skills associated with each 'building block'.

Conceptualising information literacy

For teaching librarians, the twin foundation stones of effective information literacy instruction are:

1. understanding and appreciation of how people *learn*; and

2. a personal conception and understanding of 'information literacy', as well as broader awareness of how it is defined and described in different contexts.

What does 'being information literate' mean to you? When you describe yourself as a teacher of 'information literacy', what do you mean to convey in that description? You might wonder why it is considered important to spend time in describing and reflecting on 'information literacy', when the body of knowledge and skills required for effective teaching is already so broad. For teaching librarians, expertise in information literacy can be compared with the subject expertise that academics need in order to be accepted as lecturers or professors in their fields; if we do not know the key tools, methods, theories and concepts of the 'subject' we teach, and have not acquired some degree of skill ourselves, the task of facilitating learning in others is infinitely more challenging, if not impossible. Webber and Johnston (2006) contend that 'information literacy' already meets many of the requirements of an academic discipline; they describe it as a soft-applied discipline, 'which subsumes the particular knowledge, skills and practices entailed by the [ACRL] information literacy standards' (p. 116). As teaching librarians, we must have a strong sense of what it is we are teaching, and be able to convey this to our students. Described as a 'slippery term' (Snavely and Cooper, 1997) which has eluded a universally accepted definition, Elmborg (2006) suggests that the wide variation in how information literacy is conceptualised and the contexts in which it is used have actually contributed to the identity crisis within the profession:

> Disagreements about what information literacy means are not merely a matter of semantics or technicalities: the lack of clarity has confused the development of a practice that might give shape to librarianship in the academy (p. 192).

However, it seems that it was almost by chance that the term 'information literacy' came to encapsulate a movement within LIS; as Pinto et al. point out, 'Hundreds of terms with similar meanings can also be found in the literature' (2010: 4). Coined in 1974, information literacy as a tangible concept has gradually emerged through a number of different channels:

- Through highly specific definitions that are coined either by individuals or via group consensus in collaborative settings: there are now multiple overlapping definitions of information literacy, although none is universal (e.g. ALA, 1989; CILIP, 2004).

- Through a diverse range of models, standards and frameworks, several of which depict the concept diagrammatically, or as a step-by-step process of information problem-solving and research (SCONUL, 1999; ACRL, 2000; AASL, 2007; Horton, 2008): typically, an information literacy framework begins with 'recognising a need for information' and concludes with the use of the information gathered or synthesis of an information product. A useful comparison of the three main information literacy frameworks (ACRL, ANZIIL, SCONUL) is provided by Andretta (2005: 42).

- Through empirical research which explores individual or communal experiences and understanding of information literacy (Doyle, 1994; Bruce, 1997; Webber et al., 2005; Williams and Wavell, 2006).

As teaching librarians, do we need to be aware of every single definition and model? Clearly, this would be impossible. However, from a broad perspective, teaching librarians should be aware that conceptions of information literacy fall essentially into two categories, which have implications for the ways in which information literacy instruction is structured.

1. Sets of abilities

In the first and most widely adopted category are the 'sets of abilities' and 'personal attributes' definitions, exemplified early on in Doyle's 1992 model, and later in the ACRL Competency Standards (2000), amongst similar frameworks. The approach to defining information literacy in these types of models 'is characterized by the enumeration of knowledge and skills in a series of sections', typically derived from academic settings (Webber and Johnston, 2006: 110). Although they have been criticised for embodying a somewhat rigid, 'tick-the-box' approach to information literacy that does not capture 'real-world' information behaviour, and which ignores the affective states of students engaged in research (Walton, 2010), what the models represent is an attempt to transmute an abstract concept (*'becoming information literate'*) into a more tangible construct that enables individuals to envision 'information literacy' as a state that is achievable through effort and the progressive mastery of tasks. From a teaching and learning perspective, models such as these offer concrete goals, outcomes and performance indicators, around which learning and assessment activities can be structured and which can be potentially tailored to local contexts – they enable teaching librarians to identify 'content areas' for their sessions and to specify the desired level of proficiency at each stage. However, using standards-based models as a basis for information literacy instruction is not a straightforward process – Jacobs (2008) questions the 'neatness' of such models, while noting that it is this very neatness that teaching librarians find appealing, although they do not truly represent the 'messy' world of learning, teaching and research: 'It is no wonder, then, that administrators turn to them as a way of managing the messiness of pedagogical reflection and curricular evaluation' (p. 258). Andretta (2005), however, refutes the notion that these frameworks are too linear in nature, noting that 'on the contrary, the acquisition of these competences operates on a process of reiteration' (p. 44). From a pragmatic perspective, the various information literacy standards have been adopted worldwide, as a developmental basis for information literacy programmes (Neely, 2006; Aydelott, 2007). The potential for linking the outcomes and performance indicators to institutional objectives and graduate attributes is another factor in their popularity.

2. The 'information-literate person'

The other way of conceptualising information literacy focuses on subjective experience and is decisively based on Christine Bruce's seminal phenomenographic study, the 'Seven Faces of Information Literacy' (1997). In her work, Bruce's aim was not to create a definitive model which would capture all possible ways of understanding information literacy, but rather to demonstrate how individuals conceive of information literacy in unique and variable ways, depending on their personal experiences of information use and the contexts in which information tasks are completed. Bruce's approach is known as the *relational* model, which focuses on how individuals relate to various phenomena in their lives. Webber and Johnston (2006) share a similar viewpoint; in their paper proposing information literacy as an academic discipline, they assert that they 'have shifted the emphasis more firmly from personal attributes developed mainly in educational contexts to the information literate person, situated in a range of dynamic, social and personal contexts' (p. 111). This conceptualisation of information literacy is one of self-awareness and reflection – rather than focus on a set of skills to be mastered (which may become outdated as the nature of information changes), or proficiencies to be acquired, information literacy is viewed as the individual interacting with their environment, while understanding that different contexts require different approaches. More recently, Walton (2010) rejected information literacy models on the grounds that they do not take into account the highly contextual and social nature of learning or the psychological states of students as they grapple with information problems – he notes that 'becoming information literate appears to be about an individual completing a task in a given context. This context leads to the interaction with sources (e.g. databases, e-journals, books, e-books, peer and tutors) and in so doing brings about the interplay of an individual's behavioural, cognitive, metacognitive and affective states.'

What does this duality mean for teaching and learning? As teaching librarians, **must** we choose, and strictly adhere to, one of the information literacy concepts to inform our teaching, or is there scope for both? Since we view teaching and learning as a holistic process, there is surely room for both. Each way of conceptualising information literacy offers different suggestions about how to structure the learning process.

Influence of the 'sets of abilities' definitions of information literacy

- Students, particularly adult learners, like to have a clear overview of the purpose and relevance of instruction and the tasks involved, so that they can manage their time effectively. Information literacy frameworks enable teaching librarians to provide that sense of structure through sessions that are planned around the various areas of proficiency.

- They help to motivate students by allowing the setting of targets which they view as *achievable*, through clearly identified learning outcomes and performance indicators.

- They allow students a sense of progression as they master each stage or task.

- The frameworks encompass both lower- and higher-order learning processes – contrary to appearances, a structured approach does not preclude a 'deep' approach to learning.

- The skills, abilities and attributes that are listed do not dictate the teaching and learning methods that can be used – as teaching librarians, you are still free to choose suitable learning strategies according to your perceptions of the students' instructional needs and learning preferences.

- Standards and frameworks are 'excellent places to look for ideas about your own instructional goals and objectives' (Grassian and Kaplowitz, 2009: 122).

Influence of the 'information-literate person' definition of information literacy

- In addition to fostering knowledge and skills development, teaching librarians are encouraged to assist students in constructing their own conceptions of being information literate, which are not restricted to *knowing* or *doing* certain things, but are closer to a 'state of mind'.

- It emphasises the importance of reflection and metacognition in learning, and the need to be sensitive to context, but not limited by it – aligns with the 'learning how to learn' ethos, which is process- rather than content-focused. As such, it points to the need to incorporate reflective elements into learning situations.

- It focuses on the *individual* and their interaction with the environment – each person has a unique way of addressing an information problem and should be encouraged to explore personal preferences and strategies, but also to be open to other ways of interacting with information.

- It demonstrates to students that information literacy is not just relevant to academic work, but is applicable in multiple contexts, including citizenship, personal interests, economics and culture.

- It encourages the exploration of personal values and development of a 'personal information style' (Andretta, 2005: 17).

- It supports a social approach to learning, as students are encouraged to share ideas and conceptions of information problems and information literacy.

- It is not restrictive, as it rejects the notion that there is a 'right or wrong' way of dealing with information problems, and encourages exploration of alternative strategies.

Bruce et al. (2006) also discuss the effect of different conceptions of information literacy on the teaching and learning process. In their *Six Frames* model, which we discussed in Chapter 2, they contend that there can be significant variation in how librarians, academics and students conceptualise the learning process and information literacy. In their model, each teaching and learning 'frame' is associated with a particular conception of information literacy:

- **content frame**: information literacy as knowledge about the world of information;
- **competency frame**: information literacy as a set of competencies or skills;
- **learning to learn frame**: information literacy as a way of learning;
- **personal relevance frame**: information literacy learned in context and is different for different people and groups;
- **social impact frame**: information literacy issues viewed as important to society;
- **relational frame**: information literacy as a complex of different ways of interacting with information.

As teaching librarians, you must also consider your *self-perception* as an information-literate person, and the constructs described above will surely influence your self-view. Take time to honestly reflect on what information literacy means to you and whether your conception adversely affects your self-efficacy. Are you limited by a very rigid, prescribed view of information literacy? Or do you see it as a continually evolving construct that is not defined by its 'rightness' or 'wrongness', but which enables you to interact with information in a satisfying way?

Articulating the educational mission of the library

In Chapter 2, we discussed how collaboration and advocacy are important aspects of the teaching librarian's role. Promoting the work we do, reaching out to potential collaborators and advertising our services to non-users are essential, while information literacy remains an 'add-on' rather than a core element of higher education curricula. However, being able to clearly articulate our mission does not just serve a single purpose, i.e. marketing to external parties. Rather, engaging in a thoughtful, reflective and ideally collaborative process of setting out what we currently do, and what we *can* do, empowers us with a greater sense of our own mission and purpose and gives us a clearer vision of the steps we need to take to achieve that purpose. Teaching librarians should always keep an eye on the bigger picture, even when consumed with the daily detail of planning and delivering instruction. Grassian and Kaplowitz (2005) contend that mission statements (or 'vision' statements) can serve as a unifying force within libraries when created democratically: 'When the mission statement clearly articulates a leader's vision for the future, everyone should be able to relate to it and want to work toward attaining the goals embodied by it' (p. 10).

The ACRL *Standards for Proficiencies for Instruction Librarians and Coordinators* (2008) set out this requirement in a number of the proficiencies:

- 'The effective instruction librarian describes the role of information literacy in academia and the patrons, programs, and departments they serve.'
- 'The effective coordinator of instruction investigates aligning information literacy standards with the institution's program review, departmental learning objectives, and/or accreditation standards.'
- 'The effective coordinator of instruction links instructional services to the mission of the institution and other campus planning documents and relevant off-campus documents (e.g. national standards, key publications, and reports).'

The *Oxford Dictionary of Business* (Pallister and Isaacs, 2003) defines a mission statement as 'a statement that encapsulates the overriding purpose and objectives of an organization. It is used to communicate this purpose to all stakeholder groups, both internal and external, and to guide employees in their contribution towards achieving it.' Creating an 'information literacy' mission statement is an opportunity for teaching librarians to clarify their educational role and to determine how it fits in with overall institutional goals and objectives. An information literacy mission statement typically consists of the following elements:

- a single statement capturing the overall goal or 'mission' of the library's information literacy services and/or the library in general, including the library's core values;
- a definition of 'information literacy' and/or 'the information literate student/graduate';
- 'sub-goals' or individual objectives, which support the attainment of the overall library mission;
- a statement linking the objectives to the general educational priorities expressed in the institutional mission statement or strategic plan.

Examples of information literacy mission statements can be found on the web. For example, the goal statement for the information literacy programme at Carnegie Mellon University Libraries is 'to insure that students develop fluency in obtaining, evaluating, and using information in an effective and socially responsible manner' (Carnegie Mellon Libraries, 2008). The mission statement of the Library at California State University (Los Angeles) adopts a skills-based model of information literacy for its definition, namely the CSU *Ten Basic Information Competency Skills* (CAL State LA, 2002) while the mission statement of Indiana University Libraries bases its definition on the ACRL *Information Literacy Competency Standards for Higher Education* (Indiana University Libraries, 2006).

The information literacy mission statement should describe what the library does, its core values, and its goals and objectives; however, it should also emphasise the *value* of the instructional services that are offered, and the unique contribution it can make to the education of students, e.g.: 'Librarians are ready and willing to work with faculty to provide the guidance and supporting materials needed to teach students to be information literate and successful in graduate school and careers' (Carnegie Mellon University Libraries, 2008). While mission statements are typically written every few years at most, teaching librarians should continually re-evaluate their goals and values and remain alert to any changes in the overall educational priorities of their institutions.

As writing mission statements is a task that teaching librarians may engage in relatively infrequently, why is this topic included as a core building block in the body of knowledge and skills required to teach effectively? The answer lies in the opportunity for *reflective practice* that is implied in the process. The act of thinking about missions and goals challenges teaching librarians to look beyond the purely pragmatic aspects of instruction, and to consider their broader role and contribution to the academy. Specifically, it encourages you, as teaching librarians:

- to critically compare different definitions of information literacy and to give serious thought to what information literacy *means* in a changing academic environment, for all levels of student;
- to reflect upon the educational needs of current students and to consider how best to meet those needs;
- to familiarise yourselves with the educational priorities of your home institutions and to reflect on how your library's instructional goals might support these broader objectives;

- to critically examine how instruction is currently delivered and how it might be adapted to align with broader institutional practice and best practice nationally/internationally;

- to reflect upon your *own* role in supporting higher education, an element that is frequently neglected in the professional training and daily practice of teaching librarians;

- to become familiar with the terminology of information literacy, lifelong learning, critical thinking and other essential life competencies, which you can use to communicate more effectively with internal and external collaborators.

Learning theories

'Sound instructional strategies and techniques are an important part of teaching but they must be informed by an understanding of pedagogical theory and grounded in an understanding of broader educative initiatives occurring on our campuses' (Jacobs, 2008: 257).

As a teaching librarian, every book about information literacy instruction that you read will almost certainly contain a section or chapter on general theories of psychology and learning; for some time now, information literacy educators have recognised the importance of pedagogical theory in ensuring that the choices they make regarding instructional approaches and methods are not random – instead, they are informed by at least a basic understanding of the cognitive, behavioural, affective and social processes that determine *how* and *why* people learn in different ways. Jacobs (2008) speaks of a 'theoretically informed praxis', which 'simultaneously strives to ground theoretical ideas in practicable activities and use experiential knowledge to rethink and re-envision theoretical concepts' (p. 260). In Chapter 2, we discussed the importance of a personal teaching philosophy for teaching librarians and how it is desirable to focus on *what the student does* when creating learning activities, rather than striving to master a vast range of instruction tools and methods. Biggs and Tang also define 'good teaching' as 'getting most students to use the level of cognitive processes needed to achieve the intended outcomes that the more academic students use spontaneously' (2007: 91), a definition that only makes sense when instructors *themselves* understand how those cognitive processes operate in different contexts.

However, the literature on learning theories is vast and teaching librarians are time-poor. What do we actually *need* to know about theories of learning to enable us to make good choices about our teaching approaches? A recent survey of UK-based subject librarians by Bewick and Corrall (2010) revealed an interesting finding; when asked about the knowledge that librarians need in order to teach, 'Teaching and learning theories' was deemed the least important knowledge area (7 out of 73 respondents), while 'Delivering teaching sessions' and 'Information literacy' were considered most important (46 and 32 respectively). The authors note that a few of the respondents also questioned the relevance and applicability of learning theories 'to a teaching role characterized by relatively short one-shot sessions', suggesting that practical classroom management strategies were of greater importance to practising librarians than theoretical concepts (pp. 105–6). It seems that the link between theory and practice might not have been made clear, at least to those librarians.

Theoretical concepts, when studied in the abstract, will not help teaching librarians to improve their teaching and learning practices. What we, as teaching librarians, need is for the relationship between learning theories, student behaviour and teaching practice to be made *explicit* and *relevant*, i.e. the theoretically informed praxis discussed above. Some of this we can learn formally; a lot of it will be learned through experience and observation in our 'real-world' teaching and learning situations.

So, what are the basics? Remember, what we are focusing on is the *student* and what they *do* in learning situations. The theories we learn about must give us a greater understanding of student learning processes. Teaching librarians should view learning theories in a utilitarian way, rather than see them as abstract and only partly relevant. Learning theories are useful because they give us information about how students are likely to **behave** in certain situations, and how they are likely to **react** to the learning activities and tasks we set for them. They give us clues about what will **motivate** students and, conversely, what is least likely to engage them. Theories also point us towards the approaches and methods that will most probably lead to successful outcomes in our teaching and learning endeavours.

The basics of learning theory for teaching librarians can be categorised as follows:

- **General approach to learning:** how and why students adopt a **deep-processing** or **surface-processing** approach to learning situations. Woolfolk et al. note that all the variation in learning styles displayed among students comes down to the basic difference between these two opposing approaches (2008: 147).

- Influence of the major theories: how cognitive (constructivist), behavioural, social and relational perspectives explain what the student does, and is *likely* to do, in different learning situations.

- Putting theory into practice: how different teaching and learning methods activate the desired mental, physical, affective and social states encapsulated in the above theories.

From a pragmatic perspective, these categories translate into three key questions that teaching librarians should ask for each and every set of learning outcomes:

- How do I set up my session/programme to encourage students to adopt the learning approach that will enable them to achieve the learning outcomes I have set?

- Which theory (or theories) gives me the information and guidance that I need to set up a session/programme that will engage and motivate students, and enable them to achieve the learning outcomes? What do I need to know about student learning behaviour for this particular situation?

- Based on what I know about learning approaches and theories, what actual teaching and learning methods should I choose for this session/ programme to ensure that students do what they need to do to achieve the learning outcomes?

Let us look briefly at each of the categories.

Approaches to learning

The 'deep-processing' and 'surface-processing' approaches to learning refer to the levels of cognitive activity, or type of information processing, that students engage in when approaching a learning task. Students who adopt a 'surface' approach tend to activate low-level cognitive processes, such as memorising facts, learning 'off by heart', using unevaluated and inappropriate information resources, quoting from sources without proper acknowledgment, etc. Surface-processing approaches are linked to poor motivation – students may be adopting a 'just enough' approach to gain a pass, may be overburdened with other work, or may not see the relevance and meaning of what is being taught. Deep-processing learners, by contrast, are intrinsically motivated and use higher-level cognitive processes in learning – they endeavour to *understand* material rather than simply memorise it; they look for relevance and meaning in content;

Table 3.1	Approaches to learning and teaching and assessment methods

Teaching and assessment methods which encourage a surface approach	Teaching and assessment methods which encourage a deep approach
Non-interactive lectures and demonstrations Exams which focus on content Multiple-choice quizzes 'Fill-in-the-blanks' quizzes Providing full course notes 'Following the textbook' in teaching	Problem-based learning Small group discussion and problem-solving Reflective/learning journals Concept-mapping Projects based on 'real life' scenarios and problems Webquests Annotated bibliographies (Students) creating blogs and wikis

they relate new learning to prior experience; they look for the bigger picture, rather than just focus on detail; and they critically evaluate information, rather than accept it at face value. While the surface approach can be appropriate in certain contexts, problems occur when students attempt to use low-level cognitive activities to carry out tasks which require a deeper approach – an example would be learning mathematical formulae by heart, in order to solve an engineering problem. Some of the methods which encourage deep and surface approaches to learning are outlined in Table 3.1.

Learning theories

Currently, there are four popular theories – behavioural, cognitive (constructivist), social learning, relational – each of which offers a different perspective on how people learn, although there is significant overlap between the various theoretical principles. While it might be interesting for teaching librarians to know about the origins and historical development of each theory, it is not *required* for effective teaching; rather, we need to understand what each theory suggests about the ways in which people behave in different learning situations. Let us explore each theory through the eyes of a follower.

What do behaviourists believe about learning?

In a nutshell, behaviourists believe that people change the way in which they approach tasks ('learning'), when the *consequences* of performing that task in a 'new' way strengthen the new way of behaving. Thus, if they get positive results from doing something in a certain way, they will continue doing it that way. The opposite also applies – if they achieve poor results, they will stop or change what they have been doing. Therefore, *feedback* is at the core of behaviourist learning and everything is judged in terms of behaviour – the mental processes associated with the displayed behaviours are not considered, as they cannot be observed. The behaviourist perspective has been criticised on the grounds that it offers a too-simplistic view of learning and does not capture the complexity of human information processing. However, it still forms the basis for many learning activities that are in use today. The basic principles to remember are:

- The outcome of learning is a change in *behaviour* that is brought about by interaction with the environment – the learner must visibly *do* something in a different way.

- The change in behaviour must be *observable* and *measurable* – what happens *mentally* does not count because we cannot see what's happening inside someone's head.

- *Consequences* affect behavioural change/learning; positive consequences reinforce or *reward* behaviour (reinforcers), while adverse consequences suppress it (punishers).

- However, reinforcers can be *positive* (resulting in pleasant consequences) or *negative* (removal of adverse situation).

- Frequent reinforcement increases *learning speed*.

- The student must be actively *doing things* for learning to occur, rather than thinking about tasks in the abstract.

Learning to use an OPAC the behaviourist way

The behaviourist way of learning to use an OPAC is through *trial and error* – e.g. trying the different search functions, using different Boolean combinations or alternative search terms, scanning through lists of results – until relevant information items are retrieved. A successful search is rewarded (reinforced) when relevant and useful items are retrieved; conversely, searches that do *not* work are rejected when no useful items are located (negative consequence). The *feedback* that causes learning to occur is the number and quality of items retrieved in a search.

What do cognitivists/constructivists believe about learning?

Unlike behaviourists, cognitive psychologists focus on mental processes and knowledge acquisition rather than behaviour, and explain learning in terms of how the learner processes and organises information *internally* – they assume that learners are fully instrumental in their own learning, rather than 'controlled' by environmental stimuli. Behavioural change may result from learning, but it is not automatic. According to this view 'knowledge is learned, and changes in knowledge make changes in behaviour possible' (Woolfolk et al., 2008: 294). What learners *already* know is of crucial importance in learning, since existing knowledge determines how new experiences are perceived, what learners notice, remember or ignore, and what they will pay attention to. According to the cognitive view, making sense of the world and dealing with unfamiliar experiences and phenomena is the principal driving force behind learning; new knowledge is *constructed* by the individual through active engagement with the environment, and is a highly individual process. The basic principles to remember are:

- Learning is *conceptual* change, rather than observable behavioural change or simple *acquisition* of information.

- Conceptual change may result in an overt change in behaviour.

- Learners construct new knowledge through processing information that they receive from their environment.

- New knowledge construction is based on *prior learning* – incoming information is processed and organised, according to existing knowledge or *schema*.

- There are two types of knowledge: declarative knowledge, which means *knowing that* (e.g. facts); and procedural knowledge, which means *knowing how* (to do something).

- Learners must be actively engaged in learning tasks, which must be relevant and meaningful.

Learning to use an OPAC the cognitivist/ constructivist way

Learners will start by searching their 'mental databases' for prior knowledge about the scenario – i.e. comparing the current task with information problems they have solved before. Can this task be approached the same way? What did I do in this situation before? Learners also remember the strategies they used for other databases or search engines, and examine the OPAC to see if any of the same features are present. What is different about an OPAC? They carefully consider what they are looking for and make a list of potential search terms – they might search the index of keywords to see if they can find alternatives. They analyse their task and decide in advance what the best strategy might be – are they familiar with the topic? Do they know any key authors or journals already?

What do social learning theorists believe about learning?

Social learning (or social cognitive theory) is a perspective that emphasises the influence of social interaction on the learning process. The basis of this theory is the idea of *vicarious* learning – that, through observing 'models' engaged in behaviours, we learn how to perform those behaviours, and what will happen to us in specific situations if we do perform them. A number of elements intersect to determine whether social learning is successful: (1) learners must pay close attention to the behaviour being modelled; (2) learners have to *remember* what they have observed; (3) learners have to practise the behaviour – *knowing* how to do it is not enough; (4) learners must be sufficiently *motivated* or incentivised to perform the behaviour. Observational learning is influenced by the learner's stage of development, the 'prestige' attached to the person modelling the behaviour, the learner's perceptions that success is likely, and their own conceptions of self-efficacy (Woolfolk et al., 2008: 275). Basic principles to remember are:

■ People often learn through observing others who are engaged in a particular behaviour – this is vicarious learning.

- Through observation, we learn *how* to do something and what the *consequences* of doing it might be.

- However, in order to learn from observation, we must pay attention, memorise the behaviour and practise it. We must also be sufficiently *motivated* to perform that behaviour.

- Other factors also influence observational learning, such as our belief that we can also do it and the esteem we have for the person modelling the behaviour.

Learning to use an OPAC the social learning way

The expert demonstration is at the heart of this approach to learning. An 'expert searcher', probably a librarian, talks through a 'live' search which is projected onto a screen, demonstrating the various OPAC search functions and how to combine terms using Boolean operators. The students pay careful attention to the process and mentally note each step, taking notes so as to remember everything. Then, they attempt a search themselves, taking care to stick closely to the 'expert model'. Some learners might also work through a search with their classmates, discussing each step and comparing ideas about how the task should be approached.

What do relational theorists believe about learning?

Relational theory focuses on the interaction between individuals and their environments, and acknowledges that people experience aspects of the world – including the learning process – in different ways, and at different degrees of complexity, and that this influences how they approach learning tasks. According to the relational perspective, 'learning is seen as being able to adopt . . . more complex and powerful ways of experiencing [phenomena]' (Bruce et al., 2006: 6). Thus, learning is not about mastering specific skills or competencies, but rather developing an awareness of the different ways in which it is possible to experience learning, and being able to draw on the perspective that is most appropriate in any given situation. For teaching librarians, the focus is on the different ways in which students interact with information, which might range from 'knowing about the world of information' to power relationships in society and social responsibility (Bruce et al., 2006: 6). The main principles to remember are:

- People experience phenomena and situations in unique ways, which are more or less complex.
- Learning is about being aware of the different possible ways of experiencing phenomena and being able to draw on the most appropriate perspective in any given context.
- Learning is therefore about changes in *conception*.

Learning to use an OPAC the relational way

This approach is about exploring the different ways in which the task might be approached before actually using the OPAC. The learner might be encouraged to imagine how an expert searcher, or scholar, might approach the task, as compared with the novice searcher. They might also think about the different ways that 'searching' might be perceived, based on models that have been developed through research (e.g. Edwards' 'Panning for Gold' model, 2006). Finally, they might ask themselves: How could I behave more like a researcher when I approach this task? Which way of perceiving the search process will work best here?

Applying theory to practice

As teaching librarians, the classroom activities you set up determine how the students will act, and therefore how they will *learn*. Based on what you have learned (and what you believe) about student learning, you can see how different methods activate learning in particular ways.

Learning activities which encourage a behaviourist approach:

- quizzes and standardised tests, where rapid feedback is provided;
- modularised e-tutorials or e-practicums, where students receive feedback at each stage;
- guided step-by-step demonstrations and exercises, where each 'step' is mastered before moving on;

- 'trial and error' activities, where students approach a problem from different angles until the best solution is found;
- using a classroom response system (CRS) in lectures.

Learning activities which encourage a cognitivist/constructivist approach:

- problem-solving, either individually or in groups;
- projects based on 'real life' scenarios;
- group discussion and debate; brainstorming;
- 'treasure hunts' (scavenger hunts) or webquests;
- reflective journals/portfolios;
- creating information resources – e.g. wikis, bibliographies, subject guides.

Learning activities which encourage a social learning approach:

- live interactive resource demonstrations, in computer labs with large-screen display;
- one-to-one demonstrations;
- animated or video demonstrations (e.g. YouTube);
- peer-learning: students demonstrate resources to each other and discuss approaches;
- group presentations.

Learning activities which encourage a relational approach:

- group discussion and analysis of the different ways of approaching a task or problem;
- exploration and discussion of existing models and perspectives (e.g. 'expert searcher', 'novice searcher'), and application to the task at hand;
- reflective journals or reflective 'space' embedded within practical exercises.

Broad learning frameworks

While learning activities that are based on behaviourist learning principles are appropriate in certain situations, it is approaches which draw from the more complex cognitive, social and relational frameworks which are considered more powerful for information literacy instruction. Ensuring that learning activities are engaging, relevant and meaningful for students is an important goal for teaching librarians – learning approaches must enable conceptual change rather than mere acquisition of skills; they must allow the student to be reflective and develop an awareness of their learning preferences and processes; they must take into account the potential for social learning; and most of all, they need to be *active* and absorbing, rather than passive. They must also enable students to draw on their previous experiences of learning and information use in developing new understandings and conceptions of information problems.

There are currently a number of broad learning frameworks which enable teaching librarians to incorporate all of these elements. It is important for you to be aware of them and of how they might be put into practice.

Active learning

'Active learning' is a broad, umbrella term which describes all learning activities in which students are required to *do* something, either individually, in pairs or in groups. It is in direct contrast to the more traditional, didactic approaches to learning, in which students take on the passive role of listener, rather than participating directly in the learning process. Lorenzen (2001) defines active learning as 'a method of educating students that allows them to participate in class. It takes them beyond the role of passive listener and note taker, and allows the student to take some direction and initiative during the class' (p. 1). Active learning encourages students to engage higher-order skills and to reflect on what they are doing. The role of the teacher is construed differently in active learning situations: instead of functioning as an expert 'content-provider' (as in lectures, for example), the role is more like a 'guide' or 'coach', who accompanies students on their individual journeys of discovery, offering advice where warranted, but allowing the students to work out their own strategies and make their own mistakes, where necessary. Active learning fits in with all of the theories described above, each of which stresses the need for students to *participate* in order for learning to occur; in behaviourism, it is the *consequences* of activity that reinforce or suppress behaviours; in cognitivism, active engagement supports the idea that students are instrumental in their own learning and are self-directed; in social learning, students must *practise* the behaviours modelled by the experts, in order to retain them; and in relational learning, students must participate fully in the reflective process which leads to conceptual change. For information literacy instruction, which is more about process than content, active learning is essential.

There is no single specific teaching method that is used in active learning situations – to make your learning sessions 'active', you must simply ensure that students are not just passively absorbing information, with no opportunity to put the knowledge into practice. It is possible that many of your teaching activities are *already* active, although you may not have thought of them in those terms. As long as independent or collaborative student activity is involved, active learning provides an opportunity for teaching librarians to be creative in their approach. Active learning does, to a certain degree, require teaching librarians to relinquish some control over what occurs in the classroom (or outside of it); this can be difficult for some, especially where outcomes and lessons have been carefully planned (Lorenzen, 2001: 3; Kahn and O'Rourke, 2005: 9). However, as long as learning activities are designed *in alignment* with learning outcomes, librarians should not be overly concerned about students 'going off track'.

As teaching librarians, we have a broad range of active learning approaches to choose from – and can certainly invent our own, if needed! The literature of LIS is full of examples of active learning, even though the exact term may not be used to describe the approach used in each case. Common strategies for active learning include:

- individual or group problem-solving;
- exercises or worksheets requiring the use of specific resources;
- participatory group discussion, using white boards, Post-It notes, and other visual props;
- creating annotated bibliographies;
- using pre-specified criteria to evaluate print and online information sources;
- role-playing;
- peer-coaching – having one student explain a resource or procedure to a classmate;
- in-class debates;
- reflective journals or portfolios;
- using classroom response systems in large lectures;
- stopping a lecture to invite class questions and discussion.

Enquiry-based learning (EBL)

As the term implies, EBL describes all approaches to learning 'that are driven by a process of enquiry' (Kahn and O'Rourke, 2005: 1), and falls under the umbrella of 'active learning'. Any learning situation that requires students to carry out some degree of task or problem-analysis, to discuss strategies, to search for and analyse evidence, and to offer a solution or response can be classified as EBL. Kahn and O'Rourke (2005: 2) outline some of the key characteristics of EBL:

- it requires students to engage with a complex scenario that is 'sufficiently open-ended to allow a variety of responses or solutions';
- the process is controlled and directed by the student, rather than the instructor;
- students must draw on existing knowledge and identify the learning needs associated with the problem;
- students show curiosity and are motivated to seek evidence in order to address the problem;
- students take responsibility for their learning and for analysing and synthesising evidence to solve the issue at hand.

As with most active learning approaches, the role of the instructor is assistive, rather than directive. Usually, the instructor is responsible for setting the problem or scenario and for providing some initial guidance and advice. The difference between EBL and the more traditional, content-driven forms of teaching is that the starting point is the *problem*; in traditional learning, students are provided with content first, typically in lectures; they are then required to apply theory to practice, through doing exercises or solving problems. In EBL, the students themselves must identify the type of evidence or information they will need to address the issue and then set about finding it. Thus, the process of applying theory to practice is fully holistic, as they see how content is applied in a meaningful way.

In information literacy instruction, teaching librarians can develop creative and interesting scenarios for their students, which are relevant to their everyday experiences. An EBL scenario might look like this:

Example of EBL scenario

You work for an advertising agency and have been approached by the Minister for the Environment to create a campaign which will promote energy-saving and a 'green' lifestyle to the 18–30 age group. The campaign is to run for six months and will encompass a broad range of media, including newspapers, posters in bus shelters, radio advertisements, a dedicated website and one four-minute TV advert. The Minister wishes you to supply a full strategy outline within two weeks, including an analysis of the target market, the main issues you will address in the campaign and the messages that you will focus on in the various media channels. Until now, your agency has only been involved in campaigns for retail and pharmaceutical companies. Where do you start with this new eco-campaign? The steps your group can follow in addressing this issue could be as follows:

1. Scenario analysis and discussion: what are the learning and information needs associated with this problem? For example analysing target market, key 'green' issues, effectiveness of media channels. What do we know about these issues already?

2. Initial brainstorming session to generate ideas. Concept-mapping to link ideas and develop a framework for exploring the problem.

3. Generating questions that need to be answered and a list of resources which will be useful for gathering evidence.

4. Deciding on division of labour and setting a timeline for action.

5. Evaluating evidence and synthesising information.

6. Creating the advertising strategy outline.

As teaching librarians, you might wish to provide students with an initial 'package' of material, including suggested resources, to start them off, or to have an 'expert' in the area come in to give an introductory lecture. While the process is student-directed, well-timed intervention can provide extra motivation and encouragement. Kahn and O'Rourke note that resources for EBL can include: 'specific time-tabled sessions, such as interactive lectures and seminars, workshops, laboratories, fieldwork, resource sessions and peer assisted study schemes' (2005: 7).

Problem-based learning (PBL)

PBL is 'seen as a set of approaches under the broader category of Enquiry-Based Learning' (Barrett, 2005: 13), and is well known for its application within medical education, which began at McMaster University in Canada as far back as the 1960s. Barrett emphasises that PBL is not just a teaching and learning method, but rather a 'total approach to education', in which learning results from the process of resolving a particular problem (2005: 15). The problem acts as the 'trigger' for learning and is presented to the students before any other curriculum inputs. The PBL process is highly structured, with students working on problems in small-group tutorials over a period of time. The design of the PBL 'problem' is an important process, and Barrett suggests using a curriculum matrix, which plots the problems against the intended learning outcomes for the curriculum. Problem formats do not have to be text-based; rather, PBL tutors can use a wide range of resources, including videos, posters, newspaper articles, cartoons, TV programmes, quotations and passages from literature – again, it is an opportunity to be creative and to adopt formats that will engage and motivate the students. An operational definition of PBL is presented by Barrett (2005: 15), which explains the concept clearly:

1. Students are presented with the problem at the start.
2. The problem is discussed and defined in PBL tutorials, followed by brainstorming, identifying the 'learning issues' associated with the problem and deciding on an 'action plan'.
3. Students set out independently to locate information to help with the learning issues, using a range of information resources.
4. Students reconvene in the tutorial, share what they have discovered and continue to work on the problem.
5. Students present a solution.
6. Students engage in reflection, reviewing what they have learned in the process.

PBL can be a highly effective way of fostering information literacy in students, as it engages higher-order skills and requires a great deal of critical thinking, questioning and judgement. Breen and Fallon note that 'as PBL problems always reflect "real" and current issues students can use their information skills in a meaningful way. This will help students understand the relevance and value of information literacy' (2005: 183). As teaching librarians, however, your involvement with PBL curricula unavoidably requires collaboration with academic teaching staff – as Barrett points out, it is a total approach to learning that requires the total restructuring of subject curricula, with a focus on 'concepts' and process, rather than blocks of content to be covered.

Instructional needs assessment

The process of identifying instructional needs is closely related to the next step, writing goals, objectives and learning outcomes, and is central to the planning process for teaching librarians. Although we might have a strong instinct about what a particular student group needs to learn, our basic philosophy of *'start with the student'* insists that we avoid assuming that we know best, and instead make an effort to find out exactly what these students need to learn from us. Webb and Powis (2004) refer to this process as 'auditing', and define it as 'the process of finding out what your learners need and expect from the session' (p. 60). Before we can start to design our teaching and learning activities, we need to ask ourselves some basic questions first. Using a type of question checklist can help clarify our thoughts:

- What academic programmes are the students engaged in and what kinds of assignments do they have to do?
- What do we know already about the characteristics of this group?
- What do we know about how information literate these students are?
- Is there any evidence that there are gaps in their knowledge/skills that we can help to fill?
- Is the course lecturer likely to be positively disposed towards instruction?

Teaching librarians can use an instructional needs checklist, similar to the one in Table 3.2.

Grassian and Kaplowitz (2009: 112) suggest that information about instructional needs comes to librarians in three different ways:

- *Reactively*: through noticing issues that keep coming up in the library, e.g. repeated questions at the reference desk or requests for help in

Table 3.2 Instructional needs checklist

Question	Already know?	Need to find out?
Academic programmes students enrolled in?		
Type of assignments they are doing?		
General profile (e.g. traditional/ mature? international? full-/part-time?)		
Level of information literacy?		
Knowledge/skill gaps?		
Attitude of lecturer?		

relation to a particular resource. Frequently, it come to librarians' attention that particular class groups are having problems with an assignment set by their lecturer – this can be a cue to approach the lecturer with a suggestion for a collaboratively designed information literacy session that is structured around the assignment.

- *Interactively*: through a direct request by a lecturer for instruction. In these cases, the instructional need is predefined for you, as the requester typically suggests areas that you should focus on. However, discussion with the lecturer may identify other issues that might also be dealt with.

- *Proactively*: through carrying out some exploratory research and identifying areas where information literacy instruction would be useful. Teaching librarians must bring their promotion and outreach expertise into play when in proactive mode, to persuade academics of the potential benefits of instruction.

If we find that our list of things that we 'need to find out' is longer than the things that we 'already know', we will need to consider the different means of finding the information we require. We can do this informally or formally:

Informally:

- talking with lecturers in informal settings about their class groups and curricula;

- talking with students about the areas in which they feel they need assistance;

- general background reading about the typical attributes of various student groups;
- observation of student behaviour in the library;
- informal 'polls' on the library website about students' attitudes to instruction;
- talking with library colleagues about their perspectives on students' knowledge/skills gaps.

Formally:

- surveys: print or online questionnaires distributed to students;
- focus groups held with students or with academics;
- information literacy pre-tests; developed in-house or using standardised diagnostic tests, such as Project SAILS (a commercially developed suite of standardised information literacy tests, available to higher education institutions in the US and Canada);
- student self-assessment of competence and instructional needs.

Writing goals, objectives and intended learning outcomes

The process of writing programme goals, learning objectives and, especially, intended learning outcomes (ILOs) is arguably the most important step in information literacy instruction – and not just from the point of view of the learners, but also for *you*, as teaching librarians. It serves both a pragmatic function – determining what the students will learn to do as a result of your instruction and how they will demonstrate that learning – and, crucially, a reflective function, insisting that you think deeply about how *you* will facilitate the learning outcomes that you wish your students to achieve. Every single learning session – even a one-shot, 50-minute class – must be structured around clearly articulated intended learning outcomes.

Constructive alignment

To appreciate why objectives and outcomes are so important, it is helpful to first understand the idea of *constructive alignment*, a form of outcomes-based education proposed by John Biggs (Biggs and Tang, 2007: 51).

Simply put, constructive alignment refers to learning situations in which the learning outcomes, the teaching and learning activities and the assessment are all pointed in the same direction. Biggs and Tang explain it thus: 'The "alignment" [. . .] reflects the fact that the learning activity in the intended outcomes, expressed as a verb, needs to be activated in the teaching if the outcome is to be achieved, and in the assessment task to verify that the outcome has in fact been achieved' (p. 52). Consider, for example, a session aimed at teaching students how to give effective presentations using PowerPoint. An **unaligned** session might have the following elements:

- **ILO.** 'The student uses PowerPoint effectively when giving presentations in any context.'
- **Teaching and learning activities.** Short demonstration of PowerPoint using a data show projector, followed by a 20-minute lecture on what works best and what to avoid when using PowerPoint. Handout also given, with main points.
- **Assessment.** Students do a quick multiple-choice quiz on the different functions and uses of PowerPoint.

This session is unaligned, because the teaching and learning activities and assessment tool do absolutely nothing to ensure – or demonstrate – the attainment of the learning outcome, which is that the students can **use** the software **effectively** when **giving presentations**. In order to align this session, we need to make sure that the outcome is activated in the learning activities and also that the assessment allows students to demonstrate that they have achieved the outcome – i.e. that they can actually use PowerPoint effectively when giving a presentation. So, an **aligned** session might look like:

- **ILO.** 'The student uses PowerPoint effectively when giving presentations in any context.'
- **Teaching and learning activities.** Group-work: in groups, with one laptop per group, students are given a short brief and asked to create a presentation 'cold' – they have 30 minutes to do this. Each group then shows their presentation to the class, and they are evaluated and discussed by students and instructor, using a white board to highlight points. Then, the class is shown a short video of a presentation making effective use of PowerPoint, and given a handout, with tips for good PowerPoint use.
- **Assessment.** Each group must give a 10-minute presentation on a topic of choice, using PowerPoint.

The element which holds everything together is the ILO – it determines how the learning should be facilitated by the instructor and how the students should be assessed. But most importantly, it is student-centred –it focuses on what the *students* will do after instruction, rather than on what the instructor is planning to do. This is the core of our guiding philosophy – *start with the student.*

Goals, objectives and outcomes

From a semantic point of view, there may be some confusion regarding the difference between goals, learning objectives and intended learning outcomes, as these terms are often used interchangeably. Indeed, learning objectives often appear indistinguishable from outcomes in terms of how they are phrased, while some instructors just stick to one of the terms. Biggs, as discussed above, uses the term 'intended learning outcomes' exclusively and does not refer to 'learning objectives' at all in his text, stating that the term ILO is preferred 'because it emphasises more than does "objective" that we are referring to what the student has to learn, rather than what the teacher has to teach' (Biggs and Tang, 2007: 70)

Using the terms separately, however, can be helpful in emphasising the importance of specifying *how* the students will demonstrate what they have learned, rather than just expressing the *intention* that they will learn it. The differences may be explained thus:

Goals refer to the broad, abstract aims of the programme or session – the entire programme or session target, if you like. For instance, you might state that 'The goal of this programme is for the students to become proficient library users.' Goals often seem lofty or aspirational, and don't contain any real indication of how they are to be attained in practice. They are often what you will include in your mission statements as indications of your overall instructional strategy.

Learning objectives refer to what the students will learn to *do* as a result of the learning activity. They are always active statements, using carefully chosen verbs. For instance, a learning objective related to the goal above might be 'The students will be able to locate the short-loan collection area in the library and successfully borrow an item, using the self-issue system.' There are usually a number of objectives associated with a single goal.

Intended learning outcomes (ILOs) refer to the behaviours or actions through which the students will demonstrate what they have learned – while objectives capture the *intended* outcome, the ILOs state specifically how the students show that the outcome has been achieved. So, for the

Table 3.3	Instructional intentions and intended learning outcomes

What *we* want to do	How our ILOs should look
Teach the students how to cite and reference correctly.	The students will be able to compile a bibliography using the APA referencing convention.
Demonstrate to the students how to search databases effectively.	The students will be able to select an appropriate database and retrieve relevant items using appropriate search strategies.
Show students how to critically evaluate journal articles.	The students will be able to apply evaluative criteria to any scholarly publication.

example above, an ILO might look like: '*The students will find the short-loan collection area unassisted, and will borrow two items using the self-issue system.*' ILOs, in effect, determine the assessment approach that should be used, by making it clear that certain behaviours are to be exhibited – adhering to the concept of constructive alignment.

In practice, you may choose to use both terms (objectives and outcomes), or, like Biggs, you might decide to describe what you want your students to achieve in terms of ILOs only. The key is to ensure that what you write captures what the *students* will do, and not what *you* are intending to do in the classroom. Table 3.3 shows how we should 'flip over' our instructional intentions to reflect the desired student behaviours.

The problem with 'understanding'

How do you measure or observe 'understanding'? As teaching librarians, we obviously want our students to *understand* what they are learning, rather than just mechanically repeat behaviours or memorise content. However, when our ILOs require us to describe our aims in behavioural, observable terms (so they can be assessed), it is difficult to know how to express them. To address this problem, Biggs and Tang speak about 'performances of understanding', which are based on the idea that if students truly understand something, they will *act* differently in contexts involving that concept, thereby demonstrating that understanding has occurred (2007: 75). For example, if a student really understands the difference between popular and scholarly resources, they will avoid popular resources, and instead stick to scholarly ones when writing academic essays. So, rather than use the verb 'understand' in our ILOs, we should instead think of how that understanding will be exhibited in behaviour.

> **Old ILO:** 'The students will *understand* the difference between popular and scholarly resources.'

> **New ILO:** 'The students will *choose* 10 *appropriate* resources when writing an academic essay on a given topic.'

If you feel a bit stuck in writing your ILOs, you can draw on a range of frameworks which indicate different levels of learning and understanding, as well as suggested performance indicators that you can adapt to your local context. Three frameworks in particular offer useful guidance:

ACRL Information Literacy Competency Standards for Higher Education: Each standard includes performance indicators and suggested outcomes, which are written from the student's point of view, e.g.:

Standard three:

The information literate student evaluates information and its sources critically and incorporates selected information into his or her knowledge base and value system.

Performance indicators:

The information literate student summarizes the main ideas to be extracted from the information gathered.

Outcomes include:

Reads the text and selects main ideas.

Restates textual concepts in his/her own words and selects data accurately.

Identifies verbatim material that can then be appropriately quoted.

Biggs and Collis's SOLO Taxonomy (1982): SOLO stands for 'structure of the observed learning outcomes' and is based on the idea that 'understanding' becomes more structured and complex as students reach more advanced levels. Different verbs/behaviours are associated with the increasing levels of understanding that are described by the creators of the model:

Unistructural: memorise, identify, recognise, define, name, recall, label, count, find.

Multistructural: classify, describe, list, discuss, select, outline, illustrate, separate.

Relational: apply, analyse, explain, predict, review, argue, compare, debate, construct.

Extended abstract: theorise, reflect, generate, hypothesise, create, invent, generalise.

(Biggs and Tang, 2007: 80)

Bloom's Taxonomy (1956): This famous model splits learning into three domains – cognitive, affective and psychomotor – and each domain is further divided into categories, each of which is associated with specific learning behaviours. For example, the categories under the cognitive domain include verbs such as:

Knowledge: recognise; recall; acquire; distinguish; identify.

Comprehension: convert; abstract; translate; extrapolate; interpret; transform.

Application: carry out; apply; solve; prepare; operate; plan; repair; explain; generalise.

Analysis: analyse; estimate; compare; observe; detect; classify; discover; discriminate; identify; explore; distinguish; catalogue; investigate; break down; recognise; determine.

Synthesis: write; plan; integrate; formulate; propose; specify; produce; organise; theorise; design; build; systematise.

Evaluation: evaluate; verify; assess; test; judge; rank; measure; appraise; select; check.

(EducationOasis: http://www.educationoasis.com/curriculum/LP/ LP_PDF%20Word/blooms_tax_verbs.pdf)

Selecting teaching and learning activities

While the range of teaching and learning activities available to you – the 'instructional menu' (Grassian and Kaplowitz, 2009) – is wide and varied, you will inevitably be working within a framework of limitations that will, to some extent, determine what you can and cannot do in the classroom. Factors such as class size, number and length of available slots, and staff and resource availability create very pragmatic conditions which direct our approaches. We find that we must balance these practical considerations with our desire to create teaching and learning activities that are aligned with our ILOs, and which will activate the desired learning approaches in our students. We have already discussed how certain methods foster broader approaches to learning, such as enquiry-based and problem-based learning. We have also seen how different methods are linked with different learning theories, in so far as they encourage students to learn in particular ways.

A common way of classifying instructional methods concerns whether they facilitate face-to-face (F2F) or remote learning, or whether the learning takes place in realtime (synchronous), or at a time of the student's choosing (asynchronous). Within these classifications, methods can also be paper-based or delivered online. The matrix in Table 3.4 shows different methods, classified according to these categories.

As teaching librarians, we frequently face greater restrictions in our teaching than academic lecturers; often, we have little more than a short one- or two-hour slot in which to facilitate meaningful and relevant

Table 3.4   Categories of teaching and learning activities

	Synchronous	Asynchronous
Face-to-face (F2F)	Lecture Tutorial/seminar Workshop Resource demonstration One-to-one instruction Guided library tour Group discussion/problem-solving Group/individual presentation	Not applicable
Remote	Online chat (IM – instant messaging) Video-conferencing Conference call with or without video link (e.g. via Skype) Virtual worlds (e.g. Second Life) Email, texting, posting on discussion boards Collaborative creation of wikis or other documents, using applications such as GoogleDocs and GoogleWave	Paper-based or online exercises, workbooks, quizzes e-tutorials and e-practicums Virtual library tours Video tutorials or presentations Podcasts Slide shows Paper-based guides Online help functions Many of above often hosted on learning management systems/virtual learning environments

learning activities that are aligned with our ILOs. We find ourselves caught between content that must be covered and providing an opportunity for students to engage in active demonstration of that knowledge. However, the matrix in Table 3.4 shows that we need not necessarily restrict ourselves to that single classroom-based, F2F slot: rather, we should aim to harness the resources at our disposal, to create a 'blended learning' environment, which gives us greater scope to facilitate an active learning experience for the students and 'allows you to use a combination of delivery methods in both formal and informal settings'

(Secker et al., 2007: 140–1). So, for example, you might be asked to deliver a one-hour session to a very large group of students (100+), a class size which makes it very difficult to manage active learning or group work. A blended learning approach means that, even if you are restricted to a lecture or demonstration format for the F2F session, you could also extend the learning asynchronously, through making interactive exercises available on the virtual learning environment (VLE), or through arranging a remote question and answer session using the system's online chat function, or even via email, if necessary. When choosing instructional methods, you should think not just of what might go on inside the classroom, but also *outside* of it. Technology has allowed us to broaden our conception of when and how learning takes place. When aligned with ILOs, blended learning can offer a powerful solution to the large class-size, short session problem, and take the pressure off teaching librarians to fit everything into a single session.

Creating effective learning materials

As teaching librarians, operating in a blended learning environment, creating learning materials is likely to occupy more of your time than actually delivering the sessions. Getting to grips with the different formats that are used for various learning activities is a challenge, and impossible to accomplish without training and collaboration. Among the different materials you might be required to create are:

- paper or print-based handouts, worksheets, guides, quizzes, resource lists, journal templates, webliographies, etc.;
- electronic versions of the above, using various software packages for word-processing, online quizzes and surveys, wikis, PDF documents, web pages, etc.;
- presentations (e.g. lectures) or demonstrations, using overhead transparencies, PowerPoint or other software packages;
- audio or video resources, such as podcasts or instructional videos ('vodcasts');
- blended materials, e.g. slides with audio, video embedded within resource lists, classroom response systems with PowerPoint presentations, etc.;
- e-learning tools, e.g. e-tutorials, virtual tours, webquests, full online courses, etc.;

■ social software/mobile applications – e.g. Facebook pages, blogs, smartphone applications, RSS, Twitter accounts, etc.

Effective design principles for all of these resources are impossible to cover here. However, some of the general principles which apply to the creation of instructional materials are worth keeping in mind:

1. Always start with your ILOs and constructive alignment – the materials you use to facilitate learning should enable students to engage in appropriate activities to achieve the ILOs.

2. Know what's available – Secker et al. suggest that teaching librarians should create a 'resource checklist', which requires you to audit the materials you already have at your disposal and indicate ones which could be purchased, budget permitting (2007: 140).

3. Allow sufficient time to prepare relevant teaching and learning materials. If you have been asked to provide a session at the last minute, use the tools that will allow you to create materials most quickly (while adhering to point 1 above).

4. If you don't know how to do something, don't waste time trying to figure it out from scratch yourself (unless you have lots of time to spare!) – try instead to either access appropriate training or enlist the help of a person who is familiar with the particular software or application you wish to use.

5. Think 'active learning' – for whatever resources you prepare, endeavour to include an element of interactivity. Avoid passivity – the students must be actively engaged in learning in order to encourage a deep approach. This is particularly important for materials which are mounted on VLEs – you should aim to avoid simply migrating passive content into electronic format, but instead use the various interactive options that are available (e.g. wikis, chat, discussion board, quizzes, etc.).

6. Think first, technology later – don't rush to use online or digital resources, just because they're available, or you think that you 'should'. Also consider how the physical teaching and learning environment is set up, before using technology-based materials, i.e. whether classrooms are properly equipped, whether students have access to relevant software, passwords, databases, etc.

7. If you fully 'script' a presentation or demonstration, avoid reading the script word-for-word during the session – instead, create memory prompts or short, summary points to guide you.

8. In materials that are to be given to students, always include the ILO that the resource pertains to and an explanation of how the resource contributes to achieving that ILO.

9. Aim for clarity and simplicity in all materials, whether paper-based, electronic or online – avoid clutter, overloading with content, overuse of graphics and animation, unclear guidelines or instructions, 'dead' hyperlinks, confusing site structures (for websites) and documents and programmes that take a long time to load or scroll through.

10. Always create 'storyboards' for resources such as instructional videos, e-tutorials, virtual tours, webquests and online PBL, so that you have a clear vision in advance of how they should run.

11. Don't reinvent the wheel – don't waste time reproducing documents that may be already available – e.g. online help or FAQs on databases and websites, previous materials that just need to be updated, resources that may be freely available to download and use for your own teaching, YouTube videos, podcasts, etc.

Aligning assessment with learning outcomes and activities

'[A]ssessment always begins with thoughtful consideration of appropriate teaching approaches matched to learning outcomes' (Sonntag and Meulemans, in Avery, 2003: 10).

As teaching librarians, it is not enough that we plan and deliver learning activities and hope or assume that the students will learn what we intend them to learn. The principle of constructive alignment requires that we set up assessment processes that will give students the opportunity to *demonstrate* that the ILOs have been achieved – we cannot have ILOs without also including a mechanism to determine if our learning activities have had the desired effect. *Unaligned* assessment means that the methods we are using do not actually assess the ILOs, but instead demonstrate some other form of behaviour or outcome: for instance, using a written examination to assess students' ability to search a database effectively means that what we are *actually* assessing are the students' memory, recall and writing skills (declarative knowledge) – it does not tell us whether the student would actually perform a search effectively in a real-world situation (functioning knowledge). The concept of active learning should run throughout the entire instructional development process, not just the teaching and learning activities. Sharma (2007) refers to the concept of *authentic assessment*, which is defined as 'an evaluation process that involves multiple forms of performance measurement reflecting the students' learning, achievement, motivation and attitudes on instructionally relevant activities' (p. 127). Biggs and Tang prefer the term 'performances of understanding' to distinguish between methods which assess knowledge and those which assess the application of that knowledge in practice. Underpinning authentic assessment is a desire to represent the effects of learning through student *performance* of what has been learned, anchored in a more or less 'real world' context.

In planning our instruction, we should develop our ILOs and our assessment activities *simultaneously* – they are inextricable. Traditionally, assessment has been viewed as a process that occurs at the end of instruction, rather than an integrated activity that can enhance the learning experience, as well as measure it. Many of the familiar, standard, quantitative forms of assessment – exams, quizzes, multiple-choice questions – are now considered to foster a surface rather than a deep approach to learning, as they 'are designed to test concrete knowledge and not the ability to use search skills in real life' (Avery, 2003: 2). For information literacy in particular, which is concerned more with *process* (functioning knowledge) rather than *content* (declarative knowledge), this is an issue. The problem is exacerbated by students' tendency to focus first on the assessment associated with a module or programme, and to tailor their learning approaches to what they perceive they will be examined on: Biggs and Tang refer to this tendency as *backwash*, which describes 'the effects assessment has on learning, to the extent that assessment may determine what and how students learn more than the curriculum does' (2007: 169). The existence of backwash is thus an even stronger argument for aligning assessment with ILOs and learning activities.

When we are planning our instruction, we can use a matrix to clarify our intentions and help to keep us on track in terms of aligning the ILOs and assessment methods (Table 3.5).

Other factors also influence the design and integration of assessment methods in teaching, and teaching librarians should be aware of a number of different parameters which are relevant to the timing, purpose and effect of assessment.

Formative and summative assessment

This refers to the point at which assessment is carried out.

Formative assessment refers to techniques used by instructors during a session or programme, to obtain immediate feedback on how the

Table 3.5	Constructive alignment matrix

What do I want the students to be able to do?	How can they show this?	What assessment method will enable this?
Evaluate information sources	Through selecting different information sources for a task and explaining why they chose them	Creating an annotated bibliography or resource wiki Reflective research journal
Make effective use of the library resources	Through completing a task or solving a problem which requires library use Through showing others how to use the library	Project on a specific topic Individual or group problem-solving (e.g. EBL) Scavenger hunt Preparing a library guide for a fictional group
Understand how blogging works and what it can be used for	Creating their own blogs Contributing to others' blogs Explaining blogs to others	Individual or group blogging project Preparing a 'blogger's guide'

students' learning is progressing. The results of formative feedback might be used to improve or 'realign' the learning activities, if they are veering off course. Biggs and Tang (2007) describe formative feedback as a teaching and learning activity (TLA) 'that uses error detection as the basis for error correction' (p. 164). Formative assessment is generally informal and often consists of reflective activities. Tools can range from in-class quizzes to short, reflective exercises, designed to highlight on-the-spot problems during a session.

Summative assessment occurs after learning has taken place and is designed to establish whether the ILOs have been achieved by the students. Summative assessment consists of specified activities, which provide the students with an opportunity to demonstrate attainment of the ILOs. As we have discussed above, summative assessment tools should themselves be viewed as an integral part of the teaching and learning activity. Summative tools are typically quite formal (e.g. essays, projects, presentations, examinations) and summative assessment usually carries with it a political agenda, in the sense that the data collected can be used to determine the effectiveness of a programme and thus influence the decision about whether it should continue in its present form or not.

Although the term is 'summative', it is worth reiterating that assessment tools should be planned and developed at the beginning of the instructional planning process, alongside the ILOs.

Norm-referenced and criterion-referenced assessment

This distinction refers to how judgements are made about the quality and standard of students' work or performance.

Norm-referenced assessment (the 'measurement model') evaluates the quality of students' work through *comparison* and requires that 'learning outcomes of individual students are quantified as scores along a single dimension or continuum so that individuals may be compared with each other' (Biggs and Tang, 2007: 171). Usually, this means scoring work in percentages and associating percentage ranges with particular letter grades (A, B, B+, etc.). According to this model, higher achievers are those who get the highest scores and low achievers the lowest – in other words, it places a greater emphasis on innate ability than on the effects of the teaching and learning activities. Distribution of grades among a typical class is usually expected to follow a 'bell-curve' distribution, with most students clustering around the middle – the *expectation* is that only a small number of students should achieve high scores and a small number should fail, and this is expected to remain constant. The requirement to place all students along this curve when grading means that there is little objective measurement of how well ILOs are being met – in that situation, it might be possible for *all* students to attain high scores, a situation which is not acceptable under norm-referenced grading. The negative effects of norm-referencing on student motivation are discussed by Biggs and Tang (2007: 171–6).

Unlike the norm-referencing model, in *criterion-referenced assessment* (the 'standards model'), student work or performance is evaluated based on how well it meets a predetermined standard or criterion for performance. Students are not compared with each other; rather, each student's performance is considered individually and independently from the rest of the group. As teaching librarians, we are responsible for establishing the desired standard and ensuring that students have the opportunity to demonstrate whether they can perform up to that standard or not. To do this, we can create *rubrics*, which describe the different performance standards at each level of achievement. An example of an assessment rubric for the PowerPoint session described previously can be

Table 3.6   Rubric for PowerPoint training session

ILO: 'The student uses PowerPoint effectively when giving presentations in any context.' Assessment: 10-minute group presentation on a topic of choice, using PowerPoint		
A – Excellent	**B – Very good**	**C – Good**
■ Perfect time-keeping (10 minutes) ■ Topic covered in appropriate detail ■ Excellent judgement of appropriate slide content (key words or phrases, not sentences) ■ Very clear font style and size – perfectly readable from a distance ■ Highly appropriate use of graphics to convey relevant information ■ Judicious use of animation and/or sound where appropriate	■ Very good time-keeping (more or less 10 minutes) ■ Topic covered in good detail ■ Slide content shows mostly good judgement ■ Font style and size is mostly clear and readable from a distance ■ Mostly appropriate use of graphics ■ Use of animation and/or sound mostly appropriate	■ Good time-keeping (slightly over or under 10 minutes) ■ Slide content is generally good ■ Font size and style quite clear and readable from a distance ■ Use of graphics is fairly appropriate ■ Use of animation and/or sound fairly appropriate

found in Table 3.6. Unlike norm-referenced assessment, this model fits perfectly with the idea of constructive alignment – determining what the student should *do* and to what level, facilitating appropriate learning activities and then assessing to see if they can, in fact, perform the activity to the desired standard.

Evaluation

Finally, although our primary concern is (and should be) student learning, we should not discount the usefulness of *evaluation*, which is typically undertaken after a programme or session has been completed. Unlike aligned assessment, evaluation does not give us any information about whether learning occurred or whether the ILOs were achieved; rather, evaluation tells us about student satisfaction with the learning experience and highlights any challenges that the students may have experienced in the process. Grassian and Kaplowitz refer to this type of activity as 'Level One' assessment, or 'happiness scales', which 'measure what learners think of the session' (2009: 202). Typically, student evaluation questionnaires are administered in either print or electronic format, containing both closed and open-ended questions. Closed questions frequently require students to indicate their level of agreement with a statement; for example: 'The learning outcomes for this programme were clearly defined' or 'The sessions were well-planned and organised.' Open-ended questions give students the opportunity to highlight the perceived strengths and weaknesses of the programme or session and to make suggestions for improvement.

As teaching librarians, we should never take the results of these evaluation exercises as proof that our instruction has been successful or unsuccessful. Only our aligned assessment activities can give us that information. However, we can incorporate evaluation data into our reflective practice and use what the students tell us to modify or adapt our instruction, where warranted. Evaluation data can also be useful *strategically* in demonstrating to administrators and institutional leaders that our instruction is appreciated by students and perceived as useful to their education as a whole.

Promotion and outreach

'Information literacy is not an end unto itself. Nobody aspires to it. Its habits of mind serve an individual for multiple purposes at varying times, but simply the state of being information literate has no value to anyone' (Rockwell-Kincanon, 2007: 246).

In Chapter 2, we discussed how collaborating with academics and other relevant groups is essential in order for teaching librarians to embed their instructional offerings within academic curricula and to create learning situations that are meaningful and relevant to students. However, the challenges experienced by librarians in persuading academics of the advantages of information literacy instruction were also noted. The need for teaching librarians to actively market and promote their instructional services is now an accepted fact of professional life; while the benefits of information literacy instruction may be obvious to *us*, it is true that they are not obvious to all. A teaching librarian's responsibility, therefore, is not just to ensure that meaningful student learning takes place in existing classes, but to seek out opportunities to introduce programmes and sessions where they are *needed*, in curricula and modules where they have never been embedded before. What are some of the reasons why we find ourselves having to actively promote our services? Some of the reasons have been discussed before. They include the following:

- Many information literacy programmes or sessions that are offered on an *elective* basis suffer from poor attendance, with few students signing up to participate. Sometimes it seems like the only way to get students to attend sessions is to make them compulsory or 'for credit'.

- Getting out of the starting blocks – teaching librarians often find it challenging to get IL programmes up and running in the first place, due to lack of support from administrators, academics, etc.

- 'One-shot' only – as we discussed before, establishing curriculum-integrated programmes is a huge challenge for teaching librarians, who are constantly seeking ways to initiate collaborative working arrangements with academics to gain access to the curriculum.

- 'Information literacy' is treated with scepticism outside the library community – teaching librarians sometimes have to deal with scepticism or outright criticism about the nature of information literacy and the benefits it brings to society.

Rockwell-Kincanon (2007) suggests that marketing information literacy is ultimately about helping to close the gap between current information behaviour, and habits, and what is perceived as the information-literate ideal: 'Marketing information literacy is a combination of promoting ideas (that research in a process of exploration and synthesis, for example), practices (to question an author's credentials and biases), and tools (subscription databases, workshops in genealogical search strategies)' (p. 242). It is important to present information literacy as something that is not just related to libraries, but which offers general techniques and strategies for solving problems and managing information in one's life as a whole.

Grassian and Kaplowitz (2005) contend that teaching librarians need to engage in marketing, so that they can effectively deal with their *competitors*, e.g. instructional resource developers whose products are freely available on the web, or commercial resource providers (p. 225).

For instance, an academic might choose to direct their students towards a freely available YouTube instructional video on plagiarism, rather than ask the teaching librarian to facilitate a session. However, while tackling the competition is important, there is also a strong case to be made that teaching librarians must first address the much *greater* challenge of potential service users' lack of awareness of the kind of instruction a teaching librarian can provide, or of their own instructional needs. From the marketing point of view, the starting point must also be *start with the student* – identifying what the instructional needs are and explaining how these needs can be met by the library.

As teaching librarians, we must be aware of the different 'markets' we need to target, as each will require a different strategy. In planning our marketing strategies, some of the questions we could ask include:

- Who are the target audience?
- What do they need to learn (instructional needs)?
- What aspect of our service offerings are we going to market/promote?
- Who will be the target of our campaign?
- What ultimate goal are we trying to achieve (e.g. instruction embedded in the curriculum, extra funding, etc.)?
- What form of promotion will work best with this target group?
- How can we judge when we've done enough?

For information literacy instruction, sometimes the target audience can be different from the group that we will target in our *campaign*: Rockwell-Kincanon notes that 'information literacy programmes also have dual audiences – the individual adopters and any "gatekeepers" for the institution' (2007: 244). For instance, the target group for the programme might be first-year arts and humanities undergraduates. However, if we are to try and embed our instruction into the curriculum, it is not the *students* who we are targeting from a promotional perspective; rather, we must direct our efforts towards the academics who coordinate the programmes and who are the 'gatekeepers' to the curriculum. Or, we might choose a top–down approach and target the administrators and decision-makers at the highest level in an attempt to align our programmes with the broader institutional mission. Sometimes the campaign target will be the students themselves – for instance, when we are running elective sessions, e.g. lunchtime demos, library orientations, etc.

So, who are our target markets? In academic libraries, they include those listed in Table 3.7.

Table 3.7	Information literacy target markets

Target markets	
Students	Undergraduates, postgraduates, full- and part-time, on-campus and distance learners, traditional and non-traditional
Academics	Course directors, but also teaching assistants, tutors, etc.
Researchers	Post-doctoral fellows, research fellows, research assistants
Administrators	Deans, faculty/school heads, committee chairpersons, etc.

Each target group has a different agenda and individual instructional needs, both recognised and unrecognised. How do we tap into each group? We might consider a long-established analytical tool, drawn from the field of marketing – the marketing mix, or the 'four Ps' – product, place, price and promotion.

The four Ps of information literacy instruction

Focusing each of these categories on our target market helps us to make wise decisions about how to sell our products and services.

Product

What are we 'selling'? As Rockwell-Kincanon points out, information literacy in and of itself is value-free – rather, it is up to us to demonstrate the value, or benefits that being information literate will bring to our clients' lives. In academic institutions, we might focus on particular challenges to which information literacy might offer a solution, such as plagiarism, information overload or library anxiety. Our 'product' must fill a perceived need.

Place

Place relates to the *distance* a customer must travel to obtain a product or avail of a service. For new products which are unfamiliar to an audience, a shorter distance increases the likelihood of adoption. For information literacy, bringing the learning activities directly into the classroom or onto the desktop might be a better promotional strategy than expecting them to come to *us*. For instance, mounting the learning activities on a VLE so that they are available to remote learners is a good example of 'placing' a product to make it convenient and more attractive to clients, who might not be willing to physically travel to campus to attend a session. Holding a session in the training room in the centrally located library, rather than a computer lab in a building that is at the other end of campus, is another example.

Price

Price refers to the 'cost' a customer incurs in order to obtain a product or avail of a service. This does not just mean monetary costs, but also opportunity cost, in terms of time or convenience that must be given up. For information literacy, the 'cost' for an academic might be the class sessions that they have to 'give up' for information literacy instruction, or the time they have to spend in collaborative planning with the teaching librarian. We should try to keep 'cost' as low as possible when we are trying to establish our programmes (i.e. make it easy for our clients). When the benefits are eventually perceived, we then have the flexibility to vary our 'costs'.

Promotion

Promotion refers to effective communication with the target audience. We must select the promotional tools that we think are most likely to attract the attention of our audience. We might choose from:

- pamphlets/flyers;
- posters;
- 'e-mailshots';
- short promotional videos;
- announcements on VLEs;
- electronic noticeboards;
- bookmarks, pencils, keyrings, etc., with library or information literacy logo;
- web pages;
- social networking pages, e.g. dedicated Facebook page;

- short presentation or 'pitch' to audience;

- manning a stand at open days, graduate fairs, etc.;

- testimonials from previous students (e.g. on website);

- newsletters (print and electronic);

- social events – coffee mornings, wine and cheese receptions, etc.

Must teaching librarians also become expert marketers and PR agents, on top of everything else they have to do? This is hardly realistic. However, we do have a responsibility to somehow put our products 'out there' and sell what we do to potential users of the service. What are the kinds of knowledge and skills that we need?

- clear vision of the teaching and learning mission of the library and ability to articulate it, both verbally and in writing;

- appreciation of the benefits that information literacy brings, not just to education, but to other aspects of everyday life, and the ability to convey that appreciation to potential 'clients', both verbally and in writing;

- knowledge of the different tools that can be used to gather information about our target markets, e.g. surveys, focus groups, online polling, secondary research, etc.;

- 'coolhunting' – scanning the environment to discover the latest trends and issues that have captured the interest and attention of our target groups. We can find ways of exploiting these issues to draw clients in, sometimes in quite off beat ways – e.g. offering sessions which show students how to get the most out of their smartphone applications (with academic content included, naturally!). Behen suggests that librarians should adopt themes and formats from popular culture, to engage and motivate the 'Google Generation', including reality television, game shows and movies (2006: 63–91);

- a good grasp of the 'lingo', i.e. the terms and phrases that will register with our target groups and will garner interest in what we have to offer – if 'information literacy' fails to resonate, try something different. Each group requires a different approach, e.g. you will not use the same language with academics as you would with young undergraduates;

- willingness to explore and experiment with new social networking tools to promote and generate interest in our service offerings (e.g. Twitter, Facebook, blogging, text alerts, etc.). Also, the ability to recognise when use of these tools is *not* appropriate;

- a degree of creativity, or at least a knowledge of methods that can be used to generate ideas – e.g. brainstorming sessions, idea boxes, creative workshops, etc.;

- an appreciation of the power of 'word of mouth' – exploiting local and informal channels to spread the word about our services. For example, giving an interview to the campus newspaper, making a funny YouTube video to take advantage of viral marketing, networking with non-library colleagues at social events, creating a regularly updated blog about what's happening in the library, etc.

Exercises and reflections

Choose one of the scenarios below and complete the following tasks in relation to it:

Scenario A: Teaching a class of 150 first-year arts undergraduates (freshmen), all of differing backgrounds and abilities, how to research and write academic essays (four-week programme, two hours per week).

Scenario B: Teaching a group of 30 doctoral students in the social sciences about advanced research processes (eight-week programme, one hour per week).

- Create a mission statement for your programme.

- Choose and create an instructional needs assessment instrument for the group (e.g. pre-test, focus group protocol, etc.).

- Write goals, objectives and ILOs for the programme.

- Choose (and justify) an overall learning approach.

- Choose (and justify) specific teaching and learning methods.

- Create lesson plans for the first two sessions.

- Create one or two learning materials for the programme (e.g. a worksheet, PowerPoint presentation, online quiz, webquest, handouts).

- Create a suitable assessment for the programme, including a rubric for grading.

- Devise a promotional flyer for the programme, aimed at academics.

4

Confidence-zappers and how to handle them

Abstract: This chapter highlights a number of challenging situations that can cause teaching librarians to doubt their self-efficacy and drain their confidence. Each challenge is described and analysed and solutions are suggested to help librarians deal with the difficulties they may experience, both in their day-to-day teaching work and from an overall strategic or organisational perspective. The challenges regularly faced by teaching librarians include poor student attendance at elective sessions, trying to facilitate active learning with large classes, low student motivation and poor engagement, trying to find effective ways of using a VLE to support learning activities, dealing with adult learners, and trying to create meaningful learning experiences within 'one-shot' class sessions.

Key words: confidence challenge, student motivation, one-shot classes, adult learners, virtual learning environment, active learning.

In his text on reflective teaching, Pollard (2008) notes that a significant cause of stress among (school) teachers arises from their attempts to resolve the everyday *dilemmas* which result from the conflation of numerous competing factors in their environments – for example, practical classroom matters, performance standards, personal ideals and wider educational concerns all jostle for attention in the business of teaching (p. 6). He notes that 'the resolution of such dilemmas calls for teachers to use professional judgement to assess the most appropriate course of action in any particular situation' (ibid.). As teaching librarians, we too find that we must deal with a multiplicity of factors in our attempts to teach effectively, and sometimes our feelings of confidence can be buffeted by the difficult circumstances that confront us and the recurring issues that slow us down and cause us frustration. Woolfolk et al. define self-efficacy as 'a person's sense of being able to deal effectively with a particular task' (2008: 722). The authors also draw attention to research which has shown that a teacher's sense of self-efficacy is one of the few factors that are *positively* correlated with learner achievement – the more a teacher believes in their ability to facilitate learning, the more likely they are to invest time and energy in managing and overcoming challenging situations. An important point to note is that self-efficacy is more likely to develop from *actual* concrete success experienced with learners, rather than 'cheer leading' or support from colleagues: 'Any experience of training that helps people succeed in the day-to-day tasks of teaching will provide a foundation for developing a sense of efficacy in your career (Woolfolk et al., 2008: 403). So, while encouragement is important, it is primarily through building on experience that your sense of confidence and self-efficacy will grow and enable you to face any situation, unfazed.

As we have already noted, teaching librarians face a number of challenges that are not shared by school teachers or even university lecturers, although they operate in essentially the same environment. Some of the main stress factors for teaching librarians have already been discussed in this book, including:

- being constantly overstretched – combining teaching with general library duties;
- lack of training in how to teach;
- operating in a vacuum – lack of involvement in subject curricula;
- insufficient time with students – predominance of 'one-shot' sessions;
- student motivation – unaccredited courses and sessions attract few students;
- coping with a diverse student body – every group is different;
- constant self-promotion required – 'selling' the instructional services of the library;
- feeling of having to explain role again and again.

Teacher anxiety among librarians was specifically explored by Davis (2007) in her survey of 382 academic librarians in the US. She reported the following findings:

- 63 per cent of her sample claimed to feel nervous before starting a class, with 60 per cent experiencing physical symptoms associated with that stress, e.g. sweating, upset stomach, blushing, etc.

- 65 per cent indicated that they experience mental or emotional symptoms; their worries included fears about being underprepared to deal with difficult questions (40 per cent) and public speaking (27 per cent).

- A number of respondents reported feeling anxious about librarian stereotyping (24 per cent), particularly with regard to academics' perceptions of their role.

The following sections explore several of the more challenging situations that crop up frequently in the work of teaching librarians. They represent many of the key themes that have already been discussed – motivation, active learning, classroom management, technology, relationships with academics and student diversity. Unresolved, these situations can lower motivation, increase stress and have a negative effect on perceptions of self-efficacy. Some of the situations are common to all teachers; others are specific to the circumstances of teaching librarians and relate to their unique role in the academic community. They are described in 'real' terms, designed to represent actual questions that teaching librarians might ask themselves about their work. In exploring each situation in a systematic way and applying the knowledge and concepts discussed in previous chapters, it is hoped that each section will offer you, as teaching librarians, a means to plan and develop strategies to confidently handle the issues that you face.

'Attendance at our elective information literacy workshops is poor – what can I do to encourage students to sign up?'

Elective, or 'drop-in', sessions represent a unique dilemma for teaching librarians. On the one hand, they offer a means for librarians to reach students (and academic staff) when curriculum-integrated instruction proves difficult to establish. On the other, however, they are often ignored by the very students they are designed to reach, and suffer from poor attendance. However, rather than becoming discouraged and dispirited by the lack of take-up of elective sessions, teaching librarians should endeavour to think of them in a more strategic way and to *use* them as a promotional tool, while at the same time continuing to work towards curriculum-integration and alignment with institutional objectives.

Appreciating what motivates students in educational environments is the first step in understanding why they might not attend drop-in sessions.

Typically, students' action, or inaction, arises from *extrinsic* and *intrinsic* motivational factors (Jacobson and Xu, 2004: 4–6):

■ *Extrinsic motivation* concerns factors which are *external* to the student. According to this perspective, learners respond to: a) *positive* reinforcers or rewards, which in the academic environment might include successfully passing a course, obtaining high grades, or simply gaining praise for an assignment well done; and b) *negative* reinforcers, which refer to the students' desire to avoid punishment or adverse consequences, e.g. failing a course, having to resubmit course work, angry parents, etc.

■ *Intrinsic motivation*, by contrast, derives from students' personal interest in subjects, and their innate desire to learn; they are not motivated by the promise of reward, but simply gain pleasure from the learning process itself, and are highly self-directed and independent learners. Learning which derives from intrinsic motivation is inevitably deeper and more meaningful than extrinsically motivated learning.

However, the structure of the educational process at both school and university level is typically based on *norm-referenced* assessment (see Chapter 3), which effectively pits the students against each other competitively and focuses on high grades as proof of successful learning. Students, therefore, tend to become strategic about their learning and to focus their efforts primarily on activities that they perceive will contribute to the attainment of those grades. Elective courses, if they are not mandated by lecturers, do not usually fall into this category, and are consequently perceived by students as something that can be safely ignored. Obviously, courses or sessions that are accredited, or which count towards a grade in a subject area, are less likely to suffer from attendance problems (although the problem of extrinsic versus intrinsic motivation is still an issue, from the perspective of *depth* of learning).

So, what can you, as teaching librarians, do if your sessions are not accredited? From an overall perspective, you should, of course, continue to proactively explore ways of integrating your instruction into academic curricula, where it is appropriate to do so, for the many reasons discussed in previous chapters. But, does this mean that elective sessions should be abandoned entirely? Not necessarily. When perceived in a different way, drop-in sessions can become an important marketing and promotional tool for libraries. If your elective offerings are not proving popular, it is important to look at them with a critical eye, and ask a number of probing questions:

■ *Is there a basic mismatch between what* you *think the students want or need, and what they* actually *want?* The sessions that are on offer may only represent *your* estimation of what will attract students. While we are often correct in our assumptions, there is no substitute for solid market research. When it comes to selling, drop-in sessions are like any other product or service; we must find out what the customers' needs are and try to satisfy those needs. As teaching librarians, you can adopt a proactive approach to researching your target market – for example, online surveys are now very quick and easy to create and administer, with the availability of such web-based tools as *Survey Monkey* and *Zoomerang*. Other approaches to needs assessment have been discussed in Chapter 3.

■ *Is the channel appropriate?* Most elective sessions are offered on a F2F basis, typically in an information skills laboratory located inside the library itself. Often, the idea is to 'get students through the door', so that, as a by-product of instruction, they will come to appreciate the library as *place* and the other services that are available. However, you should consider if the library is the most appropriate place to hold your instruction, or if F2F is the most suitable format. Perhaps holding a class in the campus building where the open-access computer labs are located might gain more visibility for the library, and contribute to students' perception that the library has more to offer than that which is contained within its four walls? Or creating a series of e-tutorials which can be accessed any time, any place, might best suit the needs of the target group?

■ *Are your sessions generic or 'tailored'?* Boyle describes the benefits of 'tailoring' information literacy instruction to the specific needs of defined groups, so that they can 'experience the reflection of their curriculum modules in the library sessions they attend' (2009: 74). Generic sessions are more difficult to 'sell' as they do not tap directly into students' academic concerns, and their relevance and usefulness may not be explicit. Although curriculum-embedded sessions may not be possible, drop-in sessions *can* be designed with specific groups in mind and the content tailored to their needs (and, importantly, to the *timing* of those needs). This approach does require a degree of collaboration with academics, in order to identify the most suitable time to schedule information literacy sessions.

■ *What promotional strategies are you using?* Drop-in sessions frequently suffer from low awareness, as the promotional tools fail to hit their 'targets'. Promotional tools should be highly visible to whatever target market you are trying to reach. In the case of drop-in sessions, you are often promoting at two levels: one, aimed at the students themselves, and two, aimed at the teaching staff, who might encourage students to attend. A frequently underestimated promotional opportunity is *word of mouth*, where satisfied (or unsatisfied!) customers spread the word about their experiences to family, friends and colleagues. Social networking has dramatically increased the potential of word-of-mouth promotion, as people – particularly young adults – readily air their opinions about products and services on Facebook, Twitter, and multiple Internet forums and blogs (Riegner, 2007; Godes and Mayzlin, 2004). Teaching librarians can be proactive in this regard and should not be afraid of asking students who have attended sessions to mention them on whatever social site they use, or simply to spread the word among their peers and encourage them to attend. Including testimonials (with permission) from happy customers on the library website, Facebook page or newsletter is another good way to get the word out.

- *Unique selling proposition (USP).* This is defined in the *Oxford Dictionary of Business* (2003) as 'a product benefit that can be regarded as unique and therefore can be used in advertising to differentiate it from the competition'. Have you identified the elements of your instructional sessions that make them unique? Libraries have the advantage of being the first (and often only) department on campus to provide access to useful new resources, and drop-in sessions which are focused on these resources can attract staff and students.

From a general perspective, you should treat you programme of drop-in sessions as just one element in the library's overall instructional strategy, rather than the main offering. Think of your elective programme in the same way as commercial entities think of theirs – it should be presented professionally, with clearly articulated outcomes and a statement of the benefits and value that your 'customers' will gain from attending. You could also give them something to take away (depending on the group) – for instance, a printed certificate of completion for students, which can give a sense of achievement, even though there is no actual credit attached.

'How can I facilitate active learning with such a large group of students? Is it possible to do more than lecture?'

Many teachers, not just teaching librarians, feel daunted at the prospect of engaging a large group in the learning process; often, a lecture seems the easiest option, even if purely from a class management perspective. The logistics of introducing active learning techniques into a group of 100+ students might seem overly challenging, and impossible to manage.

However, as teaching librarians, active learning is the heart and soul of what we do; the principles of constructive alignment insist that lecturing is rarely appropriate for our learning situations. From a general perspective, lecturing has long fallen out of favour as an effective learning method, although it is still widely used as a practical means of managing large groups in higher education. Biggs and Tang (2007: 108–9) describe some of the reasons (based on research) why lecturing does not facilitate deep learning:

- Unsupervised reading is actually *more* effective for presenting information to students than lecturing.
- Lectures do not stimulate higher-order thinking in students.
- Concentration is *lowered* by unchanging low-level activity (i.e. sitting and listening to a lecture).
- Students' attention span typically drops off after 10–15 minutes.
- Unless a lecture is *particularly* good, students prefer small group work.

Gibbs also famously dismantles many of the positive 'myths' surrounding the assumed effectiveness of lecturing in his paper, *Twenty Terrible Reasons for Lecturing*, published in 1981 – his arguments are still valid today.

For teaching librarians, whose instruction is most often focused on the *process* and *experience* of research rather than content, active learning is a *sine qua non*. But when we are faced with a group of 100+ students, how can we make the learning 'active' without invoking chaos in the lecture theatre? In truth, there are a great number of methods for introducing active learning to large group sessions (Biggs and Tang, 2007; Van der Meer et al., 2007). When it seems that, due to the size of your group, lecturing might be the only option, you can choose from some of the following activities to create an interactive learning experience for the students.

Buzz groups

In large classes, creating buzz groups means dividing the overall group into pairs, three, fours or fives, and giving them short tasks or problems, which involves them talking and discussing among themselves (the sound they create as they talk is the 'buzz'!), and coming up with a solution, or set of points for further discussion. Each group can then be asked to present the results of their discussion with the rest of the class, perhaps using overhead transparencies, white boards, flipcharts, or other visual props. In an information literacy context, this might involve giving the groups real-life information 'problems' to solve, e.g. 'What do you do when you need to find career information about becoming a lawyer?' or other scenarios that are directly relevant to their own lives.

Rounds

An old favourite, often used as an 'icebreaker' exercise in group sessions, this involves going around every person in the group and asking them to respond to a question, to make a statement or give an opinion. For example, students could be asked to introduce themselves, and explain why they chose the course and what they expect to get from it. Or they could be asked to state what they already know about a topic or, in an information literacy context, what kinds of resources they've used before, how much library experience they have and what skills they would like to develop. However, students should always be given the opportunity to 'pass' if they feel too shy to speak out in front of the group. Rounds work best in groups that are not too large (20–30).

Brainstorming

Brainstorming is a tried-and-tested way of stimulating the flow of ideas in a synergistic environment. Using a question as a starting point, all contributors are encouraged to shout out their ideas as they occur to them – no comments or judgements are made during the process, all ideas are treated as valid. Responses are recorded, perhaps on a flipchart, white board or blackboard, and it is only when the process is finished that discussion can occur. Students can also try to identify associations between the different ideas and perhaps try to create concept maps (mind maps), linking ideas using connectors. Another possibility would be to record each idea on a separate Post-It note, and then to cluster similar ideas by grouping the Post-Its together on a large board (or even the wall, if there is no board to hand!).

Work-along exercises

A comparatively easy way to incorporate active learning into large group sessions is to create exercises, linked to session content, which students can complete at intervals during the class, alone, in pairs or in slightly larger groups. Biggs and Tang note that, in lectures 'a short rest or a change in activity every 15 minutes or so restores performance (i.e. concentration) almost to the original level' (2007: 109). Even a short multiple-choice quiz in the middle of a session constitutes a task that requires students to be active. Information literacy offers a wealth of topics that lend themselves to hands-on exercises; for example, students could be asked to describe the differences between popular and scholarly resources through examining actual samples that are distributed; or they could be requested to create accurate bibliographic references for different information items.

It may also be possible to create interactive online activities, depending on the technology available in the classroom or lecture theatre. Nowadays, many lecture theatres are equipped with wifi, and students who own laptops or notebooks can be encouraged to bring them along and to access the relevant resources (e.g. databases, OPAC) to complete searches and exercises alongside the teacher. Alternatively, when students do not have their own laptops, many institutions now possess mobile 'laptop carts' containing a number of laptops, which can be borrowed for classes that are too large to fit into a computer laboratory.

Syndicates

Using syndicates involves small groups of students working together on specific projects (with clearly defined briefs), which require them to carry out a range of activities, including research, synthesis and presentation. Class time can be used to allow the students to progress their work, with you as moderator, moving from group to group offering support and advice where needed.

Presentations

Group presentations are activities that could run over a number of weeks. In large classes, the students can be divided into smaller groups of four to five, and each group given a different topic or problem to work on. Students must go away in their groups, gather and synthesise information on those topics, and prepare a short presentation which they will give to the rest of the class during lecture time. Depending on class numbers, one or two groups can give their presentations each week, until all groups have had a turn.

Classroom response systems (CRSs)

Classroom response systems, or 'clickers', might be familiar to readers from the 'Ask the Audience' segment of the internationally syndicated quiz show *Who Wants to be a Millionaire?*. Beatty (2004: 2) defines clickers as technology that:

- allows an instructor to present a question or problem to the class;
- allows students to enter their answers into some kind of device;
- instantly aggregates and summarises students' answers for the instructor.

In a typical lecture scenario, the software is integrated with PowerPoint; the class is presented with multiple-choice questions on the screen, and they are requested to select an answer (a,b,c,d) by pressing a button on a handheld remote device. The answers are then aggregated and appear on the screen in graphical format. Students can see if their own answer was correct; all answers are, however, submitted anonymously. As well as 'factual' questions, CRS can be used to gauge class opinion on particular issues, as interactive 'polls'.

This is an application that can grab students' attention, which they might find fun and engaging, and that can help to break up the monotony of a lecture. However, a presentation which integrates classroom response technology requires a significant amount of preparation time, and the management issues involved with the distribution and collecting of the remote devices can be burdensome. A few case studies of CRS use in information literacy classes can be found in the literature (Clobridge and Del Testa, 2008; Corcos and Monty, 2008).

Think-pair-share

Think-pair-share involves posing a question to the class, allowing each student time to consider it individually, then asking them to join with their neighbour to discuss it in pairs and, finally, sharing their thoughts with the rest of the class. For example, you could ask them a question such as: 'What are the advantages and disadvantages of using Google for academic research?' or 'How do you go about finding information on a topic you have never heard of before?' You can then record key points and perhaps create a handout based on the session to distribute to the class the following week.

Fish bowls

Fish bowls work best when the overall group is not too large. It involves a select group who volunteer to sit in the middle of the larger group and to engage in a discussion about a topic or a problem among themselves. The other students simply observe and record the discussion or task, and then afterwards any important issues may be discussed at greater length by the whole class. In an 'open fish bowl' scenario, one space in the centre group is left open, and any member of the outer group is free to take the space and join in the discussion at any point. However, one member of the inner group must volunteer to leave the fishbowl when a new member joins.

Structured note-taking

If you have chosen a lecture as your teaching method, interactivity can be introduced by providing handouts of your slides, with key words and phrases missing, that the students are required to fill in during the lecture. Also, Biggs and Tang suggest that note-taking can be useful for 'immediate review and reflection', which involves giving them sufficient time to review their notes during class, or even swapping them with their neighbour to gain additional perspective.

Jigsaw method

The jigsaw method is when different groups in the class are asked to work on separate aspects of a problem; the groups then report back to the rest of the class and the problem is discussed holistically. Van der Meer et al. suggest that: 'A benefit of the jigsaw approach is that multiple parts of a process can be studied by different groups simultaneously and then shared with the whole class, thereby using time efficiently' (2007: 51). The enquiry-based scenario which was discussed in Chapter 3 is an example of the kind of multifaceted problem that would work well in a jigsaw situation.

'I'm having trouble keeping the students interested in class – they seem bored and unmotivated. Is there anything I can do?'

Having students in class who are intrinsically motivated to learn is often perceived as a stroke of *luck* by teaching librarians and cherished for that reason. We always remember the enthusiastic students, who seemed to revel in learning for learning's sake and were endlessly interested in the subject. A more general perception is that students have to be 'persuaded' and coaxed into learning – unless they are motivated by external factors, they will not engage willingly in the learning activities that are set up for them. This perception inevitably causes stress for us, as teaching librarians, due to the feeling that motivation is something out of our control – students are either motivated to learn, or they are not, and we have to work with whatever we have.

However, Biggs and Tang flatly reject the notion that motivation in students can be lacking completely: 'There is no such thing as an unmotivated student: all students not in a coma want to do *something*' (2007: 31). They argue that the task of the instructor is to maximise the chance that what students *want* to do is to attain the learning outcomes that have been set. Becoming aware of the factors that affect motivation is a useful first step for teaching librarians. Biggs and Tang suggest that there are two major factors that influence the probability that a student wants to learn or not. They frame these factors as 'expectancy-value' theory:

1. The task must be perceived as having some *value* to the student – it must be *important* enough for them to invest time and energy (purpose of learning).

2. The student must have an expectancy of *success* – they must believe that they have the *ability* to master the task or content (self-efficacy/ learner attitude).

Webb and Powis (2004) also add the learning environment, prior experience and learning style into the mix (2004: 44), although all of these are inextricably linked to the above two.

In terms of the first main factor – the purpose of learning – the different forms of motivation have been partly discussed before. The concepts of extrinsic and intrinsic motivation have already been explained. However, students can also be *socially* motivated – learning in order to satisfy the expectations of others, e.g. to please one's parents. They can also be motivated by *achievement* – learning in order to enhance the ego, to feel good about oneself. The second factor, the expectation of success, or self-efficacy, is linked to the perception of control that a student believes they have over a topic or task. If poor performance, for example, is attributed to innate *ability* rather than effort, motivation is likely to be low, as the student might feel that no matter what they do, they cannot change their lack of ability. If they have the opposite view, however – that increased *effort* raises the probability of success – their conception of self-efficacy is likely to be much more positive.

Teachers exert a considerable influence on these factors, although they might not be aware of it. For instance, instructor feedback is highly instrumental in the development of student confidence and self-belief; a cynical, negative teacher can inflict serious damage to a student's sense of self-efficacy. The enthusiasm of a teacher for a topic can be infectious and can inspire a classroom of students; similarly, a downbeat and dissatisfied instructor can have the opposite effect. Jacobson and Xu (2004: 7) draw attention to the Keller's *ARCS* model of motivation in learning (1987), which pulls these factors together:

- Attention: capturing students' interest, stimulating desire to learn;
- Relevance: demonstrating the value of the learning outcomes to the students' own personal goals;
- Confidence: instilling in students the belief that they can master the task or knowledge at hand;
- Satisfaction: ensuring a sense of satisfaction with the learning process, in order to encourage continuing engagement.

So, bearing these factors in mind, what can we, as teaching librarians, do to stimulate and sustain student motivation? For us, the challenge is complicated further by the fact that our sessions are often unaccredited. However, based on our knowledge of the factors that motivate students, we could consider the following suggestions in our teaching:

Establish a positive teaching environment

We should endeavour to create an atmosphere in which success is attributable to effort and is perceived as achievable by the students, not something that is out of their control – in other words, we need to instil an expectation of success among our students. To explain this, Biggs and Tang refer to 'Theory X' and 'Theory Y' classrooms (2007: 37); in 'Theory X' situations, instructors assume that students are unwilling to learn and that they cannot be trusted to manage their own learning, while 'Theory Y' instructors assume the opposite – that students are positively inclined towards learning, and with the proper encouragement and intervention will do their best to achieve the learning outcomes. These beliefs naturally spill over into the teaching environment, influencing student motivation – 'Theory X' instructors are more likely to be cynical and sarcastic, to try and 'catch students out' and to display indifference to the material they are teaching, while 'Theory Y' teachers strive to create a wholly positive, encouraging environment, which brings out the best in students. As teaching librarians, it is up to you to articulate your belief to the students that all of them will be able to master the tasks or content, as long as they are willing to work.

Set achievable tasks

One of the basic tenets of self-efficacy is that the more actual success a student has in completing tasks, the more their confidence builds and the greater the sense of self-belief: 'Expectations of success are instilled on the basis of previous success' (Biggs and Tang, 2007: 33). While you shouldn't consciously 'dumb down' your class activities, it is an idea – initially at least – to set tasks and exercises for students that are *comparatively* easy to complete and which will give them a sense of control over the material, as well as the belief that they can handle more challenging assignments. You should also be very clear about what your expectations are and convey them to the students early on.

Offer encouragement

It goes without saying; you should be generous with positive feedback and encouragement; criticism should be constructive where necessary and sarcasm should be avoided at all costs. Feedback should also be as specific as possible – you should explain to students exactly what steps they can take to improve on an assignment, rather than just make general comments, such as 'You need to be more precise here,' or 'Try to narrow your topic down more.'

Show enthusiasm

The teacher's own enthusiasm and passion are powerful motivators and can inspire students to see the value of a topic or task; similarly, a teacher's obvious distaste for an activity can be equally infectious, convey the message that it has little value and is not worth doing. If you are passionate about what you are teaching, it will show. Students respond extremely well to a teacher's own interest in topics. From a social motivation perspective, this can translate into a student's desire to 'live up' to the instructor's passion and to do justice to it.

Demonstrate relevance

Unless your session is already embedded in the curriculum and linked to course content, it falls to you to make clear to students how the topics and tasks you are covering are useful and relevant to their studies. One way to do this is to frame the session in terms of realistic problem scenarios that the students might encounter, rather than enumerate the different skills and/or topics you are going to cover. For example, you might start a session by saying something like:

> So, you've just been given your first university essay assignment with strict instructions not to use Google for your research. Where do you start, if you can't use your favourite search tool?' or 'Your course instructor has asked you to prepare a two-page report outlining the key issues associated with climate change – how on earth do you summarise such a wide topic?

Place yourself on the side of the students – acknowledge their frustration with the assignments they have been set and tell them that what they learn in your session will enable them to deal with the work.

Tap into popular culture

For younger students in particular, adopting the themes and formats of popular culture is viewed by some as a means of capturing interest and motivating students to learn: 'If the popular culture of today's teens is what drives their behaviour and motivates them, why not use it to connect with them?' (Behen, 2006: 2). Popular TV shows, computer games, rock stars and movie personalities, sports and social networking applications are all popular culture elements which appeal to traditional students and can be creatively integrated into the teaching and learning experience. Behen (2006) offers numerous examples of how teaching methods can be adapted to reflect popular culture themes, including creating a series of team-based competitive library exercises, based on the reality TV show *Survivor*. Other authors have suggested the use of web-based games to teach information literacy skills (Williams, 2010; Markey et al., 2008).

'It seems like everyone on campus is using the VLE/CMS for their teaching, and I feel left behind – how can I get started with it?'

Course management systems (CMS), also known as virtual learning environments (VLE), are now used by virtually all institutions of higher education to supplement the more traditional forms of teaching and learning. Mackey and Jacobson describe some of the functions of VLEs, noting that this form of online learning 'expands the kinds of activities instructors design for an online environment, including tutorials, quizzes and surveys, as well as writing assignments (in a journal or blog, bulletin board, or online chat session)' (2008: 83). Popular VLEs at the moment include Blackboard, Moodle and ANGEL.

As teaching librarians, what is our role in regard to VLEs? Since VLE use is typically course-based, most of the time there is no obvious route for librarians, who are generalists and not usually attached to particular courses. Therefore, the first issue is gaining access. Your access to the VLE will probably be mediated by individual course instructors, who can request that you are added to their course areas. As Nickel (2007) confirms, 'Working in most course management systems requires you to have access to individual courses with a login name and password' (p. 157). The level of access you are granted determines what you will be able to do. For example, in Blackboard, there are six different course roles, which control access to the tools and content within courses. As *course builder*, for instance, you have access to almost everything, except student grades. As *instructor*, you have complete access to all areas, as this is the role that is generally designated to the course coordinator. *Students* have no access to any of the tools in the Control Panel and can only access content which has been made visible to them by the instructor. If you are involved in providing sessions for particular courses, the first step is to ask the course lecturer to add you to their course area on the VLE, preferably as *instructor,* or *teacher's assistant* at the least. That will allow you to start to upload documents and create learning activities to support your instruction (Cox, 2002).

The next step is to familiarise yourself with the functionality that is provided within VLEs, either through access to training, consulting online help manuals or through simply experimenting with the system yourself. The current versions of most VLEs offer a wide range of interactive instructional tools that are accessed through a single interface. For example, in the current version of Blackboard (9.1), in addition to document storage, instructors also have access to:

- announcements;
- blogs;
- discussion board;
- journals;
- lecture capture;
- messages;
- tasks;
- tests, surveys and pools;
- wikis.

It is important not to use the VLE simply as a 'dumping ground' for course-related materials; the principles of active learning still apply. Mackey and Jacobson emphasise that online elements should be designed carefully, so that 'they extend student learning and provide an opportunity to deepen the treatment of information literacy concepts and skills' (2008: 86). This means embracing the interactive potential of the system and using the tools to create teaching activities that align with your ILOs – just like any other instructional format.

However, you do have to start somewhere, and as you get to grips with the more complicated tools, starting simply with document upload will give you a growing sense of control over the system. For example, you can begin by embedding a small repository of general library guides, path finders and information exercises and worksheets that students can download for their own use. You might also create a 'webliography' of links to useful resources, including online tutorials, videos, slides and other multimedia resources, as appropriate to the course in question. This will allow you to establish a presence within the system. Other comparatively easy activities to set up initially include creating quick interactive quizzes or self-diagnostic information skills surveys for the students, or using the live chat function at specified times to provide a virtual reference service for the students.

When you feel that you have mastered the fundamentals of the system, you can begin to think more deeply about how it can be harnessed to support your ILOs and complement your F2F sessions, if you have them. Some suggestions for active learning within a VLE include the following:

- *Use the wiki tool.* Divide the students into groups, and ask them to create a wiki on a specific course-related topic or question. If students are already working on group projects, wiki space can be set up to allow them to collaborate without having to meet in person. One interesting exercise would be to ask the groups (or individuals) to create electronic resource guides on specified topics, encouraging them to supplement the wiki text with images, embedded audio and video files, as well as links to external websites, e-books and any other resources they consider appropriate. As the instructor, you can provide regular feedback and guidance, where required, using the comments function.

- *Use the journal or blog tool.* Students can be required to keep weekly logs of their research activities, outlining the research and reading activities engaged in, the search tools and resources accessed, the problems and challenges encountered, and just general reflection on the process. As with the wiki exercise, students can be encouraged to attach relevant documents, such as exercises completed, concept maps, lists of keywords, journal articles, or any other appendices that they consider relevant to the task. As instructor, you can provide a structured template for the journal, with clear headings and/or questions, to help the students to organise their thoughts.

- *Use the discussion board.* The VLE discussion board tool can be used to facilitate remote group-work, Q&A sessions, or just general discussion about topics of interest. However, as with most learning tools, students usually require encouragement to use them, so setting up a structured activity is likely to work best. For example, a discussion thread might be set up to analyse a specific essay topic that the students have been given – comments could range from suggesting search terms, recommending resources or simply reflecting on the assignment. To encourage participation, students could be given credit for their contributions.

An increasing number of examples of VLE use for information literacy instruction are available in the literature (Donaldson, 2010; Masters, 2009). One of the main advantages of using a VLE for this kind of instruction is that everything is accessed through a single interface – for example, you can embed easy links to resources (databases, websites, etc.) into exercises that the students are working on, so that they don't need to disrupt the flow of the activity to search for them. Text, audio and video can be located together to create a single multimedia resource. The interactive communication tools are also at hand – for example, a student working on an assignment can simply open the discussion board and post a question, or can use the online chat function if they know that you are also online at certain times of the day.

A common theme which unites all of these case studies is *collaboration with academics*, as well as IT and learning support staff. As Nickel points out: 'As librarians we need to work with teaching faculty and instructional designers in order to secure a prominent (or at least visible) position on students' radars' (2008: 153).

'I have to teach a group of adult learners and I find it intimidating – how can I live up to their expectations?'

For teaching librarians, the sense of intimidation that is sometimes felt when faced with a class of adult learners may be due to a perception that they are more knowledgeable, more life-experienced in general, more demanding of their instructors than traditional students, and less tolerant of errors. While this perception may not be *entirely* incorrect, it is, however, these characteristics, amongst others, that can make teaching adult learners such a rewarding experience. How do adult learners differ from traditional students? Many of the assumptions stem from Knowles's classic research on adult learners 30 years ago and his model of andragogical theory (adult learning theory) that derived from that. They include the beliefs that:

- Adult learners are highly self-directed and motivated to learn.
- Adult learners expect to be treated with respect.

- Adult learners expect their previous life experience to be acknowledged and view it as a strong base for their learning.

- Adult learners expect their learning to satisfy an immediate need (e.g. personal, professional) – learning must be *relevant* to be perceived as valuable.

- Adult learners often have clearly defined expectations, sometimes based on past experience, which can be positive or negative.

- Adult learners tend to have more deeply entrenched beliefs than younger students and can be more reluctant to relinquish them in light of new information.

The important things to understand about adult learners are that they have *chosen* to return to formal education, but that there are certain practical limitations, which to some extent dictate their approach to their learning. Time is at a premium for adult learners – full- or part-time work, child care, household and other family duties reduce the time available for their studies. As a result, it is important for adult learners that their time is carefully managed and that everything they do is relevant. Flexibility is also viewed as desirable. On the upside, the fact that they have returned to education voluntarily means that they are more likely to be intrinsically motivated and eager to engage with learning activities – as long as they perceive them as useful and meaningful. Currie (2000: 222) suggests that adult learning is best facilitated when:

- Learners are engaged as participants in the design of the learning.
- They are encouraged to be self-directed.
- The teacher functions as a facilitator rather than a didactic instructor.
- The individual learner's needs and learning styles are taken into account.
- A climate conducive to learning is established.
- The learner's past experiences are utilised in the classroom.
- Learning activities are deemed to have some direct relevance or utility to the learner's circumstances.

So, when you are faced with the task of facilitating sessions for adult learners, some of the key things you can do to make the session as effective as possible include the following:

- Plan and structure each session in meticulous detail, with clear learning outcomes and an outline of how the session is to be run. If there are any assessment components, bring them to the students' attention at the *start* of the session or course, and explain if and how they will be graded. Adult learners like to know exactly how a course or session will be run, as well as the deadlines for submitting course work, so that they can plan their time appropriately.

- Always check in advance, even in an informal way, what kinds of basic library and IT skills your students possess; as Gold points out, 'adult learners ... often possess neither the foundational skills nor the comfort level seen in the traditional learner' (2005: 471). Occasionally, it may be necessary to modify your lesson plans to focus on equipping the students with the basic skills that they are missing. However, it is likely that, as time goes on, this will occur less and less frequently with this demographic.

- Always give adult learners an opportunity to bring their life experiences into a class – acknowledge that they have a wealth of personal and professional experiences behind them, which can enrich and enhance their learning. This might involve something as simple as asking them to outline their previous good and bad experiences of using a library. If examples are required, give the students the chance to suggest examples from their professional or personal lives – for instance, a student might remember an episode from their working life which could have been resolved through knowledge of particular resources, or they might recall a time where they did not avail of their rights through not knowing where to go for information.

- Never teach a topic or skill without first explaining to the class *why* they are learning this particular thing. This could be as simple as including a slide in your presentation which outlines the purpose of the class. In a more hands-on scenario, if you are focusing on the use of a particular database, for example, always explain why you chose that database, and how the session will progress their learning. If you are using hands-on exercises or problem scenarios, explain the reasoning behind them – don't ask adult learners to go through the steps of an exercise without explaining how they will enhance the learning process. If the class has very practical learning outcomes, give clear examples of how the skills and knowledge can be applied in the real world.

- Don't allow time to be wasted – if, for example, you are running a session on how to search a particular resource, ensure that you provide clear written instructions on the 'mechanics' of the resource

– i.e. how to access the resource, which links to click, passwords to enter, etc., so that class time is not taken up with navigation and access issues (unless they are the point of your session!). For adult learners, time is precious and scarce, and every minute must be made to count. Equally, if you are running an individual or group exercise in your session, it often helps to provide an example of how the exercise might be approached, so that your students have a clear idea how to go about it.

■ Group-work often works particularly well with adult learners; as Webb and Powis point out: 'the development of a group ethos can help to sustain motivation and reinforce commitment' (2004: 46). Adult learners find the support and social aspect of group scenarios helpful, especially when everybody in the group has more or less similar circumstances. In groups which have a blend of adult and traditional learners, the adult learners more often prefer to work together, rather than mix with the traditionals, who have a different approach to their studies. If using group-work with mixed classes, you should consider allowing adult learners to form their own groups, rather than insist they work with the younger students.

■ Maintain flexibility in your sessions and try not to worry about 'coverage' – allow discussions to develop, if that is what your students appear to want. Very often the most rewarding and useful parts of a session are those in which students are permitted to air their opinions, to recount experiences they have had or simply to give their own take on topics.

■ Treat the learning as *collaboration*, rather than a traditional 'teacher–student' relationship. Tell the students that you expect to learn from *them* also and that you are looking forward to hearing about their experiences from the 'real world'.

It is, however, worth pointing out that many of these points might apply to traditional students also, and that they represent a common-sense approach to effective teaching. In some ways, teaching adults can often turn out to be less draining than teaching traditional students – the stories and opinions which derive from the students' life experiences can be genuinely interesting, and as teaching librarians, we often find that we can learn a lot from our sessions with adult learners.

'A lecturer has asked me to give a one-hour session with her class, but no specific idea of what she wants me to cover – how can I develop an effective session?'

'Instruction librarians often have a love/hate relationship with one-shot sessions. They are both the bread-and-butter and the bane of library instruction' (Benjes-Small et al., 2009: 38).

The 'one-shot' information literacy session is very familiar to teaching librarians – as Benjes-Small et al. point out, despite the radical changes in the information landscape, and the increasing sophistication of information technology, as teaching librarians we are still engaged in a seemingly endless struggle to increase the time allotted to us in academic curricula, and curriculum-integrated instruction is the exception rather than the norm. Badke notes that 'information literacy librarians do more one-shot instruction (either generic or subject-specific) than any other kind' (2009: 47). Frequently, all that is on offer is a single slot, typically a 50-minute class period; as this may be our only chance of contact with a particular student group, we feel immense pressure to create an engaging, impressive session that will perhaps encourage the students to seek out further training, or which might help to increase the profile of the library across the institution as a whole. The temptation is to go all out and create a memorable, bells-and-whistles session, with as much content as possible; however, this is a strategy that is ultimately counterproductive: 'While one-shot sessions remain poplar, most librarians feel pressure to include in them more content than is pedagogically sound' (Benjes-Small et al., 2009: 31). Sometimes, though, the pressure does not come from us, but rather from the academics who request the sessions and give us a long list of what they want us to include – often, they fail to appreciate the limitations of a one-hour session and what can effectively be covered in such a short time-span.

Badke (2009) proposes three possible solutions, specifically in relation to the one-shot 'orientation' sessions that are so common in libraries:

1. Cancel them and devote instruction time to something more profitable.

2. Transform them into some form of active learning.

3. Do point-of-need instruction through scheduled sessions with students, who are working on specific research projects.

While Badke rejects his first option on the grounds that it would be difficult to know what they should be replaced with, the other two options offer a lot of promise. However, the question is, how do we make the most of those one-shot sessions while ensuring that they are effective from a pedagogical perspective? The principles of good teaching still apply, but this time from a *micro*-perspective; we still want to align our ILO(s), teaching and learning methods, and our assessment – but we must find a way to do this that will fit into 50 minutes. The key is forward planning and a focus on *depth*, rather than breadth.

Planning for a one-shot session differs according to the way in which the session is requested. If you are approached by an academic, sometimes they will have very precise ideas of what they need (see Chapter 3, 'Instructional needs assessment'). Your challenge in this case is to translate their request into a solid learning outcome and plan the session accordingly – as noted, it may be sometimes necessary to negotiate a more realistic outcome, where too much has been requested. For instance, the academic might ask you to provide a session on 'database searching' for students who are beginning work on a project. Database searching is a broad topic – it could encompass basic search skills (Boolean logic, etc.), knowledge of the important databases in a particular area, critical evaluation, etc. – certainly more than can be fitted into a single session. For this class, you must find out what is the most pressing objective; do the students need to be taught how to construct searches, combining keywords with Boolean operators? Or are they experienced searchers who simply need to be familiarised with the databases that they need to do this particular project? You can also take the opportunity to offer additional, extracurricular sessions, if the instructional needs are too broad for one class, or to direct the students to online tutorials or other resources which might help them. But above all, you should avoid the temptation to try and cover everything in one hour – if you do, the students will inevitably be overwhelmed and the session will be hurried and stressful.

Another scenario that is even more challenging than the one just described is the vague request from a lecturer to 'do a library session' without specifying what the instructional needs are.

Creating an instructional menu

One solution to this challenge is to pre-empt the vague request and to return the responsibility for determining session content and structure to the academics themselves, rather than try to second-guess what might be effective. Providing academics with a ready-made list of instructional topics converted into sessions is one way of doing this and also represents good PR for the library. Benjes-Small and colleagues at Radford University had the idea of developing a 'library instruction menu' from which academics can select specific topics when requesting an instruction session from the librarians. The menu describes the instructional need that is covered by a session (e.g. 'Will your students need to evaluate websites?'), outlines the key points that will be covered in the session (e.g. 'Analysing sites for credibility') and indicates how much time is required to cover that topic (e.g. 40 minutes). Their full instructional menu can be viewed at *http://lib.radford.edu/instruction/menu.html*.

The librarians at Radford developed their menu by identifying 'commonly requested topics' based on years of instructional experience. Their sessions ranged from the 'bite-sized' (10 minutes) to much fuller sessions (up to 50 minutes). For some topics, they offered two options, a short overview or more in-depth treatment. Apart from helping librarians to develop sessions, the authors identified some other benefits that accrued from this approach. It

- proved a useful marketing tool for the library's instructional services;
- created new opportunities for academic–library collaboration;
- demonstrated to academics the limitations of a one-shot session;
- helped to standardise instruction among the librarians – everyone was covering the same objectives.

There is some evidence that this approach is increasing in popularity, although it is a recent phenomenon. In addition to reporting their own work, Benjes-Small et al. also carried out some online research to determine how many other North American libraries had created instructional menus. Their search found 47 libraries using the menu approach and a wide variation in the types of instructional offerings included on the menus. Their subsequent survey of the librarians involved showed a high degree of satisfaction with the approach, both from an instructional and a promotional perspective.

The menu approach represents a long-term solution to the one-shot challenge and requires an 'all hands on deck' approach in the library to create a list of deliverable instructional options. However, if your challenge is an immediate one, what can you do in the short term to handle these vague requests from academics? Some of the strategies include:

- If an academic asks for a 'library session', ask to see copies of the assignments that the students have to complete for the course. This may give you some idea of the areas that need to be covered, and at what point – as we already know, tailoring the instruction to course work increases the likelihood that the students will perceive it as relevant and meaningful.

- Ask the academic if they have noticed any particular difficulties among that particular group – for example, perhaps there has been an overuse of Internet sources in written assignments, or the students have not been citing sources correctly in their essays.

- Ask the students themselves to submit suggestions via email for what they would like to learn in a session. Alternatively, you could set up a short online survey for this purpose, also including a few questions to assess the students' self-perceived level of competence.

- Use your own experience and observation to put together a session that you feel would be useful to any students at any level, for example using Google Scholar, or the basics of using a reference management tool such as End Note or Ref Works.

Badke offers an interesting opinion on the effectiveness of one-shot information literacy training and suggests that teaching librarians should *lower* their expectations about what a one-shot session can achieve. He proposes that we should treat one-shot classes as 'familiarisation exercises' that introduce students to certain research tools and will hopefully lead to further training in the future: 'In fact, our profession works against real information literacy when we demand that our one-shots truly teach our students something. That's like training first graders how to read in an hour. The one-shot is not information literacy. It's a familiarization exercise that can serve as a doorway into information literacy' (2009: 49). He also suggests that replacing F2F sessions with interactive online tutorials might be a more effective approach at this level and would free up teaching librarians' time to focus on more advanced subject-specific training.

Exercises and reflections

1. You have been assigned to a cross-institutional academic librarians' 'troubleshooting task force', which has been convened specifically to assist teaching librarians in the participating institutions. As a group,

you need to be able to gather information quickly when a problem arises, so that you can suggest suitable approaches for resolution. Your task today is to create a 'problem pro-forma' which teaching librarians can complete and return to the task force when asking for help. The 'pro-forma' should include a checklist of the more common problems faced by teaching librarians, as well as scope to include unanticipated issues that arise.

2. As mentor to new library staff, consider that one of your roles is to create and maintain an induction document which offers helpful advice and tips for librarians who are teaching for the first time. Your task today is to develop an initial list of '20 top teaching tips' designed to help novice teaching librarians to effectively deal with some of the common issues that could arise in the classroom.

5

Personal and professional development as a teaching librarian

Abstract: This chapter explores the means and methods of professional and personal development for teaching librarians and describes a number of individual and collaborative strategies for self-evaluation and reflective practice. The chapter encourages teaching librarians to adopt a reflective attitude towards their instructional work and to use the results of constructive self-evaluation, and evaluation by others, to continually improve their teaching and to gradually build a 'teacher identity' that will bolster their sense of confidence and self-efficacy. The chapter also urges engagement with the wider professional community of teaching librarians, as well as other academic stakeholder groups in both formal and informal ways. The approaches to development include: student evaluation of teaching performance; peer evaluation of teaching; applying for teaching grants and awards; creating teaching portfolios; writing reflective journals and blogs; mentoring; professional learning communities; communities of practice; and publishing in academic journals.

Key words: professional development, reflective practice, peer evaluation, mentoring, teaching portfolios, teaching awards, grant writing.

[T]he acceptance of our role in teaching and learning also comes with a price. If we are to be teachers, then we need to be fully engaged in training for, and maintaining competence in, this aspect of our professional identity (Powis, 2008).

In Chapter 2, we saw how Walter emphasised the importance of establishing a 'culture of teaching' within academic libraries to promote professional development, noting that it is 'critical to any department or institutional attempt to improve the quality of instructional performance' (2005: 4). He suggests that a number of supportive structures must be in place, including interest and commitment from administrators, the full involvement of academics, frequent collegial interaction, the provision of professional development resources and the inclusion of teaching performance as a criterion for professional advancement within the institution. A similar notion is articulated by Biggs and Tang, who refer to a 'SoTL culture' – namely, an institutional culture that recognises the importance of the 'Scholarship of Teaching and Learning', which traditionally has not been afforded the same prestige as other forms of academic scholarship. The authors suggest that the existence of a SoTL culture in academic institutions 'leads inevitably to several structures that require and support transformative reflection with regard to teaching' (2007: 264).

The general importance of reflective practice has also been discussed earlier (Chapter 2). Authors such as Jacobs (2008) and Walter (2005) suggest that simply teaching librarians how to teach – by means of a pre-service module, for example – is not sufficient to fully develop an individual as a teacher; rather, such modules 'must instead be part of a larger endeavour aimed at helping librarians feel more confident in and prepared for their pedagogical work' (Jacobs, 2008: 257). However, to date there is still a comparatively small body of documentary evidence attesting to reflective practice in librarianship in general. A systematic review of the literature on reflective practice carried out by Grant (2007) identified just 13 papers which dealt with either analytical (6 papers) or non-analytical (7 papers) reflection in library and information work. Grant defines non-analytical reflective accounts as reporting on past events from a retrospective or historical perspective, while analytical accounts 'attempt to understand the relationship between past experiences and how this might impact on future practice' (Grant, 2007: 155). She however suggests that the relatively low number of articles on reflective practice might not prove *lack* of activity, but could instead mean that reflection is considered a private rather than a public process by librarians. However, in recent years, the phenomenon of blogging by librarians (Aharony, 2009) could indicate that public reflection on practice is becoming more of an accepted activity among the LIS professional community – this will be discussed later on in this chapter. In the meantime, however, as teaching librarians, we should recognise the importance of adopting a reflective approach to our work and what it can mean for our confidence and sense of self-efficacy.

As teaching librarians, some of you may be fortunate enough to work in institutions where a strong teaching and learning culture is well established and the importance of teaching is fully recognised; others among you might feel that other aspects of academic work, such as research and publication, are valued more and might feel challenged when it comes to teaching within your environments. The following sections outline the means and methods of professional development for teaching librarians. Some are individual activities; many are group-based and are dependent on the type of culture described above. Interested readers are also directed to a website set up by Scott Walter, which is specifically aimed at compiling resources for instructional improvement for academic librarians: *https://netfiles.uiuc.edu/swalter/www/instructional_improvement.html*.

Evaluation of teaching performance

A willingness to honestly examine your teaching and learning activities in a constructive way and to open these activities to the scrutiny of others is at the heart of your development as a teaching professional. Walter (2005) asserts that 'while the evaluation of library instruction may have once been the "weak link" in the overall instructional service program of academic libraries, now it is a central concern' (p. 5). Evaluation of your teaching performance is carried out through a number of different internal and external channels – a rounded overview of your performance is best obtained through using a selected mix of methods to access evidence and opinion. The following sections explore the different sources of evaluation and the methods that are associated with collecting and presenting data from each source. A clear image of your teaching performance emerges through the perspectives of a number of different stakeholder groups:

- What do *students* think? Students' opinions, as well as their success in attaining learning outcomes, are good indicators of the impact of your teaching work. To collect data from students, the methods used include paper-based or online evaluation surveys, focus groups, classroom assessment techniques and summative assessment results.

- What do your *colleagues* think? The perspectives of trusted and respected colleagues can offer useful insights into your instructional performance, through peer-observation of teaching. Sharing methods and expertise is another benefit of these mutually supportive arrangements, which will be discussed later in this chapter.

- What do *administrators, senior academics and/or national experts* think? The perspectives of outside parties and those who are charged with strategic decision-making can indicate the extent to which your teaching is aligned with institutional, or even national, educational priorities. Feedback in this context comes, for example, from applying for any teaching awards or grants that are open to educators internally, nationally or even internationally. The feedback received from both successful and unsuccessful submissions can be used to introduce improvements and modifications to your practice.

- What do you think? Your *own* perspective is the final part of the jigsaw – honest self-reflection on your teaching, acknowledgement of your strengths and areas for improvement, and your plans for future development can be captured through the use of reflective journals, portfolios or blogs, amongst other methods.

The following sections outline some of the ways in which information can be gathered from each of these stakeholder groups.

Student evaluation of teaching

Student evaluation of teaching is carried out as a matter of course in most institutions of higher education and, for academics, is an important criterion in tenure and promotion decisions. While Grassian and Kaplowitz caution against the inappropriate use of what they term 'happiness scales' to assess the pedagogical impact of information literacy instruction, they also observe that this type of evaluation provides 'valuable information about the affective effect of the instruction' (2009: 208). However, Biggs and Tang warn heavily against the use of student evaluation questionnaires as the sole measure of a teacher's performance, noting that typically 'such across-the-board measures assume that the default method of teaching is lecturing; the students rate teachers on such items as "speaks clearly," "hands out clear lecture notes" and the like' (2007: 273). Other problems associated with student feedback questionnaires are that they are also based on the students' personal rapport with the instructor, as well as their overall ease of engagement with the material. A host of environmental factors can affect students' perceptions of a learning experience, ranging from their own personal, non-learning-related challenges, to issues with the institution as a whole. Biggs and Tang suggest instead that teaching is more properly evaluated through identifying *meaningful* criteria for good teaching and through examining the evidence provided by the teacher that these criteria have been met.

This is not necessarily to suggest that the standard student evaluation questionnaire should be jettisoned entirely; rather, it can serve as a useful formative evaluation tool, providing feedback to instructors during a course, to enable modifications or improvements to be implemented in a timely fashion. Webb and Powis suggest that student evaluation could be treated as a reflective activity, in which students are asked to think about 'what they have learned, and how their learning has been shaped by the teaching session' (2004: 163). They also observe that explaining to students how the results of the evaluation will be used to effect improvement in the teaching is another means of giving them 'ownership' over the process and, consequently, a vested interest in providing thoughtful and constructive feedback.

Realistically, time and resource limitations will often mean that a hard-copy or online evaluation questionnaire is the most efficient means of gathering feedback from your students. While it is probable that your institution will already have a 'standard' questionnaire template, it is unlikely that it will be suitable to evaluate information literacy sessions and will be aimed at evaluating full academic modules. The opportunity, therefore, to design your own evaluation instrument is to be welcomed.

Most evaluation questionnaires consist of a mixture of closed or rating-scale questions and a number of open-ended questions designed to obtain more detailed feedback and suggestions about particular elements of the course or session. Often, the most interesting and revealing feedback comes through the answers to the open-ended questions, particularly if students are asked to identify what aspects did *not* work so well, and to make suggestions about how the course or session could be improved. Also, framing the questions in terms of the *students'* experience can have the effect of focusing them on the actual learning experience, rather than the teacher's performance or personality: for example, rather than asking 'In your opinion, what were the strengths of the course/session?' you might instead frame the question as 'In your opinion, which activities were most effective in helping you to learn during the course/session?' Some questions along these lines that you might use include:

■ 'In your opinion, to what extent did the defined learning outcomes for the course/session reflect your actual learning experience?'

- 'In your opinion, which learning activities were not so useful in helping you to achieve the learning outcomes for this course/session?'

- 'To what extent do you feel that the assessment for this course/session allowed you to demonstrate what you had learned?'

- 'How do you feel that the challenges that you experienced during the course/session (if any) could be overcome in the future'?

- 'To what extent (if any) do you feel that the skills and knowledge you have developed in this course/session will be useful to you in other contexts (education, professional, personal)?'

Rating scales, in which students are asked to rate their reactions to a statement along a continuum from positive to negative (usually 1–5), offer only limited insight into the effectiveness of each aspect – often, students will choose a neutral response and circle the middle digit. Closed questions such as this should generally be used to evaluate the practical aspects of the course/session, such as the physical environment, availability of resources, timetabling, etc., rather than learning effectiveness.

Using student assessment as a tool for improvement

In Chapter 3, we discussed how it is important to capture not just the *products* of student learning (essays, projects), but also the *process* that led to the attainment of the learning outcomes. It is essential not to view the results of assessment simply as measures of student learning, but also to treat them as indicators of the effectiveness or otherwise of our teaching approaches; Avery suggests that 'assessment should be student centred and proactive. The results should be used to implement positive changes in the teaching of information literacy' (2003: 2), while Sonntag and Meulemans stress the usefulness of authentic assessment in informing instructional improvement:

> Authentic assessment is, among other things, iterative. Librarians can evaluate student learning, implement changes, and continue this cycle so that improvement via assessment becomes an inherent part of the instructional process. (2003: 8)

Assignments that capture the students' learning process offer a valuable insight into what works and what doesn't work in your teaching and learning sessions. McGuinness describes how student reflective research journals in a first-year information literacy module in University College Dublin (UCD), Ireland, were used to implement modifications and improvements to the teaching and learning methods over a number of years (McGuinness and Brien, 2007). The journals, compiled by students of the module to record their experiences of researching and writing an academic essay over a number of weeks, contained a significant reflective element, which offered informal and revealing insight into the challenges faced by them in locating, evaluating and synthesising material for their essays. In particular, the final week's reflection posed a number of evaluative questions to the students, which allowed them to sum up their learning experience in a personal way:

- What was most challenging about the assignment?
- What was easiest?
- What have I learned through this assignment?
- What am I proud of with this assignment?
- What would I do differently next time I complete a similar task?
- What did I enjoy most about writing this assignment?

The advantage of this form of evaluation is that it is completely focused on the learning experience; the students are unaware that they are evaluating the module, but are rather thinking about their *own* research and learning. Based on the feedback in the students' journals, the changes made to the module included:

- The length of the journal was reduced from 10 weeks to 6 weeks.
- More hands-on lab sessions and interactive lecture content were introduced.
- The essay topics were modified from broad and unfocused topics, to narrower, more clearly defined questions.
- The 'portfolio' component of the journal was increased – more compulsory worksheets based on lecture and tutorial content were included to increase hands-on experience.
- More emphasis was placed on *activity*, rather than on pure reflection.

As teaching librarians, we should always consider the advantages of including reflective elements in our assessment, where appropriate. This does not have to be a full reflective research journal, but could also include asynchronous blog or wiki entries, or 10-minute reflections at the end of a class session.

Peer evaluation of teaching

'Peer evaluation of instruction involves librarians in conversations about what constitutes good teaching' (Middleton, 2002: 69).

The process of peer evaluation consists simply of inviting a trusted colleague or friend to observe your teaching, or to critically evaluate your teaching materials, in order to provide an outside perspective on your work and to introduce some fresh ideas about how you could modify or improve your teaching and learning approach. Grassian and Kaplowitz describe it as a 'collaborative and reciprocal relationship, the goal of which is better teaching' (2005: 126). Rather than being a critical process, the spirit of peer evaluation is mutual support, encouragement and constructive criticism, with the relationship between colleagues viewed as equal. McMahon et al. (2007) suggest that peer evaluation, or peer observation of teaching (PoT), is *most* effective when the observee retains control over certain aspects of the process, for example, choice of observer, focus of observation and the form and method of feedback. As Norbury points out, 'the whole process is owned by the person being observed, which means that it is confidential unless the observed agrees otherwise' (2001: 89).

However, although peer evaluation of teaching is an essentially 'friendly' process, it should still be treated in quite a formal way. The key to effective peer evaluation is clear advance planning, so that both parties can agree unambiguously on the procedure that is to be followed. Biggs and Tang (2007) suggest that peer evaluation of teaching can take place in four stages:

1. A pre-review or pre-observation meeting between the reviewer and reviewee, in order to set out the purpose of the evaluation, the desired outcomes of the process, and the aspects of teaching that should be particularly attended to. For example, both parties should agree on the time, date and location of the review; what the students in the session will be told about the process; what the focus of the review is, and how it will be recorded by the reviewer. Methods for evaluating teaching materials or asynchronous teaching methods should also be agreed at this point.

2. The review itself, which takes place during a live teaching session using pre-established feedback criteria (a 'feedback pro-forma') to comment on the teacher's facilitation of the session.

3. A post-evaluation meeting, to discuss the feedback generated during the session and to suggest ideas for improvement. Both parties

contribute to this meeting; the reviewee shares how they felt about the session and what went well, or not so well. The reviewer shares their observations and both parties together create a specific action plan for improvement of the teaching and learning activities.

4. The reviewee writes a post-review personal reflection on the process.

Additional steps might be the implementation of the action plan and reporting on the overall process, if required. McMahon and O'Neill (2010) suggest that a final report could be included in a professional development portfolio, a reflective journal or even published in a peer-reviewed journal to share with the wider library and academic community.

Some examples of the use of peer evaluation of teaching in academic libraries can be found in the literature. Norbury (2001) details a peer observation programme undertaken in the library at Aston University, UK, which was carried out in teams. The overall post-evaluation of the process by the librarians involved highlighted a number of important benefits, including the opportunity to exchange ideas between colleagues, increased awareness of one's own teaching and the ability to 'view the process through the students' eyes' (p. 93). Middleton (2002) describes the peer-evaluation process in the library at Oregon State University, which was established when the university made it mandatory to include 'documented evaluation of teaching by faculty peers and by students' as part of the criteria for promotion and tenure (p. 71). Peer observations of live sessions were recorded on a 'checklist for observations', which focused on key criteria, including presentation skills; clarity of presentation; content; relationship with students; relationship with classroom instructor (if appropriate). Kessinger (2004) describes how, in her role as manager, she used performance criteria to structure a peer-mentoring programme in her library. To facilitate consistency between peers, she developed a 'performance skills chart' which each mentor could use to guide their observation, highlighting areas of excellence and areas requiring improvement. The categories of observation in the chart included: organisation; presentation style; audience reactions; active learning techniques; technology; and room. Under these categories, different criteria were listed, including 'attitude' and 'energy' under 'presentation style', and 'participation' and 'body language' under 'audience reactions'.

Depending on what is viewed as important, teaching librarians are free to develop their own 'feedback pro-formas' so that the relevant aspects of the teaching and learning process are targeted in the observation. Pro-formas can include both qualitative (narrative) data, and more quantitative elements, such as 'rating scales'. It is also crucial to be clear about what will happen to the results of the evaluation – formative evaluation, which is used specifically for the purpose of improving one's teaching, is a different experience from summative evaluation, in which results might be used as part of a formal performance review to determine promotion or tenure (Middleton, 2002).

Applying for teaching grants and awards

'Institutional and national teaching fellowships offer a real chance to prove to colleagues that we can contribute to teaching and learning' (Powis, 2008).

In previous chapters, we have discussed how lack of recognition of the teaching librarian role by academic colleagues and administrators can have a detrimental effect, both on librarians' sense of self-efficacy and professional identity, *and* on the opportunities available to them to create curriculum-embedded instruction. One means of increasing your profile as a teaching librarian, and publicising the impact of what you do on the student learning experience, is to apply – either individually or collaboratively with non-library colleagues – for any teaching and learning grants, fellowships or other awards that are open to general academics. From a marketing perspective, successful grant submissions or teaching awards can showcase to the wider academic community that librarians are innovative, with a valid and important role to play in student education. From a personal point of view, the benefits are equally obvious: to start, the process of *preparing* a high-quality grant application requires you to think strategically and systematically about your teaching and how it relates to institutional or national policy. Equally, a successful application represents an opportunity to engage in exciting new activities that will expand your repertoire, will give you the invaluable experience of working on a self-contained project with clearly identified deliverables and boost your sense of self-efficacy. Grassian and Kaplowitz observe that securing teaching development grants 'offers a way to test out a new idea and even experiment with applying technology to solve a lingering problem' (2005: 182). In most cases, the grants applied for by teaching librarians are project-based, dealing with a specific problem, or using a new technology to augment teaching and learning. Biggs and Tang suggest that many teaching development projects take the form of short-term *action research* projects, applied within 'real-life' teaching and learning situations, and using the results to effect modifications and improvements in the instructional approach.

Langille and Mackenzie suggest that there are a number of barriers that affect the ability of librarians to carry out research consistently, one of which may be a lack of funds: 'One such barrier may be the inability of researchers to secure funding for this work' (2007: 24). Grants for teaching development are administered at institutional as well as national and international level; Biggs and Tang note that it is extremely important for institutions to set up their *own* teaching development funding schemes, as many teachers 'are reluctant to apply for [external] funds and go through all that form-filling to research their own teaching, because they do not consider themselves educational researchers' (2007: 264). For teaching librarians, who are already uncertain of their own professional status, the prospect of putting their instructional ideas 'out there' can be doubly intimidating. One way of overcoming this reluctance is for teaching librarians to consider applying for funds in *teams*, for example, a mixed group of librarians and academics with a common concern, or a cross-institutional or cross-sector collaboration. A good example of a cross-institutional funded project is the *Library Network Support Service (LNSS) project* in south-west Ireland, which commenced in August 2008 and was funded by the Higher Education Authority (HEA) Strategic Innovation Fund (SIF), which is 'directed towards support for innovation in higher education' and runs from 2006–2013. Under SIF Cycle II, which funded the LNSS project, a total of 31 projects were approved, for a total of €97 million in funding. The LNSS, which consists of a consortium of four higher education institutions, is focused on two areas of strategic development: first, the introduction of an online information literacy training suite for students; and second, the creation of a regional network for staff development.

Grassian and Kaplowitz (2005) and Langille and Mackenzie (2007) write extensively on the most effective ways for librarians to prepare funding applications. In particular, Grassian and Kaplowitz suggest a list of nine important questions that librarians should ask themselves when considering the possibility of applying for external funds, including clearly identifying the problem to be investigated, estimating the time that can realistically be allocated to such a project, as well as honestly assessing one's own ability to actually carry out the research to the required level (2005: 184). Among the tips for effective grant application writing offered by both sets of authors are the following:

- *Articulate a solid justification for the importance of the proposed project.* To engage reviewers, the proposal should show that the project aims to identify solutions to a real and immediate problem, or that it is significant or original in some other way, e.g. uses instructional technology in a completely innovative way. Both sets of authors suggest that the proposal should 'tell a story' – it should have a beginning, middle and end, and should be 'narrated' in a positive, enthusiastic and persuasive way. Justifying a project requires you to show that previous attempts to handle the problem have been unsuccessful. Supporting documentation should clearly demonstrate the *need* for the research; for example, survey results, a promising pilot study that has been carried out, or qualitative comments from the groups it is designed to benefit.

- *Show that the project is achievable.* Grassian and Kaplowitz note that 'grandiose promises' and 'overblown claims' should be avoided (2005: 205); instead the proposal should clearly show that resource and personnel availability has been taken into account and that the project deliverables have been tailored to what is attainable. It is important to demonstrate that the project team has access to the relevant expertise to enable the project to be carried out; i.e. are there team members with sufficient technical and research experience? Most grant proposals require the inclusion of a short résumé for each team member, proving that the relevant skills are represented. The proposal should also clarify the extent of administrative support that is available to the project team; in the case of teaching librarians, an important factor is the support of management, who can guarantee sufficient release time from other duties in order to work on the project. Finally, the proposal should reassure reviewers that the team has access to the necessary physical equipment to complete the project (other than that for which funds are being sought).

- *Prepare a clear research plan.* Much of the proposal will be given over to a description of the project itself, including a breakdown of the methodological approach that the researchers will take. As well as a brief overview of the project and its objectives, Langille and Mackenzie note that 'the research plan will include information on the sample or population, sample recruitment, data collection and data analysis' (2007: 27). The proposal should include a timeline, which clearly delineates when each stage of the research will be carried out and by whom. Possible challenges that might arise should be addressed here, as well as an explanation of how the data will be verified. The proposal should also state how any ethical issues that might arise will be handled.

- *Describe how the project results will be used and distributed.* Funding applications almost always require candidates to explain how they intend to disseminate the results of the project – for example, which journals they intend to publish in, at which conferences they intend to present the findings, or who will be the recipients of any reports that are issued. If the project is a practical, action-research-oriented one, applicants might be required to explicitly describe how and when the learning approaches will be modified in the wake of the research, e.g. the semester in which an improved module is to run, etc.

■ *Ensure that you have 'ticked all the boxes'.* Grassian and Kaplowitz strongly emphasise the importance of carefully and thoroughly reading all of the submission guidelines to ensure that you have included all of the relevant information and/or supporting documentation. Adhering to word counts is essential, as well as ensuring that all institutional signatures and stamps have been obtained in a timely fashion. Applicants must also ensure that the requisite number of copies is submitted, in the desired format(s).

Langille and Mackenzie suggest a useful grant writing timeline, starting from a year before the submission deadline, to assist in planning the process (2007: 29), while Grassian and Kaplowitz offer suggestions for tracking down specific grant opportunities (2005: 197–200).

Teaching portfolios

All of the different sources of evidence described above can be gathered together in a **teaching portfolio**, which is defined by Biggs and Tang as 'a collection of evidence about your teaching and your students' learning, and a reflection on that evidence' (2007: 266). Hochstein suggests that teaching librarians should use teaching portfolios:

■ 'To allow our training and habit of documentation to catch up with the reality of our work.

■ To provide orderly, efficient, and credible documentation of our teaching activities; this is evidence not hearsay.

■ To give us permission to stop and reflect about what we do and why we do it' (2004: 140).

She also notes that for teaching librarians, portfolios are a 'way to clearly communicate our teaching successes to those outside our immediate field' (p. 141). While the use of teaching portfolios is widespread in general teacher education and practice, it is not especially common amongst librarians. One example is the account given by Lally and Trejo (1998) of their experience of creating a developmental teaching portfolio as part of a doctoral project in which they and other librarian colleagues were invited to participate. The aim of the exercise was 'to use the portfolio to assess our growth, provide us with a mechanism for reflection, and point us towards areas for improvement' (p. 776). The items contained in their portfolios included an up-to-date curriculum vitae (résumé), a statement of teaching philosophy, an outline of teaching responsibilities, a number of samples of their teaching work and an overall written reflection.

A teaching portfolio has very obvious personal benefits; however, it can also be a useful professional development tool, which can be used to showcase your teaching work in job interviews and when applying for promotion in your current position. As our teaching role is quite unique, portfolios for teaching librarians will contain a number of items that are not usually included in general teaching portfolios. If you wish to create your own portfolio, you might consider the following structure:

Content of teaching portfolio for teaching librarians

a. Your evidence

- A statement of your personal teaching philosophy.
- Your personal understanding of information literacy and the instructional role of the librarian – how you view your current role.
- Your teaching-related qualifications – a description of the type of teaching and/or supervision you have been involved in (e.g. full courses, workshops, one-shot sessions, etc.). This might also include any continuing professional development (CPD) activities you may have undertaken relevant to teaching.
- A statement of your teaching responsibilities – sessions, modules or full programmes for which you are, or have recently been, responsible.
- Details of any teaching-related achievements – this might include teaching awards, blog awards, publications in peer-reviewed or professional journals, successful grant applications, conference presentations, seminars or workshops that you have given to professional colleagues, innovative programmes and tools you have created, e-learning initiatives you have been involved in, or supervision of research students. For teaching librarians, this might also include

participation in collaborative group initiatives or contributions to institution-wide teaching enhancements or projects.

■ Your relevant administrative responsibilities and duties (e.g. member of teaching and learning committee, academic council, etc.).

■ An account of how you keep up to date with teaching and learning and information literacy developments – e.g. journal subscriptions, membership of relevant associations, mailing lists, subscriptions to RSS aggregation services, such as *Pageflakes*, for frequently updated teaching resources on the web (e.g. blogs, sharing services, etc.), book clubs, networking events, and other similar channels.

Design and delivery of teaching – this is concerned with showcasing your teaching approaches and is supported by including self-selected samples of your work:

■ description of, or reflection on, your general approach to teaching – i.e. use of small groups, active learning methods, problem-based or inquiry-based learning, synchronous or asynchronous remote learning, etc.;

■ description of the teaching methods you use and your rationale for using them;

■ description of how you facilitate active, student-centred learning;

■ description of how you tailor your teaching to different subject curricula;

■ description of how you promote your teaching services to the academic community;

■ description of how you engage academics in collaborative teaching;

■ critical incidents that showcase particular aspects of your teaching experience.

Work samples, or 'teaching artefacts' (Lally and Trejo, 1998), that you might attach to demonstrate your teaching include:

■ course outlines;

■ lesson plans;

■ handouts;

■ worksheets;

■ pathfinders/research guides;

■ lecture slides;

■ assessments;

- DVDs with podcasts or videos of your sessions, e-tutorials, virtual tours, blogs, wikis, or other digital learning objects that you have created;

- surveys or pre- and post-tests that you have administered;

- promotional materials, e.g. flyers, leaflets, webpage screen grabs, posters, etc.

It is important to include an explanatory statement for each item that you include, explaining its significance and relevance to your teaching work.

Teaching outcomes/impact

- Evidence of constructive alignment in your teaching (aligning ILOs to assessment).

- Methods of assessment you use and rationale for their use.

- Rubrics you have developed for grading assignments.

- General facts and figures – grade distributions, attendance rates.

- Any studies you have carried out on instructional impact.

b. Evidence from colleagues and students

- Written peer feedback and evaluation of your teaching delivery and course materials.

- Student evaluations of programmes and sessions; this might include summaries of survey results, sample quotations from open-ended survey questions, notes or recordings from focus group sessions, individual (anonymised) e-mails from students praising your teaching, thank you cards, etc.

- Testimonials from colleagues: this might include 'letters of reference' from academics whom you have collaborated with, webpage testimonials, (anonymised) thank you e-mails, etc.

c. Overall reflection/statement of future plans

- Your self-perceived strengths and areas of expertise.

- The areas you feel that you need to work on.

- Your future plans: innovative approaches you intend to try, CPD that you wish to undertake, conferences you wish to attend or contribute to, ideas for research that you have, etc.

To supplement the above, Hochstein (2004) also offers a detailed and informative account of what a teaching portfolio for librarians could contain and the form it should take. Teaching portfolios can be created in hardcopy or can be maintained entirely online. The main advantage of an online format is that links to video, audio, e-learning objects and other digital artefacts are easily embedded, and a multimedia showcase of your work might be more impressive and a more accurate reflection of the teaching work that you currently do.

Reflective journals and blogs

The use of reflective journals for professional development has traditionally been associated with certain professions, such as nursing and education. Moon speculates that this could be due to the fact that 'both professions rely on interpretive knowledge which is socially constructed and not rooted in a body of "fact" [. . .] both also rely on decisions made "on the spot" with unpredictable situations being relatively common' (2006: 72). Arguably, these criteria could apply equally to library and information work, where each day brings different queries and challenges, requiring a flexible approach and rapid judgements. For teaching librarians, whose work and responsibilities are famously unpredictable, there is perhaps even *more* of a need for this type of in-depth reflective work. Moon distinguishes between two types of professional journal. In the first instance are journals which are used in the development of *self* as professional, articulated by many as 'finding one's voice' in the execution of one's work. Journal-keeping in this context encourages professionals to explore the affective side of their work, developing a growing sense of confidence as they identify and work through their fears. The other types of journal are those which enable professionals to relate theory to practice and relate what they have learned in training to real-world situations. These kinds of journals focus on making sense of real-life experiences, containing accounts of 'critical incidents' along with reflections on the significance of those events.

It is difficult to get a sense of how many librarians actually use reflective journals in their work, as the practice is not well documented. However, the spreading phenomenon of professional *blogging* has opened up a whole new channel for reflective practice and sharing one's experience with colleagues, and one which is easier to access than the private world of journal-keeping. Hall and Davison suggest that the blog can be 'regarded as the natural successor to the learning journal or learning log, because it serves as a vehicle for individual reflection' (2007: 167). Crawford describes blogs written by librarians as 'liblogs' and the overall blog collective as the 'biblioblogosphere' – defined as 'blogs written by library people or about library issues' (2010: 58). While the actual number of blogs written by librarians, or about library-related matters, is difficult to obtain, in September 2010 a simple search of the specialist blog search engine *Technorati* (using the search term 'library') retrieved 2,828 blogs; the term 'librarian' retrieved 917 blogs. Crawford's recent analysis of the biblioblogosphere suggests that there are 'certainly more than 1000 liblogs in all' (2009: 1). Although these figures are difficult to verify, they offer some insight into the size of the biblioblogosphere at the present time.

How librarians use blogs in a professional context is a topic of increasing interest. A paper by Hall and Davison (2007) identified a number of ways in which librarians have been exploiting blog applications in their work (p. 165). They include:

- the provision of news and current awareness services to the LIS community;
- as a source of competitive intelligence in the business community, through environmental scanning and monitoring of products and services;
- as an additional means of engaging library users with content;
- in commercial knowledge management to stimulate online dialogue;
- in teaching and learning, to encourage student collaboration, sharing and content creation, as well as the promotion of literacy (Hall and Davison, 2007: 165–166).

A more recent study by Aharony (2009) employed content analysis of blog tags and folksonomies to describe and classify 30 'topic-oriented blogs dealing with librarianship and information science', in order to determine what librarians use blogs for. Aharony's findings showed that while the blogs mainly reflected library-related and technology-related professional issues, there was also a significant *personal* element present; he suggests that 'perhaps the informal nature and platform of blogs enables the professional bloggers to express and share their views about personal issues, even though the platform is a professional one' (2009: 178). Many liblogs appear to be a mix of the personal and the professional, although Aharony questions whether librarians do see them as a tool of professional development:

Librarians and information scientists may assume that because of the informal nature of blogs, the information conveyed in them is only personal and casual and won't contribute to their professional development. But they should be aware of the professional potential of the blogs' content – the opportunity to exploit information on the blogs. (2009: 179)

The main difference between reflective journals and blogs is the extent to which outsiders can potentially contribute to, and shape, the direction of blogs. While blog posts are generally static, readers' comments can change a post from a personal reflection or opinion to a communal discussion, depending on the privacy settings. Librarians who are open to comment and suggestion could find this a thought-provoking exercise and an interesting way of discussing the issues and challenges that arise on a daily basis. Micro-blogging sites such as Twitter can perform a similar function, but in a much more immediate and rapid-fire way. Both forms of blogging enable networking on a scale that was impossible before the advent of social software, through the use of blogrolls and the 'follow' and 'hashtag' functions of Twitter. Many librarians avail of both, using micro-blogging to provide 'snippets' of their longer reflections and links to their blogs and other social networking sites.

An interesting recent development in the use of social software for reflection is the establishment in October 2009 of the *Library Routes Project* wiki, which 'exists to document and link to all those who have blogged or otherwise written about their library roots (how they got into the profession) and their library routes (the jobs they've had and how their career has been shaped)' (Library Routes Project, n.d.). The wiki main page provides links to existing library blog posts, or to newly created wiki entries by non-blogging librarians, containing short reflective pieces about how they came to be in their current position. The entries are highly personal and reflective. This is a good example, both of the potential of blogging for reflective practice and of the power of an online community to contribute to the understanding and development of professional identity in librarianship.

Mentoring

The traditional form of mentoring in libraries and other organisations is *hierarchical*, defined by Mavrinac as a 'dyadic relationship between a more experienced, senior employee and a less experienced, junior employee' (2005: 396). In most cases, traditional mentoring is associated with the smooth induction of new staff members into the workplace, familiarising them with professional and institutional norms, and in effect 'socialising' them to the profession of librarianship. As we noted in Chapter 1, a great deal of the acculturation process for librarians occurs through 'learning on the job' rather than the acquisition of a large body of professional knowledge, or through an extended period of scholarship. The tenure and promotion process is another situation where traditional mentoring has been used successfully (Miller and Benefiel, 1998). However, Grassian and Kaplowitz note that mentoring 'can be beneficial anytime we are changing career paths or are taking on new and different responsibilities' (2005: 118). For librarians who are new to teaching, or who never expected to have to take on an instructional role, mentoring offers potentially invaluable support as they get to grips with their new duties. However, rather than just focusing on the job at hand, the mentoring role also has quite a specific *career* focus; Bosch et al. note that 'the mentor provides the mentee with guidance and support so that they can progress in their careers and overcome professional challenges' (2010: 58). Mavrinec lists some of the benefits that can accrue to the mentee, including 'job satisfaction, career advancement, psycho-social well-being, induction to the organization, and professionalism' (2005: 396). Mentoring has been used quite extensively in academic libraries, although it is likely that much of this activity is carried out on an informal, rather than formal basis (Grassian and Kaplowitz, 2005: 119). Heinrich and Attebury (2010) provide an excellent overview of the various uses of mentoring in academic libraries.

Recently, though, there is evidence that the traditional form of hierarchical mentoring is no longer seen as a sufficient model for today's institutions, where change is rapid and continuous, where interdisciplinary collaboration is more common, and where there is increased emphasis on the 'learning organisation' and self-directed learning by the employees (Mavrinec, 2005; Bosch et al., 2010; Heinrich and Attebury, 2010). Mavrinec suggests that the 'trend is toward multiple relationships and experiences, which places the onus on learners to seek out a variety of learning opportunities to meet their needs throughout their careers' (2005: 398). Grassian and Kaplowitz also view mentoring as 'learner-centred', insofar as it is an arrangement that must be proactively sought by the prospective mentee: 'These mentoring relationships are self-initiated with individuals seeking out mentors who can assist them at different stages of their professional lives' (2005: 119). Other, flatter forms of mentoring are thus becoming more commonplace. Bosch et al. describe a new model of mentoring which 'encourages broader, dynamic networks of support and the use of multiple mentoring partners who work in non-hierarchical collaborative, cross-cultural partnerships to address specific areas of faculty activity such as research, teaching, working towards tenure and striking a balance between work and life' (2010: 58). Peer mentoring, according to Mavrinac, represents a conflation of various forms of mentoring, including co-mentoring, developmental alliances and spot mentoring, which is short term and focused on very specific objectives. Peer-mentoring arrangements constitute pairings (or larger groupings) of colleagues with the same or similar status, albeit with a knowledge or experience gap; the mentor must have something to offer the mentee. The advantage of peer mentoring arrangements is that the pool of potential mentors is much wider than in the traditional model, where there may be a shortage of experienced librarians who are willing to serve as mentors. A potential disadvantage, however, is that, since the peer mentors are usually of similar status, with comparable levels of experience, there is a natural limit to the extent of wisdom that can be shared once the initial knowledge gaps have been closed.

Group mentoring or many-to-one arrangements are also reported with increasing frequency. For example, Bosch et al. describe the approach taken at California State University Long Beach, where the *resource team model* involves a trio of senior librarians who serve as mentors to incoming library staff for the first six months of their employment. 'Mentoring circles' are another model which is described by Darwin and Palmer (2009) and used at the University of Adelaide – in this case, the 'circles' comprised a mixture of tenured and untenured faculty who met on a regular basis for six months, and represented a more fluid approach, in which members of each circle learned from each other and had access to a wider variety of perspectives than would be possible in traditional mentoring arrangements. Heinrich and Attebury (2010) describe the approach to mentoring at the University of Idaho, which more closely resembles the 'communities of practice' model, which is discussed separately later in this chapter.

For teaching librarians, a good mentor might be a colleague who has several years' instructional experience under their belt; or who has completed a teaching qualification, won a teaching award, or who has been a member of a funded educational research team. Mentors do not necessarily have to be restricted to fellow librarians; for example, seeking the counsel of an experienced academic or a member of the teaching and learning department can offer additional insights into how the academic community functions outside the library.

Professional learning communities

The professional learning community (PLC) emerges from the vision of the 'culture of teaching' described above (we might also add 'learning' to this phrase); Hord (1997) notes that the concept of a learning community was originally grounded in the recognition that 'teachers who felt supported in their own ongoing learning and classroom practice were more committed and effective than those who did not receive such confirmation' (p. 1). A PLC in the educational context is defined by Gruenbaum as 'a community of stakeholders that are all working together, focused on the best interest of the students, where results are measured in student achievement' (2010: 1). The PLC is an entirely collaborative affair and is forward-focused, targeting areas where improvement is warranted and identifying suitable responses to the challenges that are identified. In her review, Hord (1997) outlines the desirable attributes of PLCs, but in the context of the school system, as with most of the literature on this topic. However, these factors are easily translated to the academic environment and, specifically, to the academic *library* environment, where we have already identified collaboration as an essential aspect of our operations. The factors are:

- *Supportive and shared leadership.* Maliszewski et al. refer to the desirability of a 'tight–loose leadership style' in setting up PLCs, where the leader is flexible in some areas, but firm in others (2008: 4). In the academic library context, supportive leadership is interpreted on two levels; firstly, a sense of shared enterprise between library staff, academics and institutional administrators, and a recognition of the importance of collaboration and continuous learning, particularly on the part of the latter group; and secondly, on a micro-level, the support of *library managers*, whose leadership and vision is essential to the development of an operational structure within the library which facilitates the establishment of PLC-related activities.

- *Collective learning.* The recognition on all sides of the importance of continuous, shared learning within an organisation, and the fostering of a spirit of mutual inquiry and debate amongst all stakeholders in the community. In pragmatic terms, this could mean something as simple as setting aside regular time for discussion and debate in a non-threatening environment.

■ *Shared values and vision.* The primary focus of the PLC is always student learning, requiring a commitment from all stakeholders to instigate whatever actions are required to nurture potential and support student achievement. Hord observes that such a shared vision requires that the common good (i.e. student learning) 'is placed on a par with personal ambition' (1997: 4).

■ *Supportive conditions.* From a practical standpoint, the institutional environment is highly instrumental in the success or otherwise of a PLC. Hord (1997) cites structural factors, such as the size of the institution, the proximity of staff to each other and communication channels as important factors – for example, do staff members encounter each other regularly, or are they isolated in their different units? Moreover, the quality of collegial relationships is another crucial factor – is there sufficient respect and trust among staff members to permit the sharing of feedback and evaluation without rancour?

■ *Shared personal practice.* The final element relates to the concept of peer coaching, or mutual evaluation of each other's teaching practice. In a PLC, members are always willing to share and discuss their activities, as well as their challenges and successes in the learning environment. In practical terms, this requires the adoption of appropriate methods for evaluating teaching performance in a constructive way.

Hord suggests that a PLC within an educational institution brings obvious benefits for the community as a whole, including staff as well as students (1997: 5–6). However, establishing a community in an institution where different units have traditionally worked independently of one another can be challenging. Maliszewski et al. (2008) describe some of the activities undertaken in their school when the decision was taken to set up a PLC, including setting aside time for common preparation between different grade classes, attending a special summit on PLCs, and frequent meetings to work collaboratively on term plans and developing teaching and learning materials. Gruenbaum (2010) also discusses the means of establishing PLCs, but focuses on online communities. Some of the recommended strategies include:

■ *Book clubs/discussion groups.* Gruenbaum (2010) describes the use of a 'book club' to introduce staff to the concept of a PLC (p. 2) – the school in which the author was working purchased a book on PLCs for teaching faculty and staff members, and weekly reading from the book for the book club was assigned. A different person led the meeting each week, during which ideas from the book were discussed and debated in relation to the school. The author suggests that this kind of book club can also be facilitated in a remote, virtual environment, for instance using e-textbooks, online forums and instant messaging or video-conferencing applications.

- *Self-assessment surveys.* This involves members of the community taking a survey several times a year to gauge the progress of the institution towards becoming a successful PLC. She also suggests that focus groups can be useful for 'concentrating efforts where they are needed to make sure that things are on pace' (p. 2).

- *Community meetings.* In collaborative ventures, such as PLCs, meeting time is essential to foster a sense of collegiality and democracy: as Gruenbaum points out, 'the key idea is that having all members working together to craft a shared understanding of what we are working toward, and what our expectations are for student results, will make everyone feel like they are on equal ground' (2010: 3).

Creating and sustaining communities of practice

> Just as academics will use their discipline networks to explore the teaching of their subject, we should also recognise the need to develop similar opportunities within our context. (Powis, 2005: 71)

As teaching librarians, we do not work in isolation (although it may occasionally feel that way). Not only are we members of our immediate workplace or organisational community, but we are also active participants in the wider national and international community of academic teaching librarians, and teaching librarians in general. It is up to us to harness the possibilities for learning and development that exist within these communities, and to make our own contributions to the body of knowledge and experience that informs our work.

As an evolving professional role with relatively limited professional training opportunities, teaching librarianship benefits greatly from the creation of 'communities of practice' among members of the profession. The concept of community of practice (CoP) was first articulated two decades ago, by Lave and Wenger (1991), and later further developed by Wenger (1998). Wubbels defines CoP as 'the process of social learning that occurs when people who have a common interest in some subject or problem collaborate over an extended period to share ideas, find solutions, and build innovations' (2007: 226), while Bolander Laksov et al. note that 'people belonging to a community of practice are not just a group of people, or a web of interactions. They are a group who share an overall view of the domain in which they practise and mutual commitment to this' (2008: 123). The importance of *practice* is emphasised by Wenger, who observes that a CoP is essentially different from geographical communities, or even communities of interest, since the members of a CoP 'are informally bound by what they *do* together' (1998: 2).

Wenger (1998: 2) explains that a CoP is defined along three dimensions:

- *what it is about (the domain)* – refers to the *joint enterprise* that is understood and continually renegotiated by its members;
- *how it functions (the group)* – that there is a *mutual engagement* that ties members into a social entity;
- *what capability it has produced (the practice)* – this refers to the *shared repertoire* of resources that members have created over time, such as physical artefacts, routines, vocabulary, etc.

A CoP for teaching librarians might have the following characteristics:

- In addition to their normal responsibilities as librarians, the members have identified a *joint enterprise* which is the negotiation and elaboration of the instructional role as it fits into library and information work, and the relationship of this work with the overall educational mission of their institutions.
- *How it functions* – members of the group are *mutually engaged* in the facilitation of learning situations for students and find common ground based on this aspect of their role. They share the same concerns, successes, challenges and dilemmas, and relate to each other on this basis.
- Members also create a *shared repertoire* of teaching and learning resources, research publications, teaching and learning methods, presentations, problem solutions, etc.

How do we know if a CoP exists? Wenger has devised a list of indicators, which, if present, point to the formation of a CoP (1998: 125–6). Some of the indicators include:

- sustained mutual relationships;
- shared way of doing things together;
- rapid flow and propagation of information;

- no introductory preambles necessary – the process is continuous and mutually understood;
- shared perceptions of who belongs to the CoP;
- knowing what others know and what they can do;
- specific tools and other artefacts;
- local lore, shared stories, inside jokes;
- jargon and shortcuts to communication;
- shared discourse which reflects a certain perspective on the world.

Heinrich and Attebury discuss the non-formal nature of most CoPs, noting that the use of the actual term 'community of practice' to describe the grouping is not always needed: 'indeed, it is entirely possible that a community of practice may form in an organisation without its members being fully aware of its existence' (2010: 161). Wenger stresses that although CoPs do exist in most organisations, their membership is usually based on voluntary participation and, as such, they are not 'bound by organizational affiliations' and can span disciplines, departments, institutions and even sectors. In the case of teaching librarians, this broader conceptualisation of the CoP makes sense, as it is likely that the cohort of teaching librarians in most institutions is quite small. CoPs can also function well as virtual communities: Wubbels suggests that 'online communities for sharing ideas and for working on tasks fulfil conditions for creating a CoP' (2007: 228).

A good example of an attempt to create an international online CoP specifically designed to support teaching librarians is the *InfoTeach* community established by Chris Powis in 2006, which was funded by a National Teaching Fellowship award (*http://www.infoteach.org/wiki/doku.php*). Powis's plan was for 'a portal with, at its heart, a Wikipedia style information resource [which] would cover the sort of pedagogical issues that concern all those involved in teaching and learning but within a library context' (2005: 71). Like most wikis, and indeed CoPs, the overall success of the project depends on the contributions of others – as Powis states on the homepage: 'the community must own it rather than accept the received wisdom of a few.'

A more recent example of a dedicated virtual CoP is the *Librarians as Teachers Network* (*http://latnetwork.spruz.com*), a wiki set up in July 2010 by UK librarian Johanna Anderson to facilitate discussion amongst teaching librarians about their instructional experiences. The specific initial focus of the resource was librarians' experiences of completing a general teaching qualification, such as the Postgraduate Certificate in Education, available to UK instructors. However, discussion has inevitably expanded to include, amongst other topics, essential skills for teaching librarians, and general debate about the role of the teaching librarian.

Although CoPs may initially enjoy lively and active participation from their members, for any CoP to flourish and grow consistently, maintenance work is needed. Wenger notes that, although CoPs can form spontaneously and informally, the extent to which they develop depends on the quality of *internal leadership* – the individual, or individuals, who take responsibility for organising activities, gathering information, developing the social aspects of the CoP and forging links with other communities and official organisations (1998: 6). For a cross-institutional or cross-sector CoP to thrive, the following attributes can contribute to its longevity:

- A 'home' – a meeting place, be it physical or virtual, where members can assemble and interact with ease. For physical CoPs, this does not have to be a single location, but can rotate to suit members.

- A regular schedule of meetings, held at times to suit the majority of members. The CoP is more likely to continue if the meetings are scheduled in advance and all members have ample time to make arrangements to be present.

- A 'repository' which holds the resources that are created by the CoP. This can take the form of a wiki, as described above; or a CoP member could be designated the community 'curator' and volunteer to keep all documents in one secure place, making them available when requested.

- 'Showcases' – events held at regular intervals (e.g. annually) which give members an opportunity to share their experiences or resources on a wider platform and to publicise and celebrate the activities of the CoP, e.g. annual seminars, conferences, webinars, social events such as Christmas gatherings, etc.

- Informal communication channels, through which members can communicate with ease on a very regular basis and which help to maintain a sense of community and collegiality, e.g. discussion boards, online chat, mailing lists, blogs, etc . . .

Publishing in journals and presenting at conferences

'Like in any other field, it is important for librarians to continue grappling with IL issues in their research and scholarship in order to continue developing and advancing it within the profession' (Stevens, 2007: 257).

In Chapter 2, in discussing the importance of advocacy for information literacy, we have already noted the need for librarians to publish in journals outside the field of LIS, in order to promote their instructional activities and to hopefully encourage academics and other groups to collaborate with them on teaching and learning initiatives (Stevens, 2007; Weetman DaCosta, 2007). Generally speaking, writing for publication is an important activity for librarians and LIS in general; as Putnam suggests, 'journal articles edge us toward tenure; book reviews give guidance to other readers; newsletter articles share our stories' (2009: 1). Fallon emphasises that academic writing carried out by librarians 'offers the opportunity to share and disseminate experience, skills and practice that don't exist in the same framework elsewhere in the University, including a knowledge of collections, copyright, digitization, information sources and information literacy' (2009a: 421). For teaching librarians, the development of our own 'scholarship of teaching and learning' is a crucial support for our efforts, and a further means of legitimising our work. Borrowing from other fields can only take us so far: as Liles notes: 'While librarians are making progress on producing their own knowledge base regarding teaching, there is a dearth of teaching information designed specifically with librarians in mind and directed towards the unique circumstances of information literacy instruction' (2007: 114).

At present, the field is relatively healthy; Stevens points to the growing number of information-literacy-related publications, noting that the numbers are proof of 'academic librarians' sustained commitment to information literacy research and scholarship' (2007: 254). However, the culture of writing for publication in the library world is inconsistent from country to country; for example, writing in the context of Irish academic libraries, Fallon points out that while Irish librarians do engage in research, and present at national and international conferences, 'very few Irish librarians publish in the peer-reviewed literature' (2009a: 414). Mitchell and Reichel suggest that there are two key barriers which prevent academic librarians from carrying out and publishing research to the same extent as academics (1999: 233):

1. Librarians do not receive sufficient training and support for research and writing on their pre-service professional training programmes.

2. Librarians do not have enough time to carry out research, due to the day-to-day demands of their jobs, which are continuous all year round, unlike academics who use the out-of-term period to advance their research.

Another reason may be the fact that research and publication is, for the most part, not a key criterion in promotion and tenure for librarians; in their US-based study, Mitchell and Reichel found that the requirement for scholarship did *not* appear to act as a significant barrier to attaining tenure for librarians (1999: 238). In her paper, Fallon notes that the majority of librarians who publish articles tend to work in institutions where there is already a vibrant culture of research and publishing, and where it is considered important (2009a: 416).

To encourage librarians – including teaching librarians – to publish in high-ranking, peer-reviewed journals, support is required, both from a practical perspective and also a *personal* one, in terms of inspiring confidence and motivation. The mentoring and community of practice approaches described above naturally offer two potential channels for such support. Freely available online tools are another means of support; in a recent publication, Putnam provides a list of such tools, including useful blogs, meta-sites, style manuals and online writers' communities (2009). Helen Fallon's Irish-based *Academic Writing Librarians* blog[1] is another useful source that also serves as a kind of virtual community for academic librarians who are endeavouring to have their work published; although hosted in Ireland, it is very much an international resource. Another channel is continuing professional development (CPD), in the form of workshops or short courses, specifically aimed at librarians who wish to see their work in print. A good example of such an initiative is the writing support programme for academic librarians, which was established in Ireland in 2007 by Helen Fallon, a librarian in the National University of Ireland, Maynooth (Fallon, 2009a). Titled 'Introduction to Writing for Academic Publication', the programme was set up as a one-day workshop comprising 10 sessions, with each section covering a different step of the process of writing for publication; for example, sessions were included on: 'Exploring motivation to write and getting started,' 'Generating ideas' and 'Peer-review and submission'. The format of the workshop was interactive, and participants were encouraged to share their experiences and perspectives with their peers, as well as complete hands-on practical exercises and do some actual writing. The workshop was followed by two peer-review sessions, after four months and eight months respectively, for which participants were invited to send on a sample of their work in order to obtain some peer feedback; the actual feedback session was carried out in pairs during the first face-to-face meeting. In the second session, an editor from a peer-reviewed journal was invited to host a question-and-answer session for the group, which provided them with the expert, insider's view of the publication process. For an activity such as academic writing, which requires a high degree of self-motivation and persistence, the benefits of such support groups are invaluable; the subsequent publishing success of the librarians who participated in the programme described above is testament to the format's effectiveness (Fallon, 2009a).

Fallon (2009b) and Grassian and Kaplowitz (2005: 171–2) offer guidance for librarians who wish to write for scholarly publications. Fallon covers the entire nine-stage process, from 'Beginning to write' to 'Publication and celebration', describing a number of stimulating exercises at each stage which are designed to enhance creativity and confidence, and to deal with writer's block. Of particular use is her outline of the different elements of peer-reviewed journal articles (2009b: 67) and strategies for finding a suitable journal in which to publish (pp. 68–9). Grassian and Kaplowitz offer general advice about getting original research published, citing a list of tips from Bordens and Abbott (1999), including the importance of ensuring that your methodological approach is sound, and writing clearly and concisely for your target audience (pp. 171–2). Although outside the scope of this book, a useful text on research methods for librarians is *Research Methods in Information* by Pickard (2007).

For teaching librarians who are only beginning to think about writing for scholarly publications, presenting at conferences is a useful first step and an effective way both to disseminate research findings and to showcase the teaching and learning activities in your library. Most conferences these days are not restricted to the standard 45-minute long paper, but offer a range of formats for participants to present their work, including 30-minute short papers, hands-on workshops, resource demonstration sessions, symposiums, panel discussions, keynote presentations (always invited), poster presentations, and recently the rapid fire 'pecha kucha' sessions, during which presenters have 20 slides, which they display for 20 seconds each – each presenter is given just 6 minutes and 40 seconds to discuss their ideas, before it's the turn of the next presenter. If the thought of a full paper is daunting initially, you could perhaps start off with a poster presentation at one conference and then maybe a 30-minute short paper at the next, before finally giving a full paper and maybe having your contribution included as a full written paper in the conference proceedings, if that option is available. Most conferences now at least make the PowerPoint slides from each presentation available through their website afterwards, which is another good way of getting your work out there.

Exercises and reflections

1. Writing a grant proposal

(Individually or in groups)

Think of a current challenge in your workplace, or an area in which you feel that an innovative approach would be beneficial. Practise writing an application for funding, using the basic template below:

Application for funds

Project team members:

Principal investigator contact details:

Statement of role of principal investigator in project:

Associate investigator 1 contact details:

Associate investigator 2 contact details:

Project description:

Title of proposed project (maximum 100 words):

Project overview (maximum 300 words):

Starting date and duration of project:

Detailed project description (maximum 1,500 words):

1. Research question and sub-questions
2. Aims and objectives
3. Proposed research method
    i.   Research design
    ii. Population sample and recruitment
    iii. Analytical framework
    iv. Verification of data
    v.   Research ethics
4. How does the project relate to existing research, and how will it contribute to knowledge?
5. What are the proposed practical applications of the research?
6. How will the project results be disseminated?
7. Project timeline – step-by-step breakdown of the research plan, with proposed completion dates.

Budget

Total funding amount sought (specify currency):

Itemised breakdown:

Staff costs:

Travel and subsistence:

Consumables:

Equipment:

Other:

Total:

2. *Mentoring*

(Individually or in groups)

Sometimes, the reality of doing a job can be quite different from what is stated in the official job description. Based on your own experience, create a comprehensive guide or introductory PowerPoint presentation aimed at incoming teaching librarians in your library. Think of the kind of information that incoming staff members are most likely to need and/or want. You can use the following headings as a guide, or think of your own:

- current official job description;
- actual duties and responsibilities of role;
- library organisational structure – who does what;
- type of teaching carried out by library staff;
- library teaching 'philosophy' or mission;
- opportunities to develop and upgrade skills;
- tips and shortcuts;
- FAQs.

Note

1. Academic Writing Librarians Blog: *http://academicwritinglibrarian.blogspot. com/*

6

What librarians think: teaching and learning in the real world

Abstract: This chapter presents findings from a qualitative survey of 38 Irish academic teaching librarians, which aimed to explore their personal experiences of teaching, their conceptions of 'teacher identity', the challenges they face in their work, as well as their motivation and the aspects of teaching they find most rewarding. The aim of the chapter is to offer a snapshot of the 'real world' of teaching librarians in practice, and to gain an understanding of how they negotiate this aspect of their professional identity. The librarians' responses revealed several recurring themes that will be familiar to teaching librarians from all around the world.

Key words: survey, teacher identity, qualitative, teaching librarians, Ireland.

Now that we have discussed and analysed the theory and practice of information literacy instruction and teacher identity, this final chapter gives voice to real 'teaching librarians', who generously gave of their time to offer insights and perspectives on their *own* experiences of teaching in academic libraries. It is hoped that the issues and observations highlighted by the 38 Irish librarians who participated will make a useful contribution to the growing body of research that is currently being explored and extended by researchers such as Walter (2008) and Julien and Pecoskie (2009) in their investigations of librarians' subjective experience of the teaching role. It is also hoped that you, as teaching librarians, will discover that you are not alone; that your own experiences may be shared by others and that many of the issues and challenges that exist around the provision of information literacy instruction are universal. Through looking beyond the practical tools and methods of instruction, we can develop a better understanding of the factors that shape 'teacher identity' in librarians, as well as the obstacles that slow us down in our efforts to fully integrate with the teaching and learning missions of our institutions at large. We can also draw inspiration from the very positive experiences described by many of the librarians and the value they attach to this aspect of their role.

In October 2010, members of the Irish community of academic teaching librarians were invited to complete a short online qualitative survey, designed to elicit personal perspectives on the experience of facilitating learning in libraries. The questionnaire was partly informed by Walter's 2008 study, which was described in Chapter 2, and consisted of 13 open-ended, qualitative questions, with the aim of allowing participants to express themselves in detail and to reflect on their teaching experiences. The questionnaire is available to view at the end of this chapter. An invitation to participate was posted to LIR-L, the HEAnet[1] user group for librarians in Ireland, and was also forwarded to the mailing list of the *Academic and Special Libraries* section of the Library Association of Ireland (LAI). The author also sent personal emails to a number of teaching librarian contacts in universities and institutes around the country. Over a period of two weeks, 38 librarians completed the survey, providing detailed insight into their teaching experiences, role perceptions and 'teacher identity'. While not a large-scale study, the data collected is nonetheless a valid representation of the prevailing issues and concerns that affect academic teaching librarians in Ireland; much of what was said reflects themes that have arisen throughout the book and will resonate with teaching librarians in a global context.

Librarians' work roles, training and involvement in teaching

A number of the questions were designed to provide some contextual information about the librarians, in order to establish what their current work roles are, the extent and form of their involvement in teaching activities in their institutions and any instructional training they may have received, either pre- or during employment.

Work roles

The librarians describe a wide range of work roles, including subject librarians, managers, electronic resource managers, cataloguers and information service librarians. The dominant theme in their role descriptions centres on *multi-tasking* – very few of the librarians describe specialised roles, instead noting that they are required to undertake a range of duties in their jobs:

> 'Jack of all trades – so many duties I don't know where to start.'

> 'A little bit of everything – answering queries, teaching, cataloguing, dealing with invoices, processing journals and ordering documents.'

> 'Managing the library team, budget, resources. Marketing, information literacy teaching, subject liaison.'

Just three of the librarians describe themselves specifically as teaching librarians, or similar:

> 'I see myself as a teacher-librarian, who is heavily involved in teaching students and staff how to use the library resources, both at the information desk and heading up the training team.'

> 'Information skills trainer.'

The relative lack of specialist 'teaching librarians' in the survey may be a reflection of the practice of academic librarianship in Ireland; with some exceptions, Irish higher education institutions are small compared with those in nations such as the US, and the pool of library staff too restricted to permit such specialised division of roles. A full, dedicated teaching librarian or information literacy librarian in an Irish academic library is likely to be considered a luxury, rather than a necessity. Since roles tend to be defined primarily according to subject area rather than function, professional academic librarians usually find themselves in the 'jack-of-all-trades' role, into which teaching responsibilities must also fit. The challenge of juggling other library tasks with teaching duties is a theme that arises again and again in discussions of teacher-librarianship (Walter, 2008).

Involvement in teaching

The librarians describe varied and ad hoc involvement in teaching, with some providing only occasional sessions, while others are heavily involved, some in a leadership role. There is no pattern or consistency to the librarians' responses, with descriptions differing wildly. One librarian notes that last year they: 'did 154 hours of group teaching and 24 hour-long one-to-one sessions.' Some examples of the kinds of teaching facilitated by the librarians are as follows:

> 'Most terms I am asked to conduct a session with three to eight different classes, ranging from a class in the Rare Books Room where I demonstrate books, etc., to a class to more intensive classroom sessions (90 minutes long) where I instruct in the use of online resources.'

> 'I would say what I do is really more presenting than teaching. I deliver introductory sessions and also more advanced research skill sessions to both undergrad and postgrad courses – but it's usually just a one-session demonstration.'

> 'I meet with new groups of students occasionally and give them an introduction to the library services.'

> 'Lead in design and delivery of information skills learning activities embedded in medical, pharmacy and related programmes at undergraduate and postgraduate level, approx 40 contact hours per year.'

Instructional training

The librarians were asked to describe any kind of training that they had received to support their teaching work, either pre-employment or acquired on the job. Comments showed that formal instructional training is rare among librarians; the majority of librarians described ad hoc or piecemeal training, consisting of a session here and there. Very few of the librarians have formal teaching qualifications – just seven librarians stated that they had a teaching qualification of some description, or were in the process of obtaining one, usually a postgraduate diploma:

> 'I have recently completed a master's in education, which was a huge support to my teaching work.'

'I decided that it would be beneficial for me to do a course specifically for trainers which I paid for myself – Cert in Training with [institution name].'

'I recently completed a foundation diploma in Essential Trainer Skills, which was a NFQ Level 7 award.'

'Library paid for me to undertake the Postgraduate Diploma in Higher Education (PGDHE).'

A number of the librarians noted that, although they had not received training specifically in relation to information literacy instruction, they found the training that they had received in different contexts to be helpful, as well as previous experience working in a classroom:

'I already had a secondary teaching diploma.'

'I took two pedagogy courses while I was teaching English and children's literature classes at university level.'

'I have been involved in adult literacy training in the past and have trained as a tutor.'

'I had no training pre-employment to support my teaching work. I did work as an English-language assistant for one year before undertaking the MLIS so I had some classroom experience.'

The majority of librarians, however, describe their training as multifaceted and ad hoc, consisting of workshops, short courses and seminars, sometimes undertaken as part of continuing professional development (CPD). Several librarians also mentioned availing of general teaching and learning modules offered by their institution's teaching and learning departments. Some librarians had also taken an information-literacy-specific teaching module during their pre-service professional education programme. Many of the participants refer to having received some training in 'presentation' rather than teaching skills:

'I've done a number of presentation skills and large/small group teaching programmes.'

'Courses are made available by the university I work at for non-teaching staff to learn teaching skills and through library courses also I learn about teaching techniques.'

'I have used resources from the Centre for Teaching and Learning and find those excellent – I also am reading widely and then implementing some suggestions in my teaching work.'

'I have attended one-day seminars on particular resources, usually shortly after they have been launched, but I have never had any training specifically on teaching.'

Involvement in teaching networks and communities

The librarians were also asked if they are involved in any teaching and learning networks or communities, either within or outside of their own institutions. Twenty-seven of the librarians stated that they are currently not involved in any such networks, while just 10 described varying degrees of participation in internal and external communities, both formal and informal:

'A journal club is being established.'

'Yes, I am a member of a CoP on Technology in the Classroom.'

'Active member of Library Association of Ireland and engaged in some teaching activities (or activities that involve the same type of skills). Organise and speak at conferences; co-ordinating a training day and focus group at present, which I will facilitate. Member of Education Committee LAI.'

'Internal education support group of academics and related staff; participate in NAIRTL[2] and ILTA[3] activities.'

'There is a learning and development hub on the www.hseland.ie website which I am a member of.'

'Mostly in a virtual sense like the NDLR CoPs and our Centre for Learning and Teaching's mailing group on our VLE.'

'Yes, specialist diploma TLS in university. NDLR[4] IL teaching community. Academic writers' blog.'

Teaching grants and awards

In order to explore the librarians' participation in wider teaching and learning initiatives outside of the classroom, they were also asked if they had ever successfully or unsuccessfully applied for any teaching awards or grants, either individually or as part of a team.
Just five of the librarians answered yes to this question:

'Yes, the team won an in-house poster award in 2009 as sponsored by NAIRTL.'

'I was awarded Highly Commended for my teaching work by the LILAC conference.'

'Have received funding under the NDLR & SIF for IL development/ delivery.'

'Internal NDLR funding (team) – successful; Internal SIF 1 funding (team) – successful; External NDLR funding (IOTI[5] libraries) – unsuccessful.'

'Yes we applied for funding for development of IL modules in a previous job and we received it. However I moved jobs so did not see it to conclusion.'

It is not clear whether this low level of participation is due to lack of sufficient funding opportunities or to more subjective factors, such as lack of confidence or a perception that teaching and learning initiatives are the preserve of academics and researchers.

Librarians' beliefs about how role is perceived by 'outsiders'

Professional identity is partially shaped by how 'outsiders' view the profession, and how their conceptions affect the way in which they react to members of that profession. As part of the exploration of professional identity here, the librarians were asked how they believe that their work is perceived by those who are not part of the professional library community. To a significant extent, the librarians' comments suggest a degree of concern about how other parties perceive their role and work. In particular, a number of participants worry that library work is perceived as not sufficiently *challenging* – as a 'cushy number' that does not require any particular skill or expertise. This is coupled with a general lack of awareness of what the role actually entails:

'As so easy a trained monkey could do it.'

'I think some people understand the work I do but there is also a perception that if the library is quiet – not many bodies – then you must have nothing to do either. There are definitely people who wonder what it is you do all day.'

'Most people approach me with the attitude that anyone could do the job.'

'Minimal understanding of the breadth and depth of work and expertise involved. Very much seen as "admin" staff.'

Many of the librarians also believe that the traditional stereotype of the librarians still persists, despite the many changes that have transformed the profession in the past few decades.

'Outside my profession there are very strong stereotypes that we primarily sit behind a desk working with print material.'

'Majority do not have any idea of the varied roles and tasks performed by the modern librarian. They often think our role is that of shelvers/issue desk staff.'

'I think most people still see librarians as book guardians – and don't realise how technology has changed what we do.'

Significantly, in relation to this book, several of the participants suggested that 'outsiders' are frequently surprised when they learn about the teaching that librarians do, or that they do not accept that it is a valid aspect of the job. In the answers to this question, it is evident that many of the librarians are referring to *academics'* perceptions specifically – as we discussed in Chapter 1, the views of academics regarding teaching librarians are the most crucial, since it is they who are the 'gatekeepers' to the curriculum and their support is essential for curriculum-embedded learning:

'Misunderstood. Think that the consensus would be "why would librarians teach?"'

'People are sometimes surprised to hear that I teach classes. I don't think they regard it as "real teaching" but people who are familiar with the research needs of students, after they have thought about it, feel that this teaching is important for students.'

'With surprise! Most people are not familiar with the concept of teaching librarians and wonder what it is we teach.'

'As a librarian – not a teacher and limited to one-off session.'

'That's difficult because some academics don't see us as teachers; they think we've nothing to offer.'

Linked to this perception is the traditional view of librarians as 'support service' providers, rather than educators who are central to the educational mission of the institution:

'They would see me as a back-up resource to the lecturers.'

'As being primarily utilitarian in developing student information skill competencies.'

'I think they would see it as supporting teaching, learning and research in the same way as maybe tutors do.'

'This is complex. Many see it only as a supporting role.'

Tellingly, there were few positive responses to this question:

'Interesting.'

'Surprised by how varied the role is.'

'I think they would see my work as part of the bigger university picture and not just as library work.'

It is apparent that the librarians in this survey believe that their professional image – as it appears to outsiders, particularly academics – is inaccurate and undervalued, and does not reflect the reality of their role and contribution they make to student learning. How librarians *feel* about their externally projected image is crucial, although their beliefs about outsiders' perceptions may not be accurate, or even fair – without a parallel survey of non-librarians, it is impossible to verify the perceptions reported here. But it is reasonable to state that the librarians surveyed here have quite a negative conception of how they are perceived outside of the profession.

Librarians' pre-employment role conceptions compared with current role experience

The librarians were also asked to describe how the conceptions of library work that they held prior to working in libraries compared with their *actual* current experience of working in an academic library. They were asked to focus specifically on the teaching aspect in this question, inkeeping with the theme of this book. Eighteen (of 34) librarians state that the job involves a lot more teaching than they had expected. This finding tallies with our discussion of the teaching role in Chapter 1, where it was noted that many fledgling librarians are surprised by the amount of teaching they are expected to do in their jobs, and consequently feel unequipped for it:

> 'The teaching was initially a surprise and I felt unprepared for it.'

> 'It involves much more teaching than expected.'

> 'Had never considered the teaching aspect. I had thought the job would be primarily about resource management.'

> 'Teaching did not figure as part of librarians' work.'

> 'I went into librarianship because I didn't want to teach!!'

> 'I wouldn't have thought people needed to be shown how to use resources, surely they know how to do that already?'

However, many of the librarians noted that, even though they did not expect to teach, they found themselves enjoying this aspect of the job:

> 'It [teaching] is far more involved than I thought it would be but I really enjoy this aspect of my work.'

> 'I hadn't envisaged doing as much teaching as I currently do – that said, teaching is the aspect of my role that I enjoy the most.'

> 'I do like it and am happy sharing my knowledge with other staff and readers.'

A number of the librarians observe that, to them, teaching is and always has been a core element of library work. In some cases, this is what attracted them to the profession in the first instance:

'I was always aware that teaching would be part of a librarian's work, it was one of the aspects that drew me to this career.'

'It's a very large part of the work. I've been working in libraries for over 12 years so my career has developed with the teaching. It's just part of the job – it would be strange not to teach.'

'I was always aware of teaching as a core function of work as a librarian, and in all my roles, this has been the case. I would not have been interested in any role that did not involve a significant amount of teaching, training, user support or general interaction with users/clients.'

It would seem, from the answers to this question, that the teaching role is not yet viewed as a core library function by pre-service librarians, although this changes once they gain experience in the role. This raises important questions about how the profession is portrayed from a careers perspective and what motivates pre-service librarians to choose information work as a career. It also raises questions about the preparedness of the incoming librarians to undertake teaching duties. Librarians who are 'surprised' by teaching duties may feel that they have been thrown in at the deep end. Some may swim – and enjoy it, as expressed above – but equally, some might also sink. We also need to consider the issue of whether the ability to teach should constitute an 'essential' or 'desirable' competency for those entering the profession.

Librarians' confidence in teaching

In two successive questions, the librarians were asked to indicate: a) how confident they felt when they *first* took on teaching duties; and b) how confident they feel *now* about their teaching duties. Their responses are displayed in Table 6.1.

In the expanded answers to the questions, interesting themes emerged. The first, and perhaps most obvious, is the influence of *experience* on the development of confidence and perceptions of self-efficacy. The more teaching the librarians do, the more comfortable they feel.

In terms of how confident they felt at first, a number of the participants noted that their *previous* experiences of teaching in other contexts helped them when they first undertook teaching duties in their library work:

'I have quite a bit of experience in this area so it wasn't too difficult. I am comfortable with standing up in front of audiences and am fairly ok with ad-libbing if necessary. Plus I really enjoy the work!'

'Having worked in a classroom I was not worried about either my own preparation for each class or in dealing with students.'

'I felt my teaching experience would help.'

The librarians' confidence levels rise with time and practice. This is clearly shown in Table 6.1, where none of the participants said they were 'not at all confident' currently, compared with the 14 who felt they had no confidence when they started to teach:

'I've put a lot of time and work into my classes. I use my experience of action research to do the best for my students. I've also done research on how to improve your teaching and learning outcomes for students.'

'I have done this for over four years now and there are few situations I would not be comfortable in, unless, for example, I am teaching a new tool for the first time, e.g. Mendeley.'

'The more experience I have, the more confident I feel, and the more I know. I have gained a lot from the people who taught me and I find that librarianship, like most professions, is a constant learning curve, with new developments coming on stream all the time, especially in the area of IT.'

However, even with increased confidence levels, several of the librarians framed the improvement more in terms of developing 'coping skills',

Table 6.1   Librarians' confidence levels in their teaching

	At first	Now
Not at all confident	14	0
Somewhat confident	20	15
Very confident	3	19
Completely confident	0	4
Total	37 (1 skipped)	38

which they use to handle what remains a stressful situation for them:

> 'I have developed my own coping strategies, use of PowerPoint, demonstrating the library electronic resources on the projector. I also make sure I wear "nicer" clothes on the days I meet a group, as well as wear make-up and green concealer in case my face flares up!'

> 'I am far more confident in relation to preparation and interactive teaching methods as well as having far more experience. I would still not consider myself as a confident teacher though and am still not comfortable with the role.'

> 'I would never say that I'm 100 per cent confident in delivering teaching sessions, but because I am now more familiar with the theory behind teaching and learning, I feel I am a confident teacher.'

Some of the reasons behind the initial lack of confidence were discussed by the librarians in their expanded answers to the question. Several described feeling out of their depth and being uncertain as to the best way to facilitate learning sessions:

> 'I felt thrown in at the deep end. I did have one very supportive colleague without whom I would probably have sunk. It was trial and error.'

> 'I made the most basic of errors – failure to get a good idea of what would be of most benefit to the specific group I was training, and at what level. Followed by: failure to develop any kind of rapport with the group – simply launching into an over-rehearsed presentation while trying desperately to avoid questions that would put me off track. Over-reliance on PowerPoint.'

> 'My predecessor gave me some of her slides, etc., and I felt a bit daunted as they were very theoretical but as no one told me how I should do it I went with this at first.'

Others spoke of how teaching makes them aware of gaps in their *own* knowledge and skills, including subject-specific knowledge, which leads them to question their effectiveness:

> 'Confident about presentation skills, level of audience, etc., but some apprehension about my own knowledge of specific subjects, such as particular databases.'

'Enjoy lecturing and public talking, though learning curve re new subject matter sometimes quite challenging.'

'I was very nervous about standing up in front of a group of up to 200 students. I was also concerned that because I didn't have the subject background, I would be challenged on various points.'

Another worry for the librarians is their ability to correctly tailor instruction for different student groups and to pitch the sessions at the right 'level':

'As with all aspects of a job that are new, my first teaching week was difficult, I did not quite know what to expect from the class, their levels of understanding or ability.'

'When I came to the academic librarianship role, the challenge was to understand about the audience (usually students) and their needs and this was not explained to me, and hadn't really been thought about.'

'I made the most basic of errors – failure to get a good idea of what would be of most benefit to the specific group I was training, and at what level.'

From a more positive perspective, a number of the librarians suggested that their enjoyment of teaching, and the feeling that they are offering something of value, helps to overcome their nerves and to increase their confidence:

'I felt very sure of the importance, relevance and urgency of what I was teaching, and that students would be just as excited as I was about exciting databases and interesting resources. I had frequently been bored by lengthy library demonstrations, so I was confident that I could make mine much more concise and exciting.'

'The teaching was, of course, a bit daunting at first and still is sometimes, depending on the class, but I really enjoy it. I'm not sure that I'd still be working in a library, only for it.'

'I enjoy this work so I felt somewhat confident about it at the start and continue to enjoy it and feel more confident now!'

Several participants explore the issue of how they themselves learn and develop teaching competency in the course of their work. There is a strong sense of constantly wanting to improve and increase effectiveness, which in turn instils confidence. An interesting observation by one participant suggests that having mastered the 'mechanics' of teaching, they are now free to focus on how the students are *learning*:

'Over time, of course, you discover the most common questions, mistakes, etc., that students will have and you've discovered what works and what doesn't in a session.'

'[I] can still be a bit anxious – very keen to be effective. Always know when I have "connected" with students and of course when I haven't. Hope I'm improving all the time . . .!'

'While there are many information-related problems beyond my competence to teach in clinical medicine, for instance, I have learned to develop a more peer-to-peer approach which facilitates self-learning in small groups for more advanced topics.'

'Now, large groups don't bother me – what concerns me more now is how the students learn in large groups. I have also learned that it doesn't matter if I can't answer questions (especially if they need clinical expertise) – I don't have a problem admitting I don't know! And I always learn a new way of doing something, especially in a workshop. I concentrate more now on the students, rather than worrying about my performance.'

Librarians' challenges in the teaching role

A further question focused on the challenges that the librarians have experienced or which they currently face in their teaching roles. The responses to the question show that librarians perceive that their efforts to teach effectively are obstructed by environmental factors that are, to some extent, outside of their control. Perhaps unsurprisingly, the greatest barrier to teaching described by the librarians comes under the heading of 'time'; this encompasses both the time required for planning, preparation and delivery of courses and individual sessions, as well as the time needed to build up a rapport with student groups and to gradually build on content over a period of weeks.

The librarians reported that they feel torn between their teaching duties and the other responsibilities of their roles. This supports findings outlined by Walter (2008) in his similar study:

> 'Preparing and giving sessions can be time-consuming. In the light of staff reductions it is becoming more stressful to deal with competing demands.'

> 'Getting enough time to teach is always a challenge. The other challenge is that teaching is not my sole focus and I am stretched across a lot of areas.'

> 'The amount of time involved in preparation. Not enough opportunities to build experience. Not enough time to reflect on my practice.'

The other time-related challenge is linked to the prevalence of the 'one-shot' session discussed in Chapter 4 – the librarians here suggest that it is difficult to build up a relationship with their students, as they do not teach or see them on a regular basis, indeed often seeing them just the one time:

> 'Compared to teaching a class for a whole semester, where you develop a rapport with the class over a few weeks, a library class is more like a performance, where you have to capture your audience in that one show.'

> 'The one-off sessions, very hard to see a group more than once to build on what you've covered with them.'

A further challenge relates to student (and faculty) motivation. Several of the librarians observed that it can be difficult to entice students to attend information literacy sessions, or to foster independent learning behaviour when they do attend:

> 'I guess the main challenge is to convince students to attend courses, as many are not aware of the vast amount of info material out there and how important it is to be information literate.'

> 'Apathy among readers can be a problem, as can short attention spans! Readers' expectations have increased and they can also expect "spoon-feeding", but it is part of our role to teach them the skills so they can do it themselves.'

'I tend to find it frustrating that many students don't want to assume responsibility for their own learning and a lot of them seem to completely lack intellectual curiosity.'

Academics, too, are occasionally perceived as apathetic towards the instructional services offered by the librarians. The challenge of forging effective collaborative working relationships with academics is a well-established issue for teaching librarians and has been discussed widely:

'The lack of interest in the library and the resources we provide from some of the lecturers is very disheartening.'

'Teacher misunderstanding of the librarian's role. That it is not only about providing a nice space to read, with that done then there is no further need for a librarian.'

'Promoting IL and trying to get lecturers to buy into the process of IL teaching and the value it adds to academia.'

The final challenge the librarians describe concerns technical or equipment issues – for instance, classrooms that are inadequately equipped for different learning activities or learning technologies that fail in the middle of a session:

'Lack of appropriate facilities – for the training we are doing, it should be practical, hands-on and evaluative. So that requires different room structure than are available – where students can work in small groups, on laptops and I can work with them.'

'Failure of equipment, especially when giving a hands-on demonstration. Don't know where it is going to lead me.'

'Technical! The equipment that doesn't work, the network that goes down in the middle of a live session.'

What do librarians enjoy about teaching?

In contrast to the challenges, the librarians were also asked to describe what (if anything) they enjoy about their teaching role. Their comments show that interacting with and helping students are the two most rewarding aspects of teaching for them. Several of the librarians refer to the 'buzz' of a teaching session:

'Enjoy the buzz of it, the interaction with academics, with students, the sense of making a difference, guiding/facilitating students on path to self-discovery and independence as learners.'

'The buzz is good, interacting with students, hearing their perspective.'

'Student interaction. The satisfaction that you are helping and putting in the extra effort. There are creative possibilities and certainly positive feedback if you work hard at it and put the energy in'.

The librarians also describe the satisfaction of 'making a difference' with the students and facilitating them to do things they were unable to do before. Several comments describe with pleasure the 'eureka moment' when a student finally understands a concept or is able to perform a task:

'Realising that I've shown/taught them something they did not previously know that they will be able to use all their lives.'

'You definitely feel that you are making a difference when people go away happy that they have taken something away from your session that they will use in the future.'

'I find the teaching experience very gratifying. I especially enjoy teaching adults and enjoy the moment when a learner "gets it".'

'I particularly love helping students prepare for project work. I love when you can see the understanding on their faces, or when the penny drops.'

Many of these comments suggest that the librarians draw a great deal more reward from their teaching duties than the simple satisfaction of a job well done. The opportunity for direct contact with students is viewed as particularly welcome, as such involved interaction may be much less frequent in the normal course of library work. The librarians also enjoy seeing the direct impact of their instruction – i.e. when the 'penny drops'.

Some of the librarians refer again to fostering independent student learning as a source of satisfaction – helping students to help themselves:

'Seeing students being able to help themselves because of something I helped them learn.'

'I enjoy when students understand what you are teaching them and feel confident enough to be able to research the resources themselves.'

Finally, a number of the librarians observe that they enjoy the opportunity teaching affords to 'showcase' the library and promote its services to students and staff:

'Spreading knowledge about library services.'

'I enjoy telling people about our library and the fantastic services we offer!'

Librarians' conceptions of 'good' teaching

The librarians were asked to describe what they believe constitutes 'good' teaching'. Their answers can be described under four headings:

- fostering independent learning and intellectual curiosity in students;
- customisation – tailoring learning sessions to individual student groups;
- good lesson planning and clear learning outcomes;
- excitement and enthusiasm.

The librarians surveyed have a strong belief that good teaching is not about transmitting content, but rather about empowering their students to complete tasks and solve problems independently, applying the skills and knowledge they have gained in class. Their view of learning aligns closely with Biggs and Tang's *Level 3* concept of learning, which focuses on what the student *does* in class, rather than on their innate ability or the teacher's skill-set (see Chapter 2, 'Developing a personal teaching philosophy'):

'Self-directed learning. Not teaching but facilitating students on journey of discovery.'

'The idea of engaging the students, enthusing them and involving them in their own learning.'

'The idea of sharing experiences to the extent that students can become empowered and enabled.'

'Good teaching should be about giving the student enough confidence and information to be able to tackle research on their own, while also knowing they can come back to you if they need help.'

'Engaging the students so that they are immediately integrating their own questions and concerns with the material that is being presented to them.'

'Good teaching should engage the student enough to ask more questions.'

For the librarians, good teaching also means being responsive to the needs and characteristics of different student groups and 'customising' the learning sessions so that they are pitched at the correct level for the group in question:

'A deep understanding of both the information world and the students you are working with. No longer are we working with homogenous groups . . . and the material out there is diverse and growing more complex day by day.'

'Recognising that there are different learning styles and trying to cater for various styles in sessions.'

'Responsiveness, clarity, customisation of content and relevancy, interactivity and an ability to leave the group better informed than they were before the session.'

'Knowledge of what the group know already, relevant information, clarity.'

'Knowing your audience and its needs (knowing how to connect).'

Learning sessions that are properly planned, with clearly stated learning outcomes, are also a core element of good teaching practice:

'I think good teaching is structured according to definite learning outcomes.'

'Clearly identified learning outcomes that tie in with the requirements of your students. I find it more useful if you can tie in your session with a specific project/assignment they have – it makes it more practical and meaningful for them.'

'Well-executed lesson plans, and clear and measureable learning outcomes.'

Finally, a good teacher should show enthusiasm for what they are teaching and should endeavour to create a sense of excitement around the material:

'A good teacher inspires people to learn and excites them about their work. Good teaching happens when the teacher knows their area, can communicate clearly and can bring a sense of excitement and enthusiasm to the classroom. These skills translate in VLEs or in face-to-face situations.'

'The idea of engaging the student, enthusing them and involving them in their own learning.'

'I think good teaching [. . .] is delivered by someone who is enthusiastic and passionate about their subject.'

Librarians' additional comments about the teaching role

The librarians were also invited to respond to an open question, asking them if there were any further comments or observations they would like to make. Some of the comments explore interesting questions with regard to the role.

Several of the librarians took the opportunity to comment further on the lack of status and recognition they feel is afforded to them in their institutions:

'The teaching function within libraries is multifaceted and is based on political and strategic objectives as well as the educational. However, it is not always explicitly recognised within academia as being essential.'

'The role needs greater definition and support from the wider librarian community. It is one of the most demanding jobs in the library world, but the perception is that it is a cushy number, which harms any real development of the role in the professional world.'

'It's a fine line, as the lecturers' unions here are very adamant in protecting the role of lecturer. However, they are quite happy to pass the unglamorous work to the library, like citation and plagiarism.'

By the same token, teaching is also viewed by some of the librarians as a means of enhancing academic status and promoting the library to the academic community:

'It is a very valuable way to reach out to students and researchers, elevates my status in the institution to being "academic related".'

'I think this is a key growth area for library staff and is critical in ensuring that the library is part of the learning loop within our universities and colleges.'

'The teaching role of a librarian adds credibility to the role of the librarian and highlights to academics the educational role librarians do play.'

One very interesting comment referred to a perceived division within the profession itself, regarding the teaching role:

'I have been surprised at the divide between those in the profession who recognise teaching as part of our role and those who do not consider it part of their job. The profession is changing and I think that as some of the more traditional roles of a librarian will be phased out, we need to embrace new ways of promoting the skills librarians have and showing how those skills can benefit readers.'

Finally, a number of the librarians reiterated the need for, and benefits of, pedagogical training for librarians, as well as expressing concern about the lack of training opportunities:

'Based on my own experience, I think it is very worthwhile for librarians to pursue a teaching qualification. It certainly gave me a lot of confidence in my role. I know librarians can often be a bit paranoid about what lecturers make of their status, but I think this is a poor approach on the part of librarians. We need to stand equal to them – qualification-wise we usually are there or thereabouts.'

'I would mention again my surprise at the lack of training/support in the area of teaching, within the library, but also for lecturers of modules as well. It's a little bit of a concern for me that the quality of teaching is so much reliant on individuals and their personal skill-set/competencies in the area.'

Academic librarians' experience of teaching: a short survey

1. How would you describe your current role in the library (not your job title)?
2. Can you briefly outline the nature and extent of your involvement in teaching at your institution?
3. How do you think that your work would be perceived by people outside the profession?
4. How does your job – especially the teaching aspect – compare with the image of a librarian's work that you may have held prior to your employment?
5. Can you describe any training you may have had, pre- or during employment, to support your teaching work?
6. How confident did you feel when you first took on teaching duties?
   - not at all confident
   - somewhat confident
   - very confident
   - completely confident

   Can you please elaborate on your answer?
7. How confident do you feel now?
   - not at all confident
   - somewhat confident
   - very confident
   - completely confident

   Can you please elaborate on your answer?
8. What, if anything, do you enjoy about teaching?
9. What challenges, if any, have you faced, or are currently facing, in your teaching?

10. What do you believe constitutes 'good' teaching?

11. Are you involved in any teaching networks or communities inside or outside of your institution (please elaborate)?

12. Have you ever applied (successfully or unsuccessfully) for any teaching awards or grants, either individually or as part of a team (please elaborate)?

13. Are there any further comments you would like to make about your teaching role, or any other related issues?

Notes

1. Higher Education Authority Net – 'Ireland's national education and research network, providing high quality Internet services to Irish universities, Institutes of Technology, and the research and educational community' (*www.heanet.ie/about*).
2. National Academic for Integration of Research, Teaching and Learning: *http://www.nairtl.ie/*.
3. Irish Learning Technology Association: *http://ilta.net/*.
4. National Digital Learning Resources: *http://www.ndlr.ie/*.
5. Institutes of Technology of Ireland: *http://www.ioti.ie/*.

References

AASL (American Association of School Libraries). (2007). *Standards for the 21st-Century Learner*. Available at: *http://www.ala.org/ala/mgrps/divs/aasl/guidelinesandstandards/learningstandards/AASL_Learning_Standards_2007.pdf* (retrieved 20 October 2010).

AASL (American Association of School Librarians). (2003). *ALA/AASL Standards for Initial Programs for School Library Media Specialist Preparation*. Available at: *http://www.ala.org/ala/mgrps/divs/aasl/aasleducation/schoollibrary/ala-aasl_slms2003.pdf* (retrieved 20 October 2010).

AASL (American Association of School Librarians). *National Board Certification*. Available at: *http://www.ala.org/ala/mgrps/divs/aasl/aasleducation/nationalboardcer/nationalboard.cfm* (retrieved 20 October 2010).

Abson, C. (2003). The changing picture of higher education. In Oyston, E. (ed.), *Centred on Learning: Academic Case Studies on Learning Centre Development* (pp. 1–18). Aldershot: Ashgate.

ACRL (Association of College and Research Libraries). (2008). *Standards for Proficiencies for Instruction Librarians and Coordinators: A Practical Guide*. Available at: *http://www.ala/mgrps/divs/acrl/standards/profstandards.pdf* (retrieved 20 October 2010).

ACRL (Association of College and Research Libraries). (2007a). *Joint Statement on Faculty Status of College and University Librarians*. Available at: *http://www.ala.org/ala/mgrps/divs/acrl/standards/jointstatementfaculty.cfm* (retrieved 20 October 2010).

ACRL (Association of College and Research Libraries). (2007b, June). *Standards for Faculty Status for College and University Librarians*. Available at: *http://www.ala.org/ala/mgrps/divs/acrl/standards/standardsfaculty.cfm* (retrieved 20 October 2010).

ACRL (Association of College and Research Libraries). (2003). *Guidelines for Instruction Programs in Academic Libraries*. Available at: *http://www.ala.org/ala/mgrps/divs/acrl/standards/guidelinesinstruction.cfm* (retrieved 20 October 2010).

ACRL (Association of College and Research Libraries) (2000, Jan. 18). *Information Literacy Competency Standards for Higher Education*. Available at: *http://www.ala.org/ala/mgrps/divs/acrl/standards/informationliteracycompetency.cfm* (retrieved 20 October 2010).

Aharony, N. (2009). Librarians and information scientists in the blogosphere: An exploratory analysis. *Library and Information Science Research*, 31(3), 174–181.

ALA (American Library Association) Presidential Committee on Information Literacy. (1989, January 10). *Final Report*. Available at: *http://www.ala.org/ala/acrl/acrlpubs/whitepapers/presidential.htm* (retrieved 20 October 2010).

Andretta, S. (2005). *Information Literacy: A Practitioner's Guide*. Oxford: Chandos Publishing.

ASLA (Australian School Library Association). *Standards of Professional Excellence for Teacher Librarians*. Available at: *http://www.asla.org.au/policy/TLstandards.pdf* (retrieved 20 October 2010).

Avery, E.F. (2003). *Assessing Student Learning Outcomes for Information Literacy Instruction in Academic Institutions*. Chicago: Association of College and Research Libraries.

Aydelott, K. (2007). Using the ACRL information literacy competency standards for science and engineering/technology to develop a modular critical-thinking-based information literacy tutorial. *Science and Technology Libraries*, 27(4), 19–42.

Badke, W. (2009). Ramping up the one-shot. *Online*, 33(2), 47–49.

Barnes, G. (2009). Guess who's coming to work: Generation Y. Are you ready for them? *Public Library Quarterly*, 28(1), 58–63.

Barrett, T. (2005). Understanding problem-based learning. In Barrett, T., Mac Labhrainn, I. and Fallon, H. (eds), *Handbook of Enquiry and Problem-Based Learning: Irish Case Studies and International Perspectives*. Galway: CELT. Available at: *http://www.aishe.org/readings/2005-2/chapter2.pdf* (retrieved 20 October 2010).

Bawden, D. (2001). Information and digital literacies: a review of concepts. *Journal of Documentation*, 57(2), 218–239.

Beatty, I. (2004). Transforming student learning with classroom communication systems. *EDUCASE Centre for Applied Research Bulletin*, 3, 1–13.

Behen, L.D. (2006). *Using Pop Culture to Teach Information Literacy*. Westport, CT: Libraries Unlimited.

Beijaard, D. (1995). Teachers' prior experiences and actual perceptions of professional identity. *Teachers and Teaching: Theory and Practice*, 1(2), 281–294.

Benjes-Small, C., Dorner, J.L. and Schroeder, R. (2009). Surveying libraries to identify best practices for a menu approach for library instruction requests. *Communications in Information Literacy*, 3(1), 31–44.

Bewick, L. and Corrall, S. (2010). Developing librarians as teachers: a study of their pedagogical knowledge. *Journal of Librarianship and Information Science*, 42(2), 97–110.

Biddiscombe, R. (2002). Learning support professionals: the changing role of subject specialists in UK academic libraries. *Program*, 36(4), 228–35.

Biddiscombe, R. (2000). The changing role of the information professional in support of learning and research. *Advances in Librarianship*, 23, 63–64.

Biggs, J.B. and Tang, C. (2007). *Teaching for Quality Learning at University* (3rd ed.). London: Open University Press/Mc Graw-Hill Education.

Bloom, B.S. (1956). *Taxonomy of Educational Objectives*. Boston, MA: Allyn and Bacon.

Bolander Laksov, K., Mann, S. and Dahlgren, L.O. (2008). Developing a community of practice around teaching: a case study. *Higher Education Research and Development*, 13(2), 121–132.

Bosch, E.K., Ramachandran, H., Luevano, S. and Wakiji, E. (2010). The resource team model: An innovative mentoring program for academic librarians. *New Review of Academic Librarianship*, 16(1), 57–74.

Booth, A. and Brice A. (2004). *Evidence Based Practice for Information Professionals: A Handbook*. London: Facet Publishing.

Bordens, K.S. and Abbott, B.B. (1999). *Research Design and Methods: A Process Approach* (4th edn.) Mountain View, CA.

Boyle, S. (2009). Scanning, tailoring, and promoting information literacy support – another string to the liaison librarian's bow. *SCONUL Focus*, 46, 71–77. Available at: *http://www.ucd.ie/library/guides/pdf/staff_papers/boyle09_sconul.pdf* (retrieved 10 November 2010).

Breen, E. and Fallon, H. (2005). Developing student information literacy to support project and problem-based learning. In Barrett, T., Mac Labhrainn, I. and Fallon, H. (eds), *Handbook of Enquiry and Problem-Based Learning: Irish Case Studies and International Perspectives*. (pp. 179–188). Galway: AISHE and CELT, NUI Galway.

Breivik, P.S. and Gee, E.G. (1989). *Information Literacy: Revolution in the Library*. New York: Macmillan.

Briggs, L.E. and Skidmore, J.M. (2008). Beyond the blended librarian: Creating full partnerships with faculty to embed information literacy in online learning systems. In Mackey, T.P. and Jacobson, T.E. (eds), *Using Technology to Teach Information Literacy*. (pp. 87–110). New York: Neal-Schuman.

Bruce, C. (2001). Faculty–librarian partnerships in Australian higher education: Critical dimensions. *Reference Services Review*, 29(2), 106–115.

Bruce, C. (1997). *The Seven Faces of Information Literacy*. Adelaide, Australia: Auslib Press.

Bruce, C., Edwards, S. and Lupton, M. (2006). Six frames for information literacy education: a conceptual framework for interpreting the relationship between theory and practice. *Italics*, 5(1), 1–18. Available at: *http://www.ics.heacademy.ac.uk/italics/vol5-1/pdf/sixframes_final%20_1_.pdf* (retrieved 21 October 2010).

Bryan, J.E. (2007). The question of faculty status for academic librarians. *Library Review*, 56 (9), 781–787.

Burchinal, L.G. (1976). Bringing the American Revolution on-line: information science and national R & D. *Bulletin of the American Society for Information Science*, 2(8), 27–28.

California State University Los Angeles: University Library. (2002). *Information Literacy and Library Instruction: Mission Statement*. Available at: *http://www.calstatela.edu/library/1temp/infolit-what.htm* (retrieved 20 October 2010).

Cannon, A. (1994). Faculty survey on library research instruction. *Reference Quarterly*, 33(4), 524–541.

Carlson, D. and Miller, R.H. (1984). Librarians and teaching faculty: partners in bibliographic instruction. *College and Research Libraries*, 45(6), 483–491.

Carnegie Mellon University Libraries. (2008). *Information Literacy@Carnegie Mellon: Mission Statement*. Available at: *http://brie1.library.cmu.edu/Information Literacy/program.html* (retrieved 20 October 2010).

Case, D.O. (2007). *Looking for Information: A Survey of Research on Information Seeking, Needs, and Behavior* (2nd edn). London: Academic Press.

Chiste, K.B., Glover, A. and Westwood, G. (2000). Infiltration and entrenchment: capturing and securing information literacy territory in academe. *Journal of Academic Librarianship*, 26(3), 202–208.

Christiansen, L., Stombler, M. and Thaxton, L. (2004). A report on librarian–faculty relations from a sociological perspective. *Journal of Academic Librarianship*, 30 (2), 116–121.

CILIP (Chartered Institute of Library and Information Professionals). (2004). *Information Literacy Definition*. Available at: *http://www.cilip. org.uk/get-involved/advocacy/learning/information-literacy/pages/definition.aspx* (retrieved 20 October 2010).

Clayton, S.J. (ed.) (2007). *Going the Distance: Library Instruction for Remote Learners*. London: Facet.

CLIR (Council on Library and Information Resources). (2008). Prologue to a fundamental rethinking: context and topic threads. In CLIR (Council on Library and Information Resources). *No Brief Candle: Reconceiving Research Libraries for the 21st Century*. (pp. 2–7). Washington: CLIR. Available at: *http://www.clir.org/pubs/reports/pub142/pub142.pdf* (retrieved 22 October 2010).

Clobridge, A. and Del Testa, D. (2008). The World War II poster project: building a digital library through information literacy partnerships. In Mackey, T.P. and Jacobson, T.E. (eds), *Using Technology to Teach Information Literacy*. (pp. 51–82). New York: Neal-Schuman.

Colbeck, C.L. (2008). Professional identity development theory and doctoral education. *New Directions for Teaching and Learning*, 113, 9–16.

Conroy, H. and Boden, D. (2007). *Teachers, Trainers, Educators, Enablers: What skills do we need and where do we get them?* Presentation given at Umbrella, 29 June. Available at: *http://www.cilip. org.uk/get-involved/special-interest-groups/personnel/Documents/PTEGTeachersTrainers.pdf* (retrieved 21 October 2010).

Cook, M.K. (1981). Rank, status and contribution of academic librarians as perceived by the teaching faculty at Southern Illinois University, Carbondale. *College and Research Libraries*, 42, 214–222.

Corcos, E. and Monty, V. (2008). Interactivity in library presentations using a personal response system. *EDUCAUSE Quarterly*, 31(2), 53–60.

Corrall, S. (2007). Benchmarking strategic engagement with information literacy in higher education: towards a working model. *Information Research*, 12(4). Available at: *http://informationr.net/ir/12-4/paper328.html* (retrieved 22 October 2010).

Courant, P. (2008a). Scholarship: the wave of the future in the digital age. In Katz, R.N. (ed.). *The Tower and the Cloud: Higher Education in the Age of Cloud Computing*. (pp. 202–211). Boulder, CO: EDUCAUSE. Available at: *http://www.educause.edu/ir/library/pdf/PUB7202t.pdf* (retrieved 22 October 2010).

Courant, P. (2008b). The future of the library in the research university. In CLIR (Council on Library and Information Resources). *No Brief Candle: Reconceiving Research Libraries for the 21st Century* (pp. 21–27). Washington: CLIR. Available at: *http://www.clir.org/pubs/reports/pub142/pub142.pdf* (retrieved 22 October 2010).

Cox, C. (2002), Becoming part of the course: using Blackboard to extend one-shot library instruction. *College and Research Libraries News*, 63(1), 11–39.

Crawford, W. (2010). But still they blog. *Online*, 34(2), 58–60.

Crawford, W. (2009). The liblog landscape 2007–2008: a lateral look. *Cites and Insights*, 9(7), 1–48. Available at: *http://cical.info/civ9i7.pdf* (retrieved 12 November 2010).

Currie, C. L. (2000). Facilitating adult learning: the role of the academic librarian. *Reference Librarian*, 69/70, 219–231.

Curzon, S.C. (2004). Developing faculty–librarian partnerships in information literacy. In Rockman, I.F. (ed.), *Integrating Information Literacy into the Higher Education Curriculum*. (pp. 29–45). San Francisco, CA: Jossey-Bass.

Darwin, A. and Palmer, E. (2009). Mentoring circles in higher education. *Higher Education Research and Development*, 28(2), 125–136.

Davis, K.D. (2007). The academic librarian as instructor: a study of teacher anxiety. *College and Undergraduate Libraries*, 14(2), 77–101.

Dennis, N. (2001). Using inquiry methods to foster information literacy partnerships. *Reference Services Review*, 29(2), 122–131.

Dewey, B.I. (2004). The embedded librarian: strategic campus collaborations. *Resource Sharing and Information Networks*, 17(1/2), 5–17.

Dillon, A. (2008). Accelerating learning and discovery: refining the role of academic librarians. In CLIR (Council on Library and Information Resources). *No Brief Candle: Reconceiving Research Libraries for the 21st Century* (pp. 51–57). Washington: CLIR. Available at: *http://www.clir.org/pubs/reports/pub142/pub142.pdf* (retrieved 20 October 2010).

Dilmore, D.H. (1996). Librarian/faculty interaction at nine New England colleges. *College and Research Libraries*, 57, 274–284.

Divay, G., Ducas, A.M. and Michaud-Oystryk, N. (1987). Faculty perceptions of librarians at the University of Manitoba. *College and Research Libraries*, 48(1), 27–35.

Donaldson, A. (2010). Delivering legal information skills via a VLE. *Legal Information Management*, 10(2), 81–85.

Donnelly, K.M. (2000). Building the learning library: where do we start? In Bahr, A.H. (ed.). *Future Teaching Roles for Academic Librarians* (pp. 59–75). New York: Haworth Press.

Doskatch, I. (2003). Perceptions and perplexities of the faculty–librarian partnership: an Australian perspective. *Reference Services Review*, 31(2), 111–121.

Douglas, G. V. (1999). Professor librarian: a model of the teaching librarian of the future. *Computers in Libraries*, 19(10), 24–26, 28, 30.

Doyle, C. (1994). *Information Literacy in an Information Society: A Concept for the Information Age*. Syracuse, NY: ERIC Clearinghouse on Information and Technology.

Eadie, T. (1990). Immodest proposals: user instruction for students does not work. *Library Journal*, 115, 42–45.

Edwards, S. (2006). *Panning for Gold: Information Literacy and the Net Lenses Model*. Blackwood: Auslib Press.

Ellis, D. (1989). A behavioral approach to information retrieval system design. *Journal of Documentation*, 45(3), 171–212.

Elmborg, J. (2006). Critical information literacy: implications for instructional practice. *Journal of Academic Librarianship*, 32(2), 192–199.

Estrin, J.W. (1998). From bibliographic instruction to instructional management: a process-oriented approach for re-engineering library instruction programs.

Katharine Sharp Review, 6. Available at: from *http://mirrored.ukoln.ac.uk/lis-journals/review/review/6/estrin_bi.pdf* (retrieved 20 October 2010).

Eve, J., de Groot, M. and Schmidt, A.M. (2007). Supporting lifelong learning in public libraries across Europe. *Library Review*, 56(5), 393–406.

Fallon, H. (2009a). A writing support programme for Irish academic librarians. *Library Review*, 58(6), 414–422.

Fallon, H. (2009b). The academic writing toolkit: Writing for professional and peer-reviewed journals. *SCONUL Focus*, 45, 66–71.

Farber, E. (1995). Plus ça change. *Library Trends*, 44(2), 430–438.

Ferraro, J.M. (2000). *Reflective Practice and Professional Development*. (ERIC Digest, ED449120). Available at: *http://www.ericdigests.org/2001-3/reflective.htm* (retrieved 21 October 2010).

Fleming-May, R. and Yuro, L. (2009). From student to scholar: academic library and social sciences PhD students' transformation. *Portal: Libraries and the Academy*, 9(2), 199–221.

Fosmire, M. and Macklin, A. (2002). Riding the active learning wave: problem-based learning as a catalyst for creating faculty–librarian instructional partnerships. *Issues in Science and Technology Librarianship*, (34). Available at: *http://www.istl.org/02-spring/article2.html* (retrieved 20 October 2010).

Foster, A.E. (2006). Information literacy for the information profession: Experiences from Aberystwyth. *Aslib Proceedings*, 58(6), 488–501.

Foster, S. (1993). Information literacy: some misgivings. *American Libraries*, 24(4), 344,346.

Fourie, I. (2004). Librarians and the claiming of new roles: how can we try to make a difference? *Aslib Proceedings*, 56(1), 62–74.

Geck, C. (2006). The generation Z connection: teaching information to the newest Net Generation. *Teacher Librarian*, 33(3), 19–23.

Gibbs, G. (1981). *Twenty Terrible Reasons for Lecturing*. SCED Occasional Paper No. 8, Birmingham. Available at: *http://www.brookes.ac.uk/services/ocsd/2_learntch/20reasons.html* (retrieved 20 October 2010).

Godes, D. and Mayzlin, D. (2004). Using online conversations to study word-of-mouth communication. *Marketing Science*, 23 (4), 545–560.

Godwin, P. and Parker, J. (eds) (2008). *Information Literacy Meets Library 2.0*. London: Facet Publishing.

Gold, H.E. (2005). Engaging the adult learner: creating effective library instruction. *Portal: Libraries and the Academy*, 5(4), 467–481.

Grant, M.J. (2007). The role of reflection in the library and information sector: a systematic review. *Health Information and Libraries Journal*, 24(3), 155–166.

Grassian, E.S. and Kaplowitz, J.R. (2009). *Information Literacy Instruction: Theory and Practice*. (2nd edn). New York: Neal-Schuman.

Grassian, E.S. and Kaplowitz, J.R. (2005). *Learning to Lead and Manage Information Literacy Instruction*. New York: Neal-Schuman.

Grassian, E.S. and Kaplowitz, J.R. (2001). *Information Literacy Instruction: Theory and Practice*. New York: Neal-Schuman.

Gruenbaum, E.A. (2010, May 13). Creating online professional learning communities: and how to translate practices to the virtual classroom. *eLearn Magazine*, 5. Available at: *http://www.elearnmag.org/subpage.cfm?section=art iclesandarticle=122-1* (retrieved 12 November 2010).

Guevara, S. (2007). Generation Y: what can we do for you? *Information Outlook*, 11(6), 80–82.

Hall, H. and Davison, B. (2007). Social software as support in hybrid learning environments: the value of the blog as a tool for reflective learning and peer support. *Library and Information Science Research*, 29(2), 163–187.

Hardesty, L. (1995). Faculty culture and bibliographic instruction: an exploratory analysis. *Library Trends*, 44(2), 339–367.

Hardesty, L. (1991). *Faculty and the Library: The Undergraduate Experience*. Norwood, NJ: Ablex.

Haynes, E.B. (1996). Librarian–faculty partnerships in instruction. *Advances in Librarianship*, 20, 191–222.

Head, A.J. and Eisenberg, M. (2009). *Lessons Learned: How College Students Seek Information in the Digital Age*. Project Information Literacy Progress Report, 1 December. Available at: *http://projectinfolit.org/pdfs/PIL_Fall2009_finalv_YR1_12_2009v2.pdf* (retrieved 21 October 2010).

Heinrich, K. J. and Attebury, R. (2010). Communities of practice at an academic library: a new approach to mentoring at the University of Idaho. *The Journal of Academic Librarianship*, 36(2), 158–165.

Henri, J. (2001). Thinking and informing: A reality check on class teachers and teacher librarians. In P. Hughes and L. Selby (eds). *Proceedings of the Fifth International Forum on Research in School Librarianship* (pp. 119–128). Auckland: IASL.

Hepworth, M. (2000). Approaches to providing information literacy training in higher education: challenges for librarians. *New Review of Academic Librarianship*, 6, 21–34.

Hochstein, S. (2004). You mean you teach? I thought you were a librarian! Using teaching portfolios to think about and improve instruction in academic libraries. In Thomas, D.B., Tammany, R., Baier, R., Owen, E. and Mercado, H. (eds.), *Reflective Teaching: A Bridge to Learning*. (pp. 139–144). Ann Arbor, MI: Pierian Press.

Hoffmann, K., Antwi-Nsiah, F., Feng, V. and Stanley, M. (2008). Library research skills: a needs assessment for graduate student workshops. *Issues in Science and Technology Librarianship*, 53. Available at: *http://www.istl.org/08-winter/refereed1.html* (retrieved 22 October 2010).

Holtze, T.L. (2002). 100 ways to reach your faculty. *Invited presentation at the American Library Association OLOS Preconference 'Different Voices, Common Quest: Adult Literacy and Outreach in Libraries'*. Atlanta, GA, 13 June. Available at: *http://www.ala.org/ala/issuesadvocacy/advocacy/publicawareness/campaign@yourlibrary/academicresearch/reach_faculty.pdf* (retrieved 20 October 2010).

Hord, S.M. (1997). Professional learning communities: what are they and why are they important? *Issues . . . about Change*, 6(1). Available at: *http://www.sedl.org/change/issues/issues61/Issues_Vol6_No1_1997.pdf* (retrieved 12 November 2010).

Horton, F.W. (2008). *Understanding Information Literacy: A Primer*. UNESCO: Paris. Available at: *http://unesdoc.unesco.org/images/0015/001570/157020E.pdf* (retrieved 10 November 2010).

Indiana University Libraries Kokomo. (2006). *Goal and Mission Statement for the Information Literacy Instruction Program*. Available at: *http://*

www.iuk.edu/~kolibry/docs/MissionInfoLiteracy.pdf (retrieved 20 October 2010).

Ivey, R.T. (1994). Teaching faculty perceptions of academic librarians at Memphis State University. *College and Research Libraries*, 55, 69–82.

Jacobs, H. (2008). Information literacy and reflective pedagogical praxis. *Journal of Academic Librarianship*, 34(3), 256–262.

Jacobson, T.E. and Xu, L. (2004). *Motivating Students in Information Literacy Classes*. New York: Neal-Schuman.

Jenkins, P.O. (2005). *Faculty–Librarian Relationships*. Oxford: Chandos.

Jobe, M.M. and Grealy, D.S. (2000). The role of libraries in providing curricular support and curricular integration for distance learning courses. *Advances in Librarianship*, 23, 239–267.

Julien, H. and Pecoskie, J. (2009). Librarians' experiences of the teaching role: grounded in campus relationships. *Library and Information Science Research*, 31(3), 149–154.

Julien, H. and Given, L. (2003). Faculty–librarian relationships in the information literacy context: a content analysis of librarians' expressed attitudes and experiences. *Canadian Journal of Information and Library Science*, 27(3), 65–87.

Kahn, P. and O'Rourke, K. (2005). Understanding enquiry-based learning. In Barrett, T., Mac Labhrainn, I. and Fallon, H. (eds). *Handbook of Enquiry and Problem-Based Learning: Irish Case Studies and International Perspectives*. (pp. 1–12). Galway: AISHE and CELT, NUI Galway.

Kajberg, L. and Lørring, L. (eds). (2005). *European Curriculum Reflections on Library and Information Science Education*. Copenhagen: The Royal School of Library and Information Science. Available at: *http://www.library.utt.ro/LIS_Bologna.pdf* (retrieved 21 October 2010).

Kemp, J. (2006). Isn't being a librarian enough? Librarians as classroom teachers. *College and Undergraduate Libraries*, 13(3), 3–23.

Kessinger, P. (2004). Make it more than 'just' 50 minutes: improving instruction through peer mentoring. In Thomas, D.B., Tammany, R., Baier, R., Owen, E. and Mercado, H. (eds), *Reflective Teaching: A Bridge to Learning*. (pp. 125–133). Ann Arbor, MI: Pierian Press.

Kilcullen, M. (1998). Teaching librarians to teach: recommendations on what we need to know. *Reference Services Review*, 26(2), 7–18.

Kirton, J. and Barham, L. (2005). Information literacy in the workplace. *Australian Library Journal*, 54(4), 365–376.

Kraat, S.B. (ed). (2005). *Relationships between Teaching Faculty and Teaching Librarians*. Binghamton, NY: Haworth Information Press.

LaGuardia, C. and Oka, C.K. (2000). *Becoming a Library Teacher*. New York: Neal-Schuman.

Lally, A. and Trejo, N. (1998). Creating the developmental teaching portfolio. *College and Research Libraries News*, 59(10), 776–778.

Langille, L. and Mackenzie, T. (2007). Navigating the road to success: a systematic approach to preparing competitive grant proposals. *Evidence Based Library and Information Practice*, 2(1), 23–31.

Larsen, J.B. (2005). *The European LIS School Survey: A short presentation of the questionnaire-based survey*. Available at: *http://www.iva.dk/LIS-EU/LIS%20School%20Survey%20presentation.ppt* (retrieved 21 October 2010).

Larson, M.E. and Meltzer, E. (1987). Education for bibliographic instruction. *Journal of Education for Library and Information Science*, 28 (1), 9–16.

Lave, J. and Wenger, E. (1991). *Situated Learning: Legitimate Peripheral Participation*. Cambridge: Cambridge University Press.

Leckie, G.J. (1996). Desperately seeking citations: Uncovering faculty assumptions about the undergraduate research process. *Journal of Academic Librarianship*, 22(3), 201–208.

Leckie, G.J. and Fullerton, A. (1999). Information literacy in science and engineering undergraduates: faculty attitudes and pedagogical practices. *College and Research Libraries*, 60(1), 9–29.

Lester, R. (1979). Why educate the library user? *Aslib Proceedings*, 31(8), 366–380.s.

Library Routes Project. (n.d.). Available at: *http://libraryroutesproject.wikkii.com/wiki/Main_Page* (retrieved 12 November 2010).

Liles, J. (2007). Librarian readiness and pedagogy. In Curzon, S.C. and Lampert, L.D. (eds). *Proven Strategies for Building an Information Literacy Program*. (pp. 113–132). New York: Neal-Schuman.

Lipow, A.G. (1992). Outreach to faculty: why and how. In *Working with Faculty in the New Electronic Library: Papers and Session Materials Presented at the Nineteenth National LOEX Library Instruction Conference held at Eastern Michigan University*. (pp. 7–24). Ann Arbor, MI: Pierian Press.

Loomis, A. (1995). Building coalitions for information literacy. In Fifteenth Anniversary Task Force, Library Instruction Round Table and American Library Association (eds). *Information for a New Age: Redefining the Librarian*. (pp. 123–134). Englewood, CO: Libraries Unlimited.

Lorenzen, M. (2001). *Active Learning and Library Instruction*. Available at: *http://www.libraryinstruction.com/active.html* (retrieved 10 November 2010).

Luthmann, A. (2007). Librarians, professionalism and image: stereotype and reality. *Library Review*, 56(9), 773–780.

Mackey, T.P. and Jacobson, T.E. (eds). (2008). *Using Technology to Teach Information Literacy*. New York: Neal-Schuman.

Maliszewski, D., Tong, S., Chiu, J. and Huh, M.J. (2008). A professional learning community journey. *Partnership: The Canadian Journal of Library and Information Practice and Research*, 3(1). Available at: *http://journal.lib.uoguelph.ca/index.php/perj/article/view/468/833* (retrieved 12 November 2010).

Manchester Metropolitan University Library and Leeds University Library. (2002). *The Big Blue: Information Skills for Students*. Available at: *http://www.library.mmu.ac.uk/bigblue/* (retrieved 20 October 2010).

Mandernack, S.B. (1990). An assessment of education and training needs for bibliographic instruction librarians. *Journal of Education for Library and Information Science*, 30(3), 193–205.

Manuel, K., Beck, S.E. and Molloy, M. (2005). An ethnographic study of attitudes influencing faculty collaboration in library instruction. *Reference Librarian*, 89/90, 139–161.

Markey, K., Swanson, F., Jenkins, A., Jennings, B.J., St. Jean, B., Rosenberg, V., Yao, X. and Frost, R.L. (2008). Designing and testing a web-based board game for teaching information literacy skills and concepts. *Library Hi Tech*, 26(4), 663–681.

Markless, S. and Streatfield, D. (1992). *Cultivating Information Skills in Further Education: Eleven Case Studies.* (Library and Information Research Report No.86). London: British Library Research and Development Department.

Masson, A. (2009). VRE library services: learning from supporting VLE users. *Library Hi Tech*, 27(2), 217–227.

Masters, S. (2009). Exploiting a VLE to promote reading and information literacy. *The School Librarian*, 57(2), 74–75.

Mavrinac, M.A. (2005). Transformational leadership: Peer mentoring as a values-based learning process. *Portal: Libraries and the Academy*, 5(3), 391–404.

Maynard, J.E. (1990). A case study of faculty attitudes toward library instruction: the Citadel experience. *Reference Services Review*, 18(2), 67–76.

McCarthy, C. (1985). The faculty problem. *Journal of Academic Librarianship*, 11(2), 142–145.

McCartin, M. and Feid, P. (2001). Information literacy for undergraduates: Where have we been and where are we going? *Advances in Librarianship*, 25, 1–27.

McGuinness, C. (2009). Information skills training practices in Irish higher education. *Aslib Proceedings: New Information Perspectives*, 61(3), 262–281.

McGuinness, C. (2007). Exploring strategies for integrated information literacy: from 'academic champions' to institution-wide change. *Communications in Information Literacy*, 1(1), 26–38. Available at: *http://www.comminfolit.org/index.php/cil/article/view/Spring2007AR3/14* (retrieved 20 October 2010).

McGuinness, C. (2006). What faculty think: exploring the barriers to information literacy development in undergraduate education. *Journal of Academic Librarianship*, 32(6), 573–582.

McGuinness, C. (2004). *Collaborating for Information Literacy Development: Exploring the Dynamic Effect of Academic–Librarian Relationships on Information Literacy Development Programmes in Undergraduate Education.* Unpublished PhD thesis, School of Information and Library Studies, University College Dublin.

McGuinness, C. and Brien, M. (2007). Using reflective journals to assess the research process. *Reference Services Review*, 35(1), 21–40.

McLaren, B. (1999). *Changing Paradigms, New Partnerships: Information Literacy Programs in Educational Libraries.* Paper presented at Reference and Information Service Section (RAISS) Conference and Exhibition: 1999 and Beyond: Partnerships and Paradigms. Available at: *http://pandora.nla.gov.au/nph-arch/1999/Z1999-Dec-9/http://www.csu.edu.au/special/raiss99/papers/bmclaren.htm* (retrieved 20 October 2010).

McMahon, T., Barrett, T. and O'Neill, G. (2007) Using observation of teaching to improve quality-finding your way through the muddle of competing conceptions, confusion of practice and mutually exclusive intentions. *Teaching in Higher Education*, 12(4), 499–511.

McMahon, T. and O'Neill, G. (2010). *Genuine Peer-Observation of Teaching.* Available at: *http://www.ucd.ie/t4cms/ucdtld0071.pdf* (retrieved 12 November 2010).

Meulemans, Y.N. and Brown, J. (2001). Educating instruction librarians: A model for library and information science. *Research Strategies*, 18(4), 253–64.

Middleton, C. (2002). Evolution of peer evaluation of library instruction at Oregon State University Libraries. *Portal: Libraries and the Academy*, 2(1), 69–78.

Miller, J.P. and Benefiel, C.R. (1998). Academic librarians and the pursuit of tenure: the support group as a strategy for success. *College and Research Libraries*, 59(3), 260–265.

Mitchell, W.B. and Reichel, M. (1999). Publish or perish: a dilemma for academic librarians? *College and Research Libraries*, 60(3), 232–243.

Moon, J. (2006). *Learning Journals: A Handbook for Reflective Practice and Professional Development*. London: Routledge.

Moore, P. (2002). *An Analysis of Information Literacy Education Worldwide: White Paper prepared for UNESCO, the U.S. National Commission on Libraries and Information Science, and the National Forum on Information Literacy*. Paper prepared for 2003 Information Literacy Meeting of Experts. Available at: *http://citeseerx.ist.psu.edu/viewdoc/download?doi=10.1.1.130.9783andrep=rep1andtype=pdf* (retrieved 20 October 2010).

Neely, T.Y. (2006). *Information Literacy Assessment: Standards-Based Tools and Assignments*. Chicago, IL: ALA Editions.

Nickel, L.T. (2007). Collaborating with faculty and instructional technology staff. In Clayton, S.J. (ed.). *Going the Distance: Library Instruction for Remote Learners*. (pp. 153–158). London: Facet.

Nimon, M. (2000). Striking the right balance: information literacy and partnerships between librarian, lecturer, and student. In Booker, D. (ed.). *Proceedings of the Fourth National Information Literacy Conference. Concept, Challenge, Conundrum: From Library Skills to Information Literacy* (pp. 157–164). Adelaide: University of South Australia Library.

Norbury, L. (2001). Peer observation of teaching: A method for improving teaching quality. *New Review of Academic Librarianship*, 7, 87–101.

O'Beirne, R. (2006). Raising the profile of information literacy in public libraries. *Library + Information Update*, 5(1–2), 44–45.

Oberg, L.R., Schleiter, M.K. and Van Houten, M. (1989). Faculty perceptions of librarians at Albion College: Status, role, contribution and contacts. *College and Research Libraries*, 50(2), 215–230.

Oen, C. and Cooper, M. (1988). Professional identity and the information professional. *Journal of the American Society for Information Science*, 39 (5), 355–357.s.

Orr, D., Appleton, M. and Wallin, M. (2001). Information literacy and flexible delivery: creating a conceptual framework and model. *Journal of Academic Librarianship*, 27(6), 457–463.

Owens, Major R. (1976). The state government and libraries. *Library Journal*, 101 (1), 19–28.

Owusu-Ansah, E.K. (2001). The academic library in the enterprise of colleges and universities: toward a new paradigm. *Journal of Academic Librarianship*, 27(4), 282–294.

Oxford Dictionary, Thesaurus and Wordpower Guide (2001). Oxford: Oxford University Press.

Pallister, J. and Isaacs, A. (eds) (2003). *A Dictionary of Business* (3rd ed.). Oxford: Oxford University Press.

Peacock, J. (2001). Teaching skills for teaching librarians: postcards from the edge of the educational paradigm. *Australian Academic and Research Libraries*, 32(1), 26–42.

Peacock, J. (2000). From trainers to educators: librarians and the challenge of change. In Booker, D. (ed.), *Proceedings of the Fourth National Information Literacy Conference. Concept, Challenge, Conundrum: From Library Skills to Information Literacy* (pp. 182–192). Adelaide: University of South Australia Library.

Pickard, A.J. (2007). *Research Methods in Information.* London: Facet Publishing.

Pinto, M., Cordon, J.A. and Diaz, R.G. (2010). Thirty years of information literacy (1977–2007): a terminological, conceptual and statistical analysis. *Journal of Librarianship and Information Science*, 42(1), 3–19.

Pollard, A. (2008). *Reflective Teaching* (3rd ed.). London: Continuum.

Powis, C. (2008). Towards the professionalisation of practice in teaching. *Relay: The Journal of the University College and Research Group (CILIP)*, 58, 6–9.

Powis, C. (2005). Infoteach: Developing an online community of practice of librarians who teach. *SCONUL Focus*, 35. Available at: *http://www.sconul. ac.uk/publications/newsletter/35/22.rtf* (retrieved 12 November 2010).

Price, G. (1999). *User Education in Higher Education: Helping Academics Join the Learning Environment.* Paper presented at the 20th IATUL Conference: The Future of Libraries in Human Communication. Available at: *http://www.iatul.org/ conferences/pastconferences/1999proceedings.asp* (retrieved 20 October 2010).

Putnam, L.L. (2009). Professional writing and publishing: resources for librarians. *College and Research Libraries News*, 70(4). Available at: *http://www.ala.org/ ala/mgrps/divs/acrl/publications/crlnews/2009/apr/prowritepublish.cfm* (retrieved 12 November 2010).

Rader, H.B. (1997). Educating students for the information age: the role of the librarian. *Reference Services Review*, 25(2), 47–52.

Raspa, D. and Ward, D. (2000). *The Collaborative Imperative: Librarians and Faculty Working Together in the Information Universe.* Chicago: American Library Association, Association of College and Research Libraries.

Renon, F., Pychyl, T.A. and Motz, C.P. (2008). A conversation about collaboration: Using web-based video streaming to integrate information literacy into a research assignment for a large blended class. In Mackey, T.P. and Jacobson, T.E. (eds). *Using Technology to Teach Information Literacy* (pp. 29–50). New York: Neal-Schuman.

Rentfrow, D. (2008). Groundskeepers, gatekeepers, and guides: how to change faculty perceptions of librarians and ensure the future of the research library. In CLIR (Council on Library and Information Resources). *No Brief Candle: Reconceiving Research Libraries for the 21st Century* (pp. 58–65). Washington: CLIR. Available at: *http://www.clir.org/pubs/reports/pub142/pub142.pdf* (retrieved 22 October 2010).

Riegner, C. (2007). Word of mouth on the Web: the impact of Web 2.0 on consumer purchase decisions. *Journal of Advertising Research*, 47(4), 436–447.

RIN (Research Information Network). (2008, July). *Mind the Skills Gap: Information-Handling Training for Researchers.* A report commissioned by the Research Information Network. Available at: *http://www.rin.ac.uk/system/ files/attachments/Mind-skills-gap-report.pdf* (retrieved 22 October 2010).

Rockman, I. (2004). Successful strategies for integrating information literacy into the curriculum. In Rockman, I.F. (ed.), *Integrating Information Literacy into the Higher Education Curriculum.* (pp. 47–69). San Francisco, CA: Jossey-Bass.

Rockwell-Kincanon, J. (2007). Using social marketing to promote information literacy. In Curzon, S.C. and Lampert, L.D. (eds). *Proven Strategies for Building an Information Literacy Program.* (pp. 239–256). New York: Neal-Schuman.

Roes, H. (2001, July/August). Digital libraries in education: trends and opportunities. *D-Lib Magazine,* 7 (7/8). Available at: *http://www.dlib.org/dlib/july01/roes/07roes.html* (retrieved 21 October 2010).

Rowlands, I., Nicholas, D., Williams, P., Huntington, P., Fieldhouse, M., Gunter, B., Withey, R., Jamali, H.R., Dobrowolski, T. and Tenopir, C. (2008). The Google generation: the information behaviour of the researcher of the future. *ASLIB Proceedings,* 60(4), 290–310.

SCONUL (Society of College, National and University Libraries). (1999). *Information Skills in Higher Education: A SCONUL Position Paper.* Available at: *http://www.sconul.ac.uk/groups/information_literacy/papers/Seven_pillars.html* (retrieved 20 October 2010).

Scottish Information Literacy Project, The (n.d.). Available at: *http://www.gcu.ac.uk/ils/* (retrieved 22 October 2010).

Secker, J., Boden, D. and Price, G. (2007). Information literacy beef bourguignon (also known as information skills stew or i-skills casserole): the higher education sector. In Secker, J., Boden, D. and Price, G. (eds). *The Information Literacy Cookbook: Ingredients, Recipes and Tips for Success* (pp. 123–152). Oxford: Chandos.

Selematsela, D.N.S. and du Toit, A.S.A. (2007). Competency profile for librarians teaching information literacy. *South African Journal of Library and Information Science,* 73(2), 119–129.

Shapiro, J.J. and Hughes, S.K. (1996). Information literacy as a liberal art: enlightenment proposals for a new curriculum. *Educom Review,* 31(2), 31–35. Available at: *http://net.educause.edu/apps/er/review/reviewArticles/31231.html* (retrieved 20 October 2010).

Sharma, S. (2007). From chaos to clarity: using the research portfolio to teach and assess information literacy skills. *Journal of Academic Librarianship,* 33(4), 127–135.

Shonrock, D. and Mulder, C. (1993). Instruction librarians: acquiring the proficiencies critical to their work. *College and Research Libraries,* 54(2), 137–49.

Slavin, L. and Mead, J. (2008). I am not a teacher, am I? *Tennessee Libraries,* 58(1). Available at: *http://www.tnla.org/associations/5700/files/581slavin.pdf* (retrieved 20 October 2010).

Smith, R. (1997). *Philosophical Shift: Teach the Faculty to Teach Information Literacy.* Paper presented at ACRL 8th National Conference: Choosing our Futures. Available at: *http://www.ala.org/ala/mgrps/divs/acrl/publications/whitepapers/nashville/smith.cfm* (retrieved 20 October 2010).

Snavely, L. and Cooper, N. (1997). The information literacy debate. *Journal of Academic Librarianship,* 23(1), 9–14.

Sonntag, G. and Meulemans, Y. (2003). Planning for assessment. In Avery, E.F. (ed.). *Assessing Student Learning Outcomes for Information Literacy*

Instruction in Academic Institutions (pp. 6–21). Chicago: Association of College and Research Libraries.

Spitzer, K.L., Eisenberg, M.B. and Lowe, C.A. (1998). *Information Literacy: Essential Skills for the Information Age.* New York: Syracuse University, Information Resources Publications.

Starkweather, W.M. and Clark Wallin, C. (1999). Faculty response to library technology: insights on attitudes. *Library Trends*, 47(4), 640–668.

Stevens, C.R. (2007). Beyond preaching to the choir: Information literacy, faculty outreach, and disciplinary journals. *Journal of Academic Librarianship*, 33(2), 254–267.

Stiles, M.J. (2000). *Effective Learning and the Virtual Learning Environment.* Paper delivered as a Keynote at the 2000 European Universities Information Systems Congress – EUNIS 2000 – 'Towards Virtual Universities' in Poznan, Poland, April 2000. Available at: *http://www.staffs.ac.uk/COSE/cose10/posnan.html* (retrieved 21 October 2010).

Stubbings, R. and Franklin, V. (2006). Does advocacy help to embed information literacy into the curriculum? A case study. *Italics*, 5(1). Available at: *http://www.ics.heacademy.ac.uk/italics/vol5-1/pdf/stubbings-franklin-final.pdf* (retrieved 22 October 2010).

Sullivan, S. (1997). Education for library instruction: a 1996 survey. *Research Strategies*, 15(4), 271–277.

Taylor, R.S. (1979). Reminiscing about the future. *Library Journal*, 104, 1875.

Thomas, D.B., Tammany, R., Baier, R., Owen, E. and Mercado, H. (eds.) (2004). *Reflective Teaching: A Bridge to Learning.* Ann Arbor, MI: Pierian Press.

Thomas, J. (1994). Faculty attitudes and habits concerning library instruction: how much has changed since 1982? *Research Strategies*, 12(4), 209–223.

Thomas, N.P. (2004). *Information Literacy and Information Skills Instruction: Applying Research to Practice in the School Library Media Center.* (2nd edn). Westport, CT: Libraries Unlimited.

Thomas, N.P. (1999). *Information Literacy and Information Skills Instruction: Applying Research to Practice in the School Library Media Center.* Englewood, CO: Libraries Unlimited.

Thompson, G.B. (2002). Information literacy accreditation mandates: what they mean for faculty and librarians. *Library Trends*, 51, 218–241.

Van der Meer, P.F., Ring, D.M. and Perez-Stable, M.A. (2007). Engaging the masses: library instruction with large undergraduate classes. *College and Undergraduate Libraries*, 14(1), 39–56.

Virkus, S. (2003). Information literacy in Europe: A literature review. *Information Research*, 8(4), Paper 159. Available at: *http://informationr.net/ir/8-4/paper159.html* (retrieved 20 October 2010).

Wallace, R. and Carter, N. (2008). Evidence based library and information practice. *Tennessee Libraries*, 58(1). Available at: *http://www.tnla.org/associations/5700/files/581wallace.pdf* (retrieved 22 October 2010).

Walter, S. (2008). Librarians as teachers: a qualitative inquiry into professional identity. *College and Research Libraries*, 69(1), 51–71.

Walter, S. (2006). Instructional improvement: building capacity for the professional development of librarians as teachers. *Reference and User Services Quarterly*, 45(3), 213–218.

Walter, S. (2005). Improving instruction: what librarians can learn from the study of college teaching. In Thompson, H.A. (ed.). *Currents and Convergence: Navigating the Rivers of Change: Proceedings of the Twelfth National Conference of the Association of College and Research Libraries, 7–10 April, Minneapolis, Minnesota* (pp. 363–379). Chicago: Association of College and Research Libraries.

Walton, G. (2010). *Demolishing the Seven Pillars: A Warning from Research?* Paper presented at LILAC (Librarians' Information Literacy Annual Conference) in Limerick, Ireland, on 30 March. Abstract available at: *http://www.lila cconference.com/dw/programme/parallel_sessions_detail_3.html*; Slides available at: *http://www.lilacconference.com/dw/programme/Presentations/Tuesday/City_View_Suite/Walton_Demolishing.pdf* (retrieved 20 October 2010).

Webb, J. and Powis, C. (2004). *Teaching Information Skills: Theory and Practice.* London: Facet Publishing.

Webber, S. (2003). *An International Information Literacy Certificate: Opportunity or Dead-end?* Paper presented at the 2003 IFLA Conference. Available at: *http://dis.shef.ac.uk/literacy/webber-ifla2003.pdf* (retrieved 20 October 2010).

Webber, S., Boon, S. and Johnston, B. (2005). A comparison of UK academics' conceptions of information literacy in two disciplines: English and marketing. *Library and Information Research*, 29(93), 4–15.

Webber, S. and Johnston, B. (2006). As we may think: information literacy as a discipline for the information age. *Research Strategies*, 20, 108–121.

Webber, S. and Johnston, B. (2000). Conceptions of information literacy: New perspectives and implications. *Journal of Information Science*, 26(6), 381–397.

Weetman DaCosta, J. (2007). Preaching to the non-converted: the art of promoting information literacy to academic staff. Paper presented at LILAC (Librarians' Information Literacy Annual Conference), 26–28 March, Manchester Metropolitan University. Available at: *http://www.lilacconference. com/dw/archive/resources/dacosta07.ppt* (retrieved 10 November 2010).

Weiss, S.C. (2004). The origin of library instruction in the United States, 1820–1900. *Research Strategies*, 19(3–4), 233–243.

Wenger, E. (1998). Communities of practice. Learning as a social system. *Systems Thinker*, June. Available at: *http://www.co-i-l.com/coil/knowledge-garden/cop/lss.shtml* (retrieved 12 November 2010).

Westbrook, L. (1999). Passing the halfway mark: LIS curricula incorporating user education courses. *Journal of Education for Library and Information Science*, 40, 92–98.

White House, The. (2009). *National Information Literacy Awareness Month, 2009: By the President of the United States of America: A Proclamation.* Available at: *http://www.whitehouse.gov/the_press_office/Presidential-Proclamation-National-Information-Literacy-Awareness-Month/* (retrieved 20 October 2010).

Wilder, S. (2005). Information literacy makes all the wrong assumptions. *Chronicle of Higher Education*, 51(18), B13.

Wilkinson, J. (2000). From transmission to research: librarians at the heart of the campus. In Bahr, A.H. (ed.), *Future Teaching Roles for Academic Librarians*. (pp. 25–40). New York: Haworth Press.

Williams, D.A. and Wavell, C. (2006). *Information Literacy in the Classroom: Secondary School Teachers' Conceptions.* Final report on research funded by

Society for Educational Studies. Aberdeen: Robert Gordon University. Available at: *http://www4.rgu.ac.uk/files/ACF4DAA.pdf* (retrieved 10 November 2010).

Williams, P. (2006). Against information literacy. *Library + Information Update*, 5 (7–8), 20.

Williams, P. and Rowlands, I. (2007). *Information Behaviour of the Researcher of the Future: The Literature on Young People and their Information Behaviour* (Work Package II). London: British Library/JISC. Available at: *http://www.ucl .ac.uk/infostudies/research/ciber/downloads/GG%20Work%20Package% 20II.pdf* (retrieved 21 October 2010).

Williams, S. (2010). New tools for online information literacy instruction. *Reference Librarian*, 51(2), 148–162.

Wilson, K.M. and Halpin, E. (2006). Convergence and professional identity in the academic library. *Journal of Librarianship and Information Science*, 38(2), 79–91.

Woolfolk, A., Hughes, M. and Walkup, V. (2008). *Psychology in Education*. Harlow: Pearson Education.

Wubbels, T. (2007). Do we know a community of practice when we see one? *Technology Pedagogy and Education*, 16(2), 225–233.

Zurkowski, P. (1974). *The Information Service Environment: Relationships and Priorities*. Washington, DC: National Commission on Libraries and Information Science. (ERIC Document Reproduction Service No. ED100391).

Index

AASL (American Association of
School Librarians) 10
'Academic champions' 19, 59, 60
Academic-librarian collaboration 17,
19–24, 58–62
barriers to collaboration 22–24,
59–60
'disconnect' between academics
and librarians 59–60
forms of working relationships 59
faculty culture 23
importance of collaboration
18–21
instability of collaborations with
individual academics 61
Strategies for collaboration
60–62
'Top-down' approach 61–62
Academics:
collaboration with librarians 17
Ellis's model of information
behaviour 13, 50
expert researcher model 13, 50
as gatekeepers to the curriculum
116
information behaviour 13
information competence
15–16
perceptions of teaching librarians
18–24, 188
unrealistic expectations of student
information behaviour 13

willingness to teach information
literacy 15–16
Academic Writing Librarians blog
177
ACRL (Association of College &
Research Libraries) 6, 26
and faculty status for
librarians 18
Guidelines for Instruction
Programs in Academic
Libraries 58
Information Literacy Competency
Standards for Higher Education
6, 29, 75, 103
list of library instruction courses
for librarians 26
Standards for Proficiencies for
Instruction Librarians and
Coordinators 8, 28–29, 58
Action Research 55–58
action research cycle 56–57
definition of 56
Active learning 92–93, 108
and large groups 126–132
Adult learners 47, 139–142
Advocacy 62–67
and need to target non-LIS
audience 66
and Scottish Information Literacy
Project 63–65
and Social networking 66–67
strategies 65–66

CPSIA information can be obtained at www.ICGtesting.com
Printed in the USA
268771BV00002B/1/P